The Word Rides Again

*Rereading the Frontier
in American Fiction*

J. DAVID STEVENS

Ohio University Press

Athens

Ohio University Press, Athens, Ohio 45701
© 2002 by J. David Stevens
Printed in the United States of America
All rights reserved

Ohio University Press books are printed on acid-free paper ⊗™

10 09 08 07 06 05 04 03 02   5 4 3 2 1

Library of Congress Cataloging-in-Publication Data

Stevens, J. David, 1969–
 The word rides again : rereading the frontier in American fiction. /
J. David Stevens.
  p. cm.
 Includes bibliographical references and index.
 ISBN 0-8214-1417-8 (cloth : alk. paper) — ISBN 0-8214-1418-6 (pbk.
: alk. paper)
  1. American fiction—History and criticism. 2. Western stories—
History and criticism. 3. Frontier and pioneer life in literature.
I. Title.

PS374.F73 S74 2001
813'.087409—dc21

2001033931

For Janet, with love

CONTENTS

Preface: A Personal Beginning   ix

Acknowledgments   xxi

Introduction: The "Origin" of the Popular Western
and Some Themes   1

1   *Hobomok:* A Brief Case Study from the Beginning
    of the Genre   34

2   "She war a woman": Family Roles, Gender, and Sexuality
    in Bret Harte's Western Fiction   50

3   "Don't forget the cowboys, Sandy": Mark Twain
    and the Western Myth   74

4   A Man's Role: Literary Influence and *The Virginian*   95

5   (Re)Writing a Native American Western: John Rollin Ridge
    and Zitkala-Sa   112

6   Riders of the Papal Sage: Willa Cather's "Western"   134

7   The Many Echoes of *The Man Who Killed the Deer*   154

Epilogue: Reading the Western and the
Importance of History   173

Notes   181

Works Cited   221

Index   233

A Personal Beginning

Like many American boys, I watched TV westerns religiously from ages seven to fourteen. Every Saturday, a local cable station reran episodes in an eight-hour chunk, and when my mother allowed it, I would watch the shows start to finish: *The Rifleman, The Lone Ranger, Sugarfoot, Cheyenne, Bronco, Wagon Train, The Virginian, The Guns of Will Sonnet,* and *Gunsmoke.* It did not matter to me, even in the late seventies and early eighties, that the programs aired mostly in black and white or that many of the actors were, in reality, near death. I was drawn to the men and their guns, their rough but honest lives, their air of immortality, their unswerving commitment to do the "right" thing even when it meant placing themselves in jeopardy.

Put that way, I cannot recall why I stopped watching the shows. I'd like to say that I stopped because of the stereotypical and unfair way the shows treated any characters who were not white men: the Indians, the Mexicans, the women. But truth to tell, Indians and Mexicans did not appear very often on the screen. And women, in those rare moments when they did appear, occupied roles that seemed consummately decent to a kid: love interests, moral touchstones, sources of maternal wisdom to be protected by their male counterparts.

Rather, I think that I stopped watching TV westerns because at some point they stopped making fundamental sense. Most of the plotlines revolved around a hero trying to stay out of trouble for the first fifty broadcast minutes only to be forced into a violent confrontation in the last ten. In this sense, the shows pretended to value dialogue and compromise while still providing the entertainment of a showdown as their climax. Growing older—and learning to avoid fights myself—I began to notice this fundamental disconnect in the western hero's world. Here were men who claimed to want nothing more than to "live and let live," yet who were "forced" into violence on a weekly basis. Either they were the unluckiest guys in the world, I figured, or they were bit-players in a hypocritical game that sought to promote peace and violence at the same time. Even at age fourteen, I knew that western heroes could not have their bullets and use them too. They lived in a world that was ultra-violent ultra-often, a world where lethal confrontation was infinitely predictable even as it purported to be random and unexpected. It was not my world. Though I suspected that physical force was sometimes necessary to defend oneself and others—a belief I still hold—I also realized that the western hero did not think very hard about the issues involved in using such force. He merely played a part in a formula where a showdown was inevitable, a formula that for me was increasingly distant from reality.

My return to the western was, therefore, a gradual process and one that occurred in backdoor fashion. As a junior at Duke University, I took a course with Arnold E. Davidson—a well-known scholar of Canadian literature—who talked about the way that Canadian Western novels differed from their American counterparts. Rather than looking to the future, Davidson explained, Canadian Western writing looked backward in an attempt to articulate a historical identity and, in turn, to qualify what it meant to be "Canadian." The Canadian novel contained few graphically violent confrontations between whites and Indians, outlaws, or other enemies. Instead, it explored humanity's confrontation with the land itself and the inherent difficulty of coming to terms with the "surrounding silence" of the wilderness.[1] In fact, Davidson continued, there was nothing in American western novels to match the introspection and retrospection of Canadian fictions. Almost all American westerns proceeded from the fact of a frontier, its rapid western movement under the banner of Manifest Destiny, and the resultant violence between Euro-Americans and Indians or Mexicans (the classic battle of "civilization versus savagery"). Even the finest American westerns—often called anti-westerns or revisionist westerns[2]—evolved out of this frontier ethos and were created as an explicit response to the more traditional narratives sanctioning frontier violence.

Oddly, my sense of patriotism was roused. Even though my own experiences with the western suggested a lot of truth to what Davidson was saying, I felt confident that at some point America must have yielded authors whose accounts of the West were more complex and even-handed than those focusing on a cowboy-gunfighter bringing justice to a savage land. Indeed, as I continued my work on the western through graduate school, I encountered many of those scholars who had already questioned Hollywood's vision of the West and whose research had helped to demarcate the serious discipline of Western Studies: John Cawelti, Richard Slotkin, Henry Nash Smith, Patricia Nelson Limerick, Gerald Haslam, Leslie Fiedler, John R. Milton, Christine Bold, and countless others. They had all contributed different elements to the field. They had defined the popular western and traced its cultural history. They had explored responses to the mythic West. They had (re)discovered much Western literature that had been ignored through the mid-twentieth century. And they had shifted critical debate toward subjects previously ignored in discussions of the West (the roles of women, the importance of Indians and other minorities, the development of postfrontier Western regionalism, ecocriticism, and others). In fact, by the time I started writing seriously about the West in the early nineties, the field of Western Studies had been firmly established, and most writers who could be considered "Western" had already been introduced to the critical public, their works examined and classified.

That last word, "classified," was an important one for me, though, because as I read the criticism I began to notice a method of classification that seemed peculiar to Western Studies. Because much of the discipline evolved as a reaction to Western images in popular culture, there developed an almost necessary "us-versus-them" mentality in Western critical circles. Writers, scholarly and otherwise, often saw themselves debunking a mythic West that centered on white male gunfighters, violent performance, and the advance of "civilization." These writers, by contrast, worked to uncover the "real" West—striving for a greater degree of factual accuracy in Western history, for better publicity for the many Western texts that deviated from the mythic model, and for a greater sense of inclusion (cultural, racial, and gendered) in accounts of the West. Even critics who dealt seriously with the mythic West addressed it as a cultural phenomenon, an American self-image inscribed in a body of texts that owed its existence more to our values and desires as a nation than to historical authenticity.

As a result—and sometimes without even knowing it—Western Studies critics began to partition Western literature into two distinct camps: the popular, formula, or mythic western on the one hand (the genre where white male heroes carry the day for "civilization"), and the anti-western, revisionist western, or Western writing on the other (the genres that challenge the historical imprecision and biases of the popular western). On its face, this system seemed self-evident. After all, no one was going to mistake Willa Cather for Luke Short. But at the same time, the exclusive categorization of texts created problems, especially in Western literature where plotlines and characters were often more complex than in the movies or the most hastily produced pulp novels. Suddenly works that seemed to have a lot in common—James Fenimore Cooper's Leatherstocking Tales and Lydia Maria Child's *Hobomok,* Bret Harte's stories and Mary Austin's novels, Owen Wister's *The Virginian* and Stephen Crane's "The Bride Comes to Yellow Sky"—were being read antithetically and holistically, with little attention given to the subtler tensions contained within them. Differences between writers were emphasized while similarities were overlooked. And problematic characters, themes, or passages in individual works were discounted for the sake of an overall impression. Indeed, this process cut to the core of how literate readers were going to address Western novels. Were they going to focus on the debates occurring between novelists while ignoring the dialogues occurring within the novels themselves? Were they going to rely on identity politics to determine where an author "stood" on the "Western issue"? Were they going to use authorial intention as a determining factor in understanding how a particular novel should be read?

Even today the answers to these questions, like all things literary, remain complex and conditional. Certainly some books lend themselves to more singular interpretations than others. Some authors (and their works) wear politics more conspicuously on their sleeves than do their peers. But in their zeal to compensate for a hundred years of biased reportage and criticism, contemporary scholars have sometimes swung the pendulum too far the other way, dismissing mythic western narratives that share cultural concerns with more "deserving" cousins and overlooking "problems" in nonmythic narratives for the sake of distinguishing them from the popular West. One of the feats of Western scholarship has been to confirm that, in Western fiction, the good guys do not always wear white hats, nor the bad guys black, as we once believed. Ironically, though, that paradigm has shifted to authors themselves—with critics playing judge, jury, and haberdasher. The idea that authors, with rare exceptions, can be read so exclusively is preposterous. While critics have opened the gap between Western fictions so much that the debate has become part of the popular consciousness—echoing the political battle of "conservative values" and "liberal progressivism"—the time has come to revisit the centrist possibilities in Western/frontier writing and to reassert the continuum that slopes one side of the debate irrevocably into the other.

Consider, for example, the case of Hamlin Garland.

In the early years of Western Studies, Garland was often classed with writers like Cooper and Twain as an exemplar of American Western fiction. Born in 1860, Garland grew up in Wisconsin and South Dakota, setting most of his early work in these places and focusing on the difficulties (bad weather, inhospitable terrain, and economic injustices) that plagued the lives of farmers and other settlers. While not a frontier writer per se, most of Garland's fiction—including *Main-Travelled Roads* (1891), his best-known work—was set in the period just after the frontier had been tamed, with the first wave of immigrants traveling from the east to create settlements. In addition, later in his career, Garland took up the cause of American Indians and wrote several romances set in the Rockies that portrayed Native life both sympathetically and accurately. Despite its uneven quality, the canon of his work established him as a literary writer, a Western regionalist, and a serious realist. As contemporary critics have noted, his fictions belong most properly to the category of literary "western novels"[3] and should not be considered "[popular] Westerns under any circumstances."[4]

But for all that, Garland's stories demonstrate a nagging tendency to anticipate the thematic tensions of many popular western novels. "Under the Lion's Paw," the best-known story from *Main-Travelled Roads,* is a good example. The story follows an immigrant farmer, Haskins, who agrees to lease a farm for a term of three years with an option to buy the land when the lease expires. At the end of the lease period, Haskins goes to Butler (the farm's owner) to purchase the property, but Butler tells him that the price will be three times what they had originally discussed. The reason for the price hike is "the land's increased value," a result of the many improvements that Haskins has sacrificed to make but that are, technically, the property of Butler. Without legal recourse, Haskins considers killing Butler but, in the end, pays the price he asks.

This theme of economic victimization is reiterated in Jack Schaefer's popular-western classic *Shane* (1941), where a greedy rancher attempts to force a group of homesteaders off their farms, which he wants for grazing land. The details of the story are much like those of "Under the Lion's Paw." The struggling farmers have made the land valuable by making it viable, and now Fletcher, the powerful valley aristocrat, is determined to wrest it from them through threats of both legal and physical violence. Unlike Garland's Haskins, however, the homesteaders are saved by the arrival of Shane, a man of unknown origin who keeps a well-oiled pistol tucked in his saddle blanket and agrees to help the homesteaders for reasons only he knows. Despite his reluctance to use violence, Shane is eventually forced into battle with Fletcher's hired guns, where he triumphs, then departs the Wyoming valley as quickly and mysteriously as he came.

The principal, and obvious, difference between Garland's story and Schaefer's is the presence of the man with the gun—in Shane's case a man of mythic proportions. But, acknowledging that difference, one cannot help noting the many similarities between the two texts. Both take place on land that was recently frontier, where the forces of white America are internally contesting the direction that the nation will take economically. Far from a civilization/savagery conflict, this struggle is a matter of class, pitting the democratic—if less profitable—ideal of the yeoman farmer against the ruthless and dehumanizing forces of big business and industry. Both authors come down firmly on the side of the farmers struggling for self-determination, and even the works' endings are ideologically similar, the pitiable Haskins and the irreproachable Shane both suggesting that American schemes of democracy and morality sometimes require recourse beyond the strictly legal. Despite Shane's decision to shoot it out in the end, the striking parallels between the two works suggest at least a minor flaw in the critical logic that labels Garland's story a western "under no circumstances" while proclaiming Schaefer's novella "a self-conscious classic of the form."[5] In short, the labels with which they have been branded fail to account for the complex and largely sympathetic cultural relationship that exists between the two.

Granted, even the people who use such categories admit their inadequacies. James H. Maguire warns that generalizations "about popular Westerns should be suspect, partly because it is unlikely that any critic could read them all, but mainly because all sorts of popular writers have varied the pattern, and some have occasionally broken out of the formula."[6] And even Richard Etulain concedes that attempts to categorize Western texts are like "shovelling fleas through a barn door—more escape than are captured."[7] To these arguments, one might add the obvious theoretical observation that it is dangerous to classify books based either on the author's intention (because authors' intentions change and multiply during the construction of a book) or on the authority of a single voice in a novel (because novels are, by nature, places where many voices compete for le-

gitimacy).[8] More obvious still is Don D. Walker's extended admonition
about the dangers of critical reduction:

> Suppose I find that a certain novel reduces to a certain formula. What do I
> then know about the book? Very little, since most of its bookness has been
> stripped away and tossed into the trash bin. . . . What finally matters is what
> goes on within the form. To find this, one has to give up the form charts,
> the field guides to Western formulas, the reading glasses that have guide-
> lines set like hairs across the lenses. One has to give up all this and go back
> to the task of reading, letting words, sentences, and paragraphs work their
> special way.[9]

Walker's New Critical stance may seem reductive in itself, especially for a
genre like the western that often relies on standard conventions encountered by readers across various texts. But at the same time, he reminds
critics that each book must be read individually to avoid the hasty pi-
geonholing that sometimes accompanies the creation of larger categories.
As Michael Kowaleski has argued more recently, "certain critical categories seem 'memorized' ahead of time such that their premises frequently
dictate many of their conclusions." Indeed, he continues, the "most fruitful recognition of cultural diversity in the West will be one that complicates our conception of both mainstream *and* marginal cultures—
questioning along the way the usefulness of thinking about centers and
margins in western writing rather than about interdependence, hybridity,
and overlap."[10]

These cautionary notes are especially important in a discipline that
has become increasingly bipolar and political. In the early years of Western Studies (from the 1950s to the 1970s), this critical gap existed between
intellectuals who wanted to view the West as a cultural space—that is, the
enduring frontier—and those who wanted to view the West as a contemporary geographic region. However, since the rise of interdisciplinary and
multicultural movements (American Studies, the New Western History,
and so forth),[11] the fight over how the western should be viewed and
which books should qualify as westerns has become increasingly personal,
relying heavily on identity politics and close associations of so-called popular westerns with right-wing movements of the larger world.[12] One does
not have to go far to find such connections. In her introduction to the edited collection *Old West—New West: Centennial Essays,* Barbara Howard
Meldrum draws explicit parallels between Owen Wister's *The Virginian*
and the Persian Gulf War. "Trampas and the Virginian," she writes, "were

recast as Saddam Hussein and George Bush, who 'would rather die than settle the argument by talking to one another'—but, of course, others would do the dying for them."[13] And Susan J. Rosowski ends her article on the western hero with deliberate "political terms" when she denounces such heroes as "appealing to emotion and holding reason in suspicion. Power that resides absolutely within a single authority is despotism; an appeal to emotion and prejudice plus hostility to reason is demagoguery."[14] More poetically, Ann-Janine Morley-Gaines concludes her article on frontier sexual tension with the observation that the "gender antagonism which currently infuses American fiction betokens one of the most profound failures of the questing American spirit."[15] And Susan Lee Johnson, in a deliberate call for greater unity within Western Studies, gives her readers a rather one-sided statement about the dangers of disunity:

> Before we devolve into rival camps . . . we ought to convene in a spirit of interdisciplinary engagement and, ultimately, of political coalition. This is a crucial moment at which to fortify alliances. In the western states, where many of us live and work, we watch as Affirmative Action programs are dismantled; as violence is perpetrated against people of color and against gay, lesbian, and transgender people; and as global forces of capital wreak havoc on our local environments and especially on the poor and working class people who reside there.[16]

For Johnson, to study the New Western History is to engage in the overtly liberal task of "advanc[ing] insights that all of us who study western places and peoples ignore, not only at our peril, but at the peril of progressive politics both within and beyond academia."

Of course, I am not stumping for the political right here. Recent Western scholars have made important observations about how popular western fiction often marginalizes women and minorities, and their work deserves further consideration. Indeed, as Jan Rousch notes in her 1999 column for *Western American Literature*, the number of books to explore Western writing has increased exponentially over the last twenty years (from "19 titles in 1967 to 239 in 1999"), and most of these books have served to redefine "the three major themes in the field (Native American; women, gender, and race/culture; concerns about the land)."[17] Key books in the last decade—in particular, Jane Tompkins' *West of Everything: The Inner Life of Westerns* (1992) and Lee Clark Mitchell's *Westerns: Making the Man in Fiction and Film* (1996)—have definitively explored the construction of gender in western texts.[18] And those books are accompanied by hundreds of articles on various issues of difference ranging broadly across the American frontier.[19] Important as these works are, though, to transmute them (as some scholars have done) into a denouncement of the popular western as a form—moreover with little consideration given to what books should rightfully be called "westerns"—is to invite a climate of recrimination in which scholars, afraid of landing on the wrong side of the political line, refuse to take up certain texts because of their ideological ambiguities. Such moves limit debate rather than encourage it. And they achieve the inverse of what Rosowski, among others, claims to fear: a discipline guided by demagoguery, only this time a demagoguery created in the name of interdisciplinarity, multiculturalism, and political progressivism.

The Word Rides Again seeks to pull back on these political reins. Rather than engaging in the contest described above, this book reevaluates a number of fictions about the West, focusing on problems of classification and asking simple questions about why books that have much in common are often read in opposition. This study purports to be neither exhaustive (it deals with roughly a dozen works at length) nor exclusive (certainly there are Western texts that defy the ambiguous or unconventional readings that I offer here). But in providing the close readings that I do, I hope to suggest a loose template that other critics may bring to those Western fictions not considered here—a template that emphasizes a book's content over authorial intention or reputation and that stresses the dialogues occurring on the printed page over the supposed debates occurring between writers. The results of such readings may be political, after all, because they will suggest a literary genre more complicated than the simple binaries on which some contemporary critics rely. And given how the western has affected U.S. culture, to complicate our sense of that genre is by necessity to complicate our sense of ourselves as Americans. Explicitly, however, my interest is less in such extratextual connections than in the texts themselves. I take on the modest challenge of reading books that, somewhat like guns, have often been only as dangerous as the people who have wielded them.

The introduction offers some conventional definitions of the popular western, as well as a brief history designed to introduce readers to the genre and to the way it fits into the larger discipline of Western Studies. Before that, however, several important points must be made about the construction of this volume.

First, I use the words "frontier" and "West" almost interchangeably, pursuant to the settings of the books that I consider. Almost all of my subjects are set in an historical era in which the frontier represents the farthest westward expanse of the United States or its agents—hence, in which "frontier" and "West" are synonymous. It is important to remember, of course, that more than a century has passed since Frederick Jackson Turner declared the frontier closed and that, in the interim, a wealth of literature devoted to the West as a geographic region has been written. None of the novels considered herein, however, were produced after 1942, and even the ones produced after 1900 reflect on a time before the continent was completely settled, as per Turner's Thesis. My reason for choosing such books is simple: frontier novels have undergone critical scrutiny for almost two hundred years, beginning with Cooper. They are the books that have been treasured and trashed, distinguished and dismissed, by scholars, and even today they are the books that cause the greatest consternation in Western Studies circles. While not all frontier novels are popular westerns, all popular westerns *are* frontier novels, so it is impossible to talk about the ideological continuum that exists within Western literature without consuming a hearty dose of frontier works. And, frankly, it is impossible to talk about the impact of the western on American culture, for better or worse, without conceding the point that in the popular consciousness "Western novel" and "frontier novel" mean almost the same thing. I am not dismissing Western-region writing in any sense, as my use of Hamlin Garland suggests. But the frontier novel casts a long shadow across the field of Western Studies, forming a subgenre that both includes popular westerns and Western writing, and remains broad enough to offer the variety of texts that I need to make my points.

Second, I have limited my use of literary theory in this book, such that most "theoretical" items appear in notes in support of more general observations drawn from the primary texts. Obviously my notions of internal dialogue, multivoiced narratives, and indeterminacy owe a great deal to Bakhtin, among others.[20] But I have tried to eschew jargonized philosophical posturing for close textual study, writing what follows in unspecialized—albeit intellectual—language. Western literature, so closely associated with popular ideas about what it means to be American, deserves to be treated directly—in words that any literate person could understand and from which any interested reader could form an opinion about the subject matter. Perhaps I am too optimistic about the number of "interested readers" this book will enjoy. But like some western characters, I am skeptical of words that rely on elusiveness for their effect. Better to talk straight, even if an audience ultimately disagrees with what I have to say.

Finally, I will deal only with books here, no films. It has become fashionable in recent studies to combine the two media, viewing movies as a natural extension of the books that preceded them. But while movies partake of a certain cultural legacy derived from frontier novels, it is also clear that this legacy is extremely narrow, piecemeal, and too often one-dimensional. Unlike novels, films often lack ambiguity. The good guys *do* often wear the white hats, the bad guys black. When the hero struts down the celluloid street, there is little question about with whom the audience is supposed to sympathize. In fact, I would argue that it is our contemporary immersion in film and TV westerns—being accustomed to the simplistic paradigms of those media—that has caused us to read earlier Western literature in the single-minded and bipolar way that we have.[21] Granting again that some novels are pure pulp, most book westerns are nonetheless more complex than film westerns will ever be. This idea is particularly true for books predating 1940, before film had so thoroughly engaged the Western writer's imagination that he had little choice other than to reenact the mass-media version of the frontier in his books or to challenge that version. In this sense, the relatively recent development of Western Studies could be seen as the product of a slightly less recent wholesale cultural acceptance of the popular western myth. This is not to say that the West and its heroes did not strongly influence American cultural trends before the advent of film. But it is to say that film crystallized and codified the qualities of the western hero in a way that books could not, delivered that hero in a package more accessible and more easily consumed than a book, and marketed that package so aggressively as to ensure the image of Americans as cowboy-gunfighters throughout the world. The mythic West may have started with James Fenimore Cooper and been refined by Alfred Beadle and Owen Wister. But it achieved its pinnacle in the persons of Gary Cooper and John Wayne, the direction of John Ford and Howard Hawkes, and the public-relations machinery of every major Hollywood studio. Western film, finally, should be viewed as a genre unto itself, far more contemporary than many Western novels, and it should be read in conjunction with Western fiction only with a great deal of care and qualification.

Indeed, care and qualification are two features that should accompany any discussion of Western literature, especially when deciding how specific books should be read. Literature and history are not synonymous, of course. While critical study may complicate our sense of American culture, it cannot reverse the outcome of past tragedies in the West—turn industrial blight back into wilderness, revive animal species now extinct, compensate for violence against Native Americans and other minorities that often reached genocidal levels. But for all that, reading novels reminds us of what our best and brightest minds were once thinking about. It is to deepen our sense of the complexity of ideological debates occurring in the past, even if we abhor the practical or political actions that were taken simultaneously. Critical responses to Western novels should be more complex than having to choose between a conservative or liberal stance because, put simply, the way we understand those old texts says a lot about how we define ourselves in the present. Recognizing moments of overlap, interdependence, and hybridity in Western fiction (to paraphrase Kowalewski) places those works along an ideological spectrum rather than in two distinct camps. It emphasizes moments of cultural convergence as much as divergence. And it reaffirms the individuality and nuance inherent in each literary text. We are so accustomed to grouping Western fiction—as popular western, anti-western, and so forth—that it may be difficult to start viewing books as individuals again. But such a move will prevent the easy platitudes and invectives that critics launch from both sides of the Western divide. It will avoid casual labeling. And it will suggest a model for Western Studies, if not Cultural Studies, in the future—where diversity can be explored without automatic division, and where the things that draw us together are as important as the things that drive us apart.

ACKNOWLEDGMENTS

Thanks to my family—Janet, Lindsey, and Mom and Dad—who sometimes wondered when it would end.

Thanks to Cris Levenduski, for her good-natured advice and continued support.

Thanks to Seton Hall University, for its generous approval of course releases and a Summer Research Stipend that greatly facilitated this manuscript's production.

Thanks to Ohio University Press and, in particular, David Sanders and Nancy Basmajian, for their faith in this project and their patience (even when I did not deserve it).

And in memoriam to Ted Davidson, without whom I would have never begun this journey.

The Word Rides Again

Introduction

The "Origin"
of the Popular Western
and Some Themes

A myth itself, the Old West begins—structurally and thematically—in the many myths preceding it. Scholars have linked the modern popular western to portions of the Bible, classical epic, the chivalric tradition of Malory, Renaissance tragedy, the British romances of Sir Walter Scott, the frontier romances of James Fenimore Cooper, and dime novels of the 1840s and '50s, among others. It stands to reason, then, that any professed "origin" for the popular western is both approximate and arbitrary, designed to emphasize a particular viewpoint: the western's relation to uniquely American patterns of development versus the western's place in a cultural evolution dating from the dawn of European civilization; the close ties of popular western themes to isolated American political trends versus a view of the western as symptomatic of governmental strategies since the founding of European colonies. Such linkages have their place, of course, but none can be called definitive. The western partakes of all of these earlier traditions, knowingly or not, and its evolution involves a scheme of literary borrowing and echoing as complex as that of any other genre.

But while it is impossible to say for sure when the western began as a form, or what cultural forces gave it earliest rise, scholars largely agree on when it became central to American cultural life—or at least when Americans began to consciously view the western myth as the most defining element of their cultural history. The period between 1890 and 1910 oversaw the codification of the western myth in the public imagination.[1] During these years, radical shifts in American demographics, the political and military landscape, literary and artistic values, and gender and race relations combined to produce a climate ideal for the rise of the western.

The End of the Frontier

At the center of the 1890s "westernist" movement was Frederick Jackson Turner. A relatively unknown history professor before 1893, Turner would produce what has commonly been called the Frontier Thesis—or Turner's Thesis—a phrase variously used by critics to mean a simple idea about the importance of the West in American history, a slightly more complex idea about land use on the frontier, or the four-hundred-odd page book in which both of these ideas are contained and on which Turner would base the majority of his career. Most simply, Turner was the first among several prominent historians (many of them his students) to argue that American history had been governed less by frictions between North and South—as was commonly believed—than by the existence of a frontier and its gradual movement westward. As Turner contended, the availability of an unending supply of "free land" at the frontier provided sustenance first to poorer people who emigrated from the East to settle it—and then to the entire nation in the form of an agrarian-based economy that kept America both well-fed and economically self-reliant.[2]

More importantly, the character of the farmers who settled that frontier —courageous, independent, and self-sufficient—acted as a touchstone for American values as the country rose to international prominence. While cities of the eastern seaboard slowly evolved to resemble cities in Europe (replete with their "cosmopolitan" values and vices), there were always hard-working men and women at the frontier to remind the government, the media, and other public-policy makers of what differentiated America from Europe: the purity of its democracy, its commitment to universal human equality, and its unerring emphasis on the individual's right to define his own future.[3] Turner envisioned a nation where any man worth his salt could go to the frontier and succeed by his own devices, a scenario impossible in Europe where all of the desirable land had been effectively used up. As he writes,

> In short, at the frontier the environment is at first too strong for the man. He must accept the conditions which it furnishes, or perish, and so he fits himself into the Indian clearings and follows the Indian trails. Little by little, he transforms the wilderness, but the outcome is not the old Europe, not simply the development of Germanic germs, any more than the first phenomenon was a case of reversion to the Germanic mark. The fact is, that here is a new product that is American. (4)

For Turner, independence was an idea rendered in largely economic terms. Because land at the frontier was free, the new settlers—regardless of their various backgrounds—could all restart their lives on equal footing, struggling against the same landscape to create civilization. European issues of class (defined for centuries in terms of land ownership, lineage, and money) would cease to exist at the frontier, because abundant land was available to whomever was willing to take it and because a social pedigree meant very little to marauding Indians, inhospitable weather, or land in need of cultivating. Finally, Turner's frontier was a place that necessitated a new kind of order simply for survival's sake; it was a place where American ideals of democracy, egalitarianism, and self-reliance not only could but also had to be put into practice.

Lost in this romantic rhetoric was a more ambiguous reality. In order to accentuate the positive aspects of the frontier, Turner often overlooked its more egregious problems. While acknowledging that white settlement had required Indian removal, for instance, Turner referred to the process obliquely as "the Indian problem" and often examined the frontier after such dispossession had occurred, with "the frontier army post, serving to protect the settlers from the Indians" (16).[4] He downplayed the fact that much of the West's finest land had been claimed by the railroads, corporations, and land barons. He tacitly endorsed the processes that pitted settlers against one another, often violently, as they made their land claims (moreover, he ignored the issues of fraud and theft that were rampant during mass settlements, especially land or mining rushes). And despite his belief that slavery played an important role in the frontier's development, he never quite grasped the irony created by his theoretical paean to individual freedom juxtaposed against the residual oppression of African Americans in reality.[5]

But despite its defects, Turner's Thesis accounted for much of the complexity of American history in straightforward fashion, and its oversights regarding race were largely ignored by an audience whose cultural assumptions paralleled Turner's own. Turner presented a version of several historic frontiers in which European Americans from various national, ethnic, and class backgrounds had worked toward the common goal of creating a new life—personal and civic—for themselves. It was a model that not only played on the ideal of a "composite nationality for the American people" (22) but also that, untroubled by the specter of race, approximated many immigrants' experiences. Turner was even quick to recognize the drawbacks of the frontier ethos, namely that "the democracy born of free land, strong in selfishness and individualism, intolerant of administrative experience and education, and pressing individual liberty beyond its proper bounds" (32), often bred individuals who were reluctant to submit to the democratic will. In his defense, however, Turner noted the way that education and religion had naturally tamed these excesses in areas of the country where "civilization" had been long established. His conclusion was that, given time, all parts of America—even those most recently frontier—would revert to a natural brand of order, and individuals incapable of following society's rules would either die off, be incarcerated, or depart for foreign places that more closely resembled the less restrictive frontier for which they yearned.

In fact, if Turner recognized any serious problem with the frontier, it was a simple matter of demographics. His famous thesis was first presented at the Chicago World's Exposition of 1893, only three years after the U.S. government had declared the frontier officially closed. As the Superintendent of the Census wrote,

> Up to and including 1890 the country had a frontier of settlement, but at present the unsettled area has been so broken into by isolated bodies of settlement that there can hardly be said to be a frontier line. In the discussion of its extent, its westward movement, etc., it can not, therefore, any longer have a place in the census reports.[6]

But the literal exhaustion of the frontier did not deter Turner. Instead, he attempted to enshrine the frontier as a set of guiding, even mythic, principles that could be conveyed to successive generations. His idea held that the moralities and social structures of the frontier could be preserved in theory and taught at American universities as a model for training future leaders. While this vision did not literally come to pass, it underscored the point that the frontier (particularly its last bastion, the West) had been removed from the realm of facts, if it had ever really existed there, and handed over completely to the realm of imagination.[7]

It was in this last effort that Turner made his greatest contribution to Western literature. Whereas before 1890 Americans had recourse to journalistic accounts of the frontier and even to the reality of pioneer life itself, Turner's romantic history of the disappearing frontier installed it at the center of a debate that began to value interpretation over experience, myth over reality.[8] Granted the attributes of the frontier had always been embellished, even fictionalized, to serve the purposes of those who had a stake in the frontier's development.[9] But the inescapable truth remains that before Turner there had always been an actual frontier to refer to, while after Turner there were only textual sources about the frontier, rife with propaganda and mythologizing. Turner may not have been the first thinker to recognize the importance of the frontier, but he was the first to recognize it as a part of the past rather than the present. Fittingly, his theories were adopted wholesale by a number of writers who would become the first practitioners of the "pulp western" in the twentieth century. For if Turner's central point was that the frontier's existence had been the most decisive factor in American development, then his secondary point held that it was not only the prerogative but also the responsibility of American intellectuals to perpetuate that dying landscape in their work.

The Strenuous Age

Turner may have been the first person to "codify" public opinion about the importance of the frontier, but he was by no means alone. At the end of the nineteenth century, numerous American public figures in various fields latched onto the frontier as a vital symbol of national characteristics and values. Of these, three figures deserve special note because, despite the academic credibility that Turner offered the frontier, Frederic Remington, Owen Wister, and Theodore Roosevelt arguably did more to spread the myth of the frontier, both its good and bad points, than any other people in American history.

Turner, Remington, Wister, and Roosevelt are often classed together in Western Studies because of the contemporaneous and seminal influence that they exerted over the field. But even more important is the fact that Roosevelt, Wister, and Remington were friends who mutually influenced each other's vision of what the frontier had to offer. Remington and Wister, for instance, corresponded through letters much of their adult life. And Roosevelt and Wister had been friends at Harvard (Wister would later pen a biography of his university chum). After Wister's initial trip west, both Remington and Roosevelt encouraged him to return—in particular exhorting him to create a version of the cowboy in literature that the nation would take seriously. Wister felt rejuvenated in the West, and he began to see in the region a universally therapeutic property, the same property that helped Roosevelt to overcome the deaths of his wife and mother in the same year (1884) and to prepare for the political challenges that lay ahead. Both men came to see westerners as uniquely American individualists, though Wister more adamantly identified this property in cowboys in particular, making them into veritable supermen. In this sense, he was closely akin to his friend Remington, who held the same view of the U.S. cavalry.

Of course, none of the three had been born in the West. Remington and Roosevelt grew up in New York State, Wister in Philadelphia. Wister and Roosevelt, for that matter, did not spend extended time in the West until their mid-twenties. But that absence, in one sense, made them perfect representatives of Turner's ideal. Not only did their Western experience convince them that rugged individualism could be learned by anyone willing to embrace a "frontier" lifestyle; it also convinced them that such ideals could be transmitted textually—in a political speech, a novel, a painting—in much the same way that Turner had hoped to disseminate his ideas through public universities. Along with others, the influence of this trio in the fields of politics, art, and literature helped to insinuate the frontier into serious public debate. No longer the stuff of traveling shows and dime novels, the West became a serious business, a blueprint for political and cultural greatness.

Remington

The most prominent American artist to agree with Turner's ideas, Frederic Remington had already established himself as one of the preeminent painters and writers of the West by the final decade of the 1800s. Remington's rise to fame had been meteoric. A relative unknown in 1885, he sold more than thirty-seven drawings to *Harper's Weekly* in 1887 and by 1890 was one of the most sought-after illustrators in America. He exhibited an unparalleled gift for rendering the West in single emblematic moments, which he captured most effectively in painting and sculptures, despite dabbling in fiction. Like Turner, Remington had early recognized the inevitable decline of the frontier and set himself on the path of preserving it in art. Unfortunately, in 1885, the year he set to wandering through New Mexico, Colorado, and Arizona, the West had already become a landscape starkly different from the one that he believed himself to be chronicling.[10] The frontier had all but disappeared, adequate farmland and the railroads had caused a massive influx of settlers from the east, and the Indian wars had been fought and (at least from a federal perspective) won. So certain were United States prospects all over the West that William Tecumseh Sherman could deliver a final report in 1883 about his tenure as General of the Army that declared the West completely settled and safe from large-scale military uprisings.[11] While "spasmodic and temporary alarms," as Sherman put it, would continue to trouble the country into the next decade (most notably, the Ghost Dance episodes of 1890 and the Wounded Knee Massacre), his belief that the United States was now in undisputed control of the continent proved accurate. The West that Remington encountered on his trip in 1885 was a somewhat pale shadow of the West that Sherman had been dispatched fifteen years earlier to conquer, and while the landscape was hardly developed in full, neither was it the combination of blood and guts, romantic adversaries, scenic wonder, and derring-do that Remington had imagined. As a result, he resolved himself to the task of not only chronicling the scenes he encountered but also extrapolating from those scenes into an earlier "strenuous age," simultaneously depicting events to which he had been only a partial witness (if he had seen them at all) and elegizing those same events as if to reaffirm their palpable place in American history and cultural lore.[12] His imagined subjects came to pass for one version—if not the single defining version—of what the West was and could be again, and his fictions were soon given as much public credence as more factual accounts.

David McCullough recounts a humorous though highly symbolic anecdote of how far Remington's influence went in defining public perceptions of the West. In 1890, Remington toured Montana, at one point joining several members of the Eighth Cavalry in their encampment on the Tongue River. Among the soldiers was Lieutenant Alvin H. Sydenham, an admirer of Remington who himself possessed artistic aspirations. As McCullough writes,

> One morning before dawn, Sydenham was awakened by a prolonged scratching at the flap of his tent. It was Remington asking for a "cavalryman's breakfast." Sydenham didn't know the expression. "A drink of whiskey and

a cigarette," Remington said. The story quickly made the rounds, to the advantage of Remington's already considerable popularity with the men.

To Sydenham, Remington was "a fellow you could not fail to like the
first time you saw him," and others would say much the same. Though
never a cowboy or soldier, never a good shot, often bothered by the sight
of blood, he relished the comradeship of "hard-sided," plainspoken men,
"men with the bark on," who loved the outdoors as he did and welcomed
his high spirits and fund of stories. Nothing gave him such pleasure, Remington said, as sitting about with good companions "talking through my hat."[13]

The irony of the scene is inescapable: Remington, the man with none of
the "cowboy's" attributes, who weighed close to three hundred pounds
and rode into camp wearing "yellow English riding breeches, and fancy
Prussian boots," asks Sydenham, a bona fide cavalry officer, for the "cav-
alryman's breakfast," of which Sydenham has never heard. Yet even more
ironic is Sydenham's quick adoption of the phrase, not to mention its
adoption by the entire troop. Life imitates art as the actual cavalry officers
allow their identity to be defined by not only a civilian but a poor speci-
men of the rugged survivalists which Remington purported cavalry troops
to be. Later, in 1892, Remington would paint a scene entitled "A Cavalry-
man's Breakfast on the Plains," which depicts a group of horse soldiers
preparing their morning meal and provides an interesting counterpoint
to Sydenham's story.[14] In this picture, only a few of the score of men portrayed are smoking, a bottle of whiskey is nowhere to be seen, and generous portions of meat and coffee are warming over the cooking fires. In the
background, a soldier carries a water bucket down a line of tethered
horses, while another salutes a caped officer presiding over the scene. The
marked difference between this painting and his remark to Sydenham
suggests that Remington's art was a highly opportunistic one, his works
profoundly affected by his intended audience, his world-view derived
from a highly selective (if not entirely conscious) blending of fiction and
fact, and reproduced, basically, through his "talking through his hat." Perhaps more importantly, though, Sydenham's reaction suggests the readiness, even the eagerness, of Americans to accept the version of the West
that Remington was offering them, despite their access to an often closer
and contrary reality.

As it had been for a century, the West in 1890 was defined through
symbols and narratives not always commensurate with the experiences of
its inhabitants. But the official closing of the frontier seemed to make the
public's affection for myth even stronger, their cynicism about the valid-

ity of tales like Remington's countered by an intense sense of loss over a
region by which they had defined themselves as Americans from birth.
The frontier, it seemed, needed to be preserved at all costs in order to preserve the nation, and Frederic Remington, despite—or perhaps because
of—his tendency to hyperbolize, was just the man to immortalize it "cor-
rectly."

Remington's artistic cause was helped considerably by his political
stances, which were violent and racist yet couched in terms of American
imperial glory and of the glorious characteristics of Anglo-Saxons who
had forged a nation from a wilderness. Such stances fell on sympathetic
ears in his native East, where the growing industrial economy was resulting in mass immigration by rural Americans and poor Europeans to the
nation's urban centers. More than ever, white Easterners felt threatened
by racial or cultural Others and distanced from the heritage of their white
ancestors who had "tamed" the landscape inch by inch. Whether or not
there was much truth to these self-images mattered less than the themes
they suggested—themes that Remington was more than happy to exploit
in his art. Like Wister and Roosevelt, he saw the Anglo-Saxon community in America growing soft, losing its sense of identity in the murky
waters of a capitalist and increasingly industrial economy.[15] His response
to this quandary was to hearken back to the heyday of Anglo-Saxon conquest, to celebrate the violent primitivism of the West as opposed to the
refined "peace" of the East, and to proclaim innovations in the art of warfare as the greatest accomplishment of whites in American history. He
celebrated Indians insofar as they offered a violent and militarily skilled
adversary, but in reality "his nostalgia for lost red savagery [was] really a
disguised lament for the loss of the primal, and hence 'savage,' essence of
Anglo-Saxon virtue."[16]

In fact, Remington's dislike of Native Americans reflected his hatred
of other groups, whose inclusion in society he largely blamed for the demise of Anglo-Saxon greatness. Consider, for instance, this excerpt from
"Chicago Under the Mob" (*Harper's Weekly*, July 21, 1894), written around
the time of the Pullman riots and describing the complex role of the federal soldiers sent there:

> Our statesmen fail to understand that soldiers are not police, and that
> police-work deteriorates troops. Soldiers only know their trade—that's
> fighting. . . . They should never be expected to associate with a mob, except
> after their manner, which is to get strategically near enough and then shoot.
>
> In consequence, the easy-going soldier mind out here has been strained

to its utmost. When infantry must walk through a seething mass of smells, stale beer, and bad language, as my picture indicates, they don't at all understand. The soldier idea would be to create about eleven cords of compost out of the material at hand. And again, the soldier mind doesn't understand this Hungarian or Polack, or whatever his stuff is; he will talk to a real American striker in an undertone, and tell him it is best to go home and not get shot, but he tells me in his simple way, "Say, do you know them things ain't human?—before God I don't think they are men."[17]

The Chicago riots provided Remington with abundant "evidence" of the detrimental effects of urban existence, specifically of the debilitating way in which city demographics necessitated the commingling of "incompatible" races and cultures. In a private letter to Owen Wister, he echoes this chief point of his *Harper's* article, only in far more specific terms:

Jews, Injuns, Chinamen, Italians, Huns—the rubbish of the earth I hate—I've got some Winchesters and when the massacring begins, I can get my share of 'em, and what's more, I will. . . . Our race is full of sentiment. We've got the rinsin's, the scourin's, and the Devil's lavings to come to us and be *men*—something they haven't been, most of them, these hundreds of years.[18]

Underlying the vitriol of these words is Remington's conviction that competition with non-Anglo-Americans would compel Anglo-Americans to be stronger in a physical sense than they had ever been—that is, as strong as their frontier ancestors. Alexander Nemerov describes Remington's belief in this way: "Even if immigrants endangered 'American ideas and institutions' . . . they also excitingly transformed the urban world, heretofore the place of feminized enervation, into a new kind of frontier."[19] Remington longed for a palpable replication of that frontier he had only rendered in fiction and art (but which to him was as "real" as any version of history). He longed for violent conflict between the races that would ultimately raise Anglo-Americans to a "renewed" martial readiness. And lacking the literal frontier, he saw American cities as the site in which such a contest could take place. As Nemerov continues:

If Chicago was a primitive place, Anglo-Saxons had an unexpected opportunity to rediscover the race's martial spirit. Various rhetorical stratagems were produced to continue the frontier experience—and in that way stave off the threat of a fully civilized (feminized) country. Mechanical engines were referred to in terms of horse-power. In a 1908 *Everybody's* article, workers on Manhattan skyscrapers were called cowboys of the skies. . . . An actual urban war in Chicago would have made a modern-day frontier. There was no more Hayes City, no more Klondike, but there was this jungle with its rivers of lard and "savage" inhabitants. Remington's Pullman coverage makes it clear that here, he felt, was a chance to fight again the glorious racial wars of the nation's past. . . . Like earlier frontiers, Chicago had become a place to develop Anglo-Saxon masculinity. (122–23)

In this way, Remington's depictions of the frontier became a call to arms sounded along none-too-subtle racial or ethnic lines. And his desire for "race warfare" was a quite literal one.

Remington's racism alone did not propel him to prominence in American popular culture. Initially, viewers were attracted by the style and subject matter of his art, with the cultural implications of paintings and sculptures becoming apparent only through a review of the larger canon of his work. Remington's art focused on *men:* usually white, often soldiers, single or in groups, and always in action. Most of the time the action involved fighting, with other men, animals, or the elements. It was this straightforward and relatively unchanging style that acted as the perfect vehicle for Remington's central message. The glory of the United States and of the Anglo-Saxon race that founded them was the product of a perpetual physical struggle in which white men destroyed the obstacles in their path. The terms of the battle were simultaneously personal and universal, for it was certain that whatever way the white soldier, hunter, or explorer went, so went the nation.[20]

Despite its questionable thematic tenor, Remington's technique of depicting white men involved in various rugged pursuits was intriguing, coupling his simplistic stance on racial superiority to representations of subjects as "free" of cultural restraints as they are of complicating background images. Remington's paintings and sculptures were evocative, forceful, exciting, alluring, and triumphant, especially to the male viewers who could fantasize themselves into the position of the artist's subjects. His art offered viewers a version of self: not a sweeping landscape which bespoke the "greater" realities of the West, but a close representation of vicarious individuals who suggested the potential of what each viewer might be. His art invited viewers to partake of the hunt, the gunfight, the pitched battle, the most elemental aspects of human experience, and to emerge victorious. His was an uncluttered version of white male strength, even invincibility, which in the ongoing angst-ridden and eco-nomically complex transition to an urban-industrial society offered many Americans the touchstone they had been seeking. Of course within this equation was an undeniable contradiction, for even as Remington invited viewers to partake of the Anglo-Saxon martial spirit, he did so by means of a highly static medium. Viewers were invited to *observe* the violence Remington valorized, not necessarily to participate in it. As Nemerov asks, "Was not the den- or gallery-bound examination of art as distant from the activities of an intrepid soldier as one could imagine? By asking people to look at art, of all things, Remington seemed to perpetuate the enervated social behavior that the example of the Old West was meant to oppose" (124).

Remington responded to such contradictions largely by ignoring them, believing that he was at least keeping alive some version of the Anglo-Saxon spirit in his audience even if they were not completely ready to act upon it. Naïve as this belief may have been, there is no denying that his art was infused with an intensity that invited an almost savage emo-tional reaction, an intensity Remington failed to detect in other artists' work. In one sense, he can even be said to have bridged the gap between painting and film, that burgeoning form whose valuation of movement and forward progress in a literal sense provided an appropriate artistic model for an American public which valued the same things. Even after he acknowledged certain advantages to Impressionism in the late 1890s, Remington's works, notable for their meticulous attention to detail, re-mained thematically minimal. If he did sketch in a background, it was a background populated by many of the same figures and structures that occupied the foreground. As Christine Bold notes,

> Many of [Remington's] studies of single horses, cavalrymen, or cowboys are given no background at all. Only in his later years, as the effects of Impres-sionism finally began to interest him, did he shape his background creatively. Even then, he was concerned not with detail or shape but with contrasts of shade, color, and texture. When Remington did fill in his background at all, he did it with figures of animals, men, or buildings, smaller echoes of the shapes which occupy the foreground of the picture, not with elements of a natural landscape.[21]

Indeed nature—that foreign entity with whom the frontier hero had to contend—featured most prominently in the figure of the horse, whose initial wild resistance to man suggested the primal values Anglo-Saxons needed to rediscover and whose ultimate submission demonstrated the triumph which a return to such beliefs would bring about. With Remington, nothing was allowed to obfuscate the active figures at a work's center. And in this respect, he differed radically from his contemporary Western artists, who either celebrated nature as a greater force than man or produced scenes more complicated in terms of their imagistic range or ethnographic import.[22] Such differences worked almost exclusively to Remington's advantage. By focusing on men in action, and by bucking the largely Romantic trends of Western art, he created a perfectly "boiled down" version of American existence, where the only thing that could hinder an Anglo-Saxon reconquest of the nation was the race's own resolve.

Wister

These sentiments were echoed almost verbatim in the writing of Remington's friend and counterpart Owen Wister, who shared with Remington a central belief in the power of the West to rejuvenate Anglo-Saxon greatness. Wister first traveled to the West in 1885 at the recommendation of a family doctor attempting to cure the young man's depression, much of which could be attributed to pressures placed on the twenty-five-year-old by his father, who required his son to give up artistic aspirations in order to pursue a more lucrative career. This patriarchal insistence—coupled with the rejection of Wister's first novel manuscript by William Dean Howells—only depressed the young writer more, and despite his voluntary acquiescence to his father's wishes (he became a banker), Wister's psychological problems began to take a physical toll. The West, however, seemed to refresh him, and it was on his second trip in 1887 that he actually began to consider "cowboys" not only as adequate subjects for fiction but as heroes of a uniquely American landscape who could restore public virtue just as Wyoming had restored his health. Increasingly, as Remington's art became more popular and Turner's frontier thesis received acknowledgment, Wister turned to the cowboy as a source for his art that earlier had met with only lukewarm success. In "The Evolution of the Cow-Puncher," an essay published seven years before his great novel, *The Virginian* (1902), he compared the cowboy to Lancelot, arguing that the range-riding icon was "a lineal descendant of the Anglo-Saxon knight-at-arms, a man in whom the rugged outdoor life of the West [had] brought out the latent courage, heroism, and toughness of his kind."[23] Such overtures to myth self-consciously populated the entire canon of Wister's work, for more than valuing the actual life of range hands (*The Virginian* is often derided as "a cowboy novel without cows"),[24] Wister took up the "self-chosen task to define the 'historic yesterday' through which the cowboy continued to ride."[25] And, importantly, he rendered this mythic history in narrative fiction. As he wrote,

> Why wasn't some Kipling saving the sage-brush for American literature, before the sage-brush and all that it signified went the way of the California forty-niner, went the way of the Mississippi steam-boat, went the way of everything? Roosevelt had seen the sage-brush, had felt its poetry; and also Remington, who illustrated his articles so well. But what was fiction doing, fiction, the only thing that has always outlived fact?[26]

Clearly Wister always recognized his work as deviating somewhat from reality; indeed he created it to do just that. His goal, like Remington's, was to render the West in such a way as to prove Anglo-American superiority. He once wrote, "[T]o survive in the clean cattle country requires spirit of adventure, courage, and self-sufficiency; you will not find many Poles or Huns or Russian Jews in that district; but the Anglo-Saxon is still forever homesick for out-of-doors."[27]

Despite his personal politics, though, Wister's fiction did not feature much overt racism or ethnocentrism. His design was to uphold the greatness of the Anglo-Saxons, and it was the literary form he created to convey such sentiments, as much as the sentiments themselves, that made his art so important. Although he wrote only a few works of consequence, *The Virginian* by far the most notable, Wister synthesized the styles and ideas of various writers who preceded him—Scott, Cooper, the dime novelists, even Remington and Roosevelt. And this synthesis helped to establish the basic tenets of the "formula" western as they have been understood through most of the twentieth century.

Two of those tenets were a belief in Anglo-Saxon indomitableness, as already noted, and its representation in a single archetypal hero. *The Virginian*'s first chapter is entitled "Enter the Man," a phrase that lingers throughout the narrative as Wister's protagonist either literally appears or is the topic of conversation in virtually every paragraph of the novel. Though the book portrays the Virginian at a variety of pursuits—from mundane activities like fence repair and storytelling to a vigilante lynching and final gunfight—the story overall can be divided into two basic parts: the Virginian's running battle with and eventual victory over his enemy, Trampas, and his wooing of the town's new schoolmistress, Molly Wood. In both pursuits, Wister reveals the Virginian as the perfect fron-

tier type, a man who can skillfully deploy a savage violence against his
enemy even as he champions civilization through his relationship with
Molly and his staunch defense of "domesticity" as the cornerstone of
white advancement. By painting his hero thus, Wister cut against the cur-
rent of more literary writers, who expressed their doubts about the ability
of violent frontiersmen to integrate into civilization. The frontier character, their logic maintained, was a savage being whose complete existence
was framed by his ability to contend with unmitigated nature, whether
the external physical world or the darker impulses of the human soul. For
these writers—the Naturalists especially—it was only a matter of time before the frontier male surrendered to the advance of an irrepressible domesticity, as does Stephen Crane's Scratchy Wilson in "The Bride Comes
to Yellow Sky," or lashed out against the world in the only savage manner
available to him, as does the title character of Frank Norris's *McTeague*.[28]
For Wister, however, the Virginian represented the best of both worlds.
Unlike his frontier predecessors who could not remain in civilized society
too long—Natty Bumppo who chooses to die on the prairie facing West,
or even Huck Finn who must "light out for the Territory ahead of the
rest"—the Virginian represents an odd brand of individual, raised in the
East, matured by the West, capable of surviving and becoming a leader in
both civilized and natural worlds. Richard Slotkin observes how "Wister
[saw] the primary achievement of the Frontier as the production of a new
racial type, selected from among the Anglo-Saxon 'democracy' and
trained by the frontier experience in the skills and psychology of command."[29] In this sense, the two plotlines of *The Virginian* are related
through the theme of the Anglo-Saxon hero's superiority on all fronts.
Molly Wood bends to the advances of the Virginian and eventually accepts him as her guide and protector because she senses the inexplicable
power that raises him above other men. He is *her* promised leader just as
he is the kind of man who will eventually lead the nation at large. Though
she cannot rationally condone the violence he employs, she likewise recognizes the one-sidedness of her "complacent" Eastern upbringing, causing her to advocate peace at all costs, which in the end is as dangerous to
national health as the equally one-sided and unchecked Western savagery
represented in the outlaw Trampas.

By uniting the best qualities of East and West in his hero, Wister
broke sharply with Remington's ideas about the role of the frontier in
American life. For Remington, the East represented the apathy and racial
tolerance that had begun to weaken America, but for Wister, the East offered an ingredient of moderation, the civilizing influence that prevented

a Western leader from operating completely unchecked (as does the morally bankrupt Trampas). In this regard, Wister more properly adhered to the Western tradition as set forth in the novels of James Fenimore Cooper, whose hero is fundamentally committed to both wilderness and civilization.[30] Unlike Cooper, however, Wister had no trouble balancing the seemingly oppositional forces of frontier and city in his characters, a circumstance largely attributable to the time periods in which the two authors were writing. Cooper's frontier was a fact, an expanse of land that stretched from the Ohio Valley to the Pacific Coast, and as each section of that terrain disappeared, it was only natural that he should come to view the frontier as a landscape completely incompatible with the demands of civilization. Wister's frontier, by contrast, was contrived, a psycho-mythic terrain intended to ensconce "Western" virtues forever in the consciousness of American society. Where Remington believed in the possibility of the West's literal resurrection on various fronts, Wister understood that the West as he and Remington valued it could only be maintained through cultural artifacts: literature, art, song. And as with Remington, the absence of an actual frontier worked to Wister's advantage, for it largely precluded a literal referent against which his images of the West could be judged. The landscape he created was not supposed to be a place to which readers might have literal access; rather, it offered a stage where a largely stock cast of characters could (and would) perform a strangely American morality play time and again on a variety of cultural levels. This kind of West readily appealed to Americans regardless of regional bias, for it was not a locale in either a spatial or historical sense, but a set of guiding principles, a frontier of the mind that never changed despite the rapid national evolution occurring around it.

To ensure the appeal of his characters and themes, Wister took several ingenious steps in constructing *The Virginian*. The first of these was to make his hero an Easterner who moved west rather than a Westerner by birth.[31] The Virginian's migration, which takes place prior to the novel's beginning, suggests the largely Anglo-Saxon links uniting all regions of America. The Virginian is a character tempered by experience, shaped partially by each American landscape through which he travels: Virginia, Vermont, Wyoming. He is a Southern aristocrat without an aristocratic lineage, a New England intellectual whose arrogance has been bled from him through honest toil and sweat, an ironic Western democrat poignantly aware of (if rarely expressing in words) his own superiority to the world around him. He handles himself with decorum in social gatherings in Vermont and with a savage resignation during his final showdown with Trampas. In Wister's day, the Virginian seemed like the American Everyman, and it was certainly the strong identification of various regional qualities within him that first allowed a national readership to accept the Virginian as a version of itself. For Wister, the West would always be the Virginian's figurative home, for only there could his innate physical and intellectual acuity enjoy their most perfect expression. But even so, his trek through the American sociopolitical map and his ability to function with grace and certainty in whatever circumstance he finds himself suggest the transregional qualities with which the author hoped to endow him.

The Virginian's marriage to Molly Wood at the novel's end represents the culmination of these transregional unions, in terms of both geography and cultural sensibility. Unlike Natty Bumppo, the Virginian is not denied a mate, and the favorable resolution of the novel's romance plot symbolizes a negotiation of civilized and savage worlds that Cooper's protagonist could never manage. Aside from reasserting the Virginian's commitment to the idea of family, the marriage works generically to unite various literary forms of the late nineteenth century—in particular, frontier and sentimental novels. Molly Wood, appearing throughout *The Virginian* as a voice of rationalism, moderation, tolerance, and understanding, is a variation on the sentimental heroine, that character who arguably dominated American popular literature through 1900. Of course, *The Virginian*'s sentimental plot is somewhat thwarted as no real tragedy occurs to evoke the kind of pity or self-pity common to such novels. Trampas's death can hardly be mourned, and even if it could, the narrative moves quickly to Molly and the Virginian's nuptials in order to dispel any residual pathos and to reinforce the idea of victorious justice begetting social tranquility. Nevertheless Molly's presence acts as a lingering whisper in the ears of readers. When she questions the validity of a lynching led by the Virginian or protests the final gunfight, Wister's audience is compelled to recognize the tragedy of such scenes. In fact, Molly's voice is so prevalent throughout the text that John Seelye, among others, can identify her as the book's true agent of change, the character who compels the Virginian toward a life of familial order over self-serving anarchy.[32] Such a reading must obviously be balanced against the question of how much the Virginian actually changes throughout the text. Nevertheless, Molly does act as a conscience for the Virginian, much as sentimental novels strove to act as a conscience for the nation. The particular brand of sympathy which she brings to the text, coupled with the romance plot overall, provides *The Virginian* with a moral touchstone and feminine sensibility absent in many earlier frontier narratives. Despite the fact that the Trampas plotline is resolved in a fashion largely inimical to the tenets of sentimental fiction, Molly's presence invites female readers into the novel and even allows them, as Seelye's interpretation suggests, to posit femininity's civilizing influence as the most important "message" in the book.

Wister's skill as writer and mythmaker turned on his subtle ability to play off opposing cultural forces—East and West, men and women—in a way that managed to valorize whichever side a particular reader favored. In part, this ability stemmed from his own divided loyalties on the question of which region or regional character was best suited to lead the nation. Despite the admirable skill with which Wister drew his protagonists, many Americans might have found it difficult to believe in the apparent split-personality (ideological, geographical, and cultural) that his theory of leadership required had it not been for a growing population of actual Americans cut from the same cloth as the Virginian. Mostly politicians and business leaders, these men had been born and raised in the East but traveled to the West at an early age in order to experience the kind of vitality and raw power celebrated in fiction, art, even journalism of the day. Their imperial vision of the world, and of America's central place in it, was profoundly influenced by their embrace of the indomitable Western spirit, an outlook espoused no more vigorously than in the statements of that most accomplished transregional citizen, Theodore Roosevelt.

Roosevelt

Roosevelt was the first among his associates to spend an extended period "out West." An accomplished scholar and politician at an early age—by twenty-three he had been elected to the New York State Assembly and published his first book with G. P. Putnam's Sons—he nonetheless retreated in 1884 to a family ranch in North Dakota, consumed with grief over the near-simultaneous deaths of his mother and wife.[33] In the West, Roosevelt devoted himself assiduously to the alternate activities of working his ranch and writing, as Ben Merchant Vorpahl notes:

> He stayed on the ranch for about two years, writing more or less steadily, even while he also practiced the strenuous life that transformed him from a frail asthmatic into a robust outdoorsman. Three books came directly out of the North Dakota experience—*Hunting Trips of a Ranchman* (1885), *Ranch Life and the Hunting Trail* (1888), and *The Wilderness Hunter* (1893).[34]

Unlike his first attempt at writing—*The Naval War of 1812*, a historical study—the three books which grew out of Roosevelt's North Dakota experience were straightforward and uncomplicated, presenting a version of human progress that was subject only to a few "natural" laws.[35] Shirking the scholarly tone and complex analytical strategies of his first book, Roosevelt used events from ranch life as metaphors for the functioning of civilization at large, outlining a mostly Darwinist view of the world scented with a few idiosyncratic moral dictums.

Whether an attempt to eradicate his grief by dissociating himself from his former beliefs, or an honest (if epiphanic) change in philosophical outlook, the social and managerial strategies advocated by Roosevelt, especially in *Ranch Life*, operated on the simple caveat of being "hard, yet honest" and provided a blueprint for the governmental strategies that would follow him through the rest of his career. These beliefs recur in all of his later works but, in many respects, can be summarized by his 1899 speech, "The Strenuous Life," which I quote at length here:

> I wish to preach not the doctrine of ignoble ease, but the doctrine of the strenuous life, the life of toil and effort, of labor and strife; to preach that highest form of success which comes, not to the man who desires mere easy peace, but to the man who does not shrink from danger, from hardship, or from bitter toil, and who out of these wins the splendid ultimate triumph.
>
> A life of slothful ease, a life of that peace which springs merely from lack either of desire or of power to strive after great things, is as little worthy of a nation as of an individual. I ask only that what every self-respecting American demands from himself and from his sons shall be demanded from the American nation as a whole. Who among you would teach your boys that ease, that peace, is to be the first consideration in their eyes—to be the ultimate goal after which they strive? . . . We do not admire the man of timid peace. We admire the man who embodies victorious effort; the man who never wrongs his neighbor, who is prompt to help a friend, but who has those virile qualities necessary to win in the stern strife of actual life. . . .
>
> As it is with the individual, so it is with the nation. It is a base untruth to say that happy is the nation that has no history. Thrice happy is the nation that has a glorious history. Far better it is to dare mighty things, to win glorious triumphs, even though checkered by failure, than to take rank with those poor spirits who neither enjoy nor suffer much, because they live in the gray twilight that knows not victory or defeat. If in 1861 the men who

loved the Union had believed that peace was the end of all things, and war and strife the worst of all things, and had acted up to their belief, we would have saved hundreds of thousands of lives, we would have saved hundreds of millions of dollars. Moreover, besides saving all the blood and treasure we then lavished, we would have prevented the heartbreak of many women, the dissolution of many homes, and we would have spared the country those months of gloom and shame when it seemed as if our armies marched only to defeat. We could have avoided all this suffering simply by shrinking from strife. And if we had thus avoided, we would have shown that we were weaklings, and that we were unfit to stand among the great nations of the earth. . . . Let us, the children of the men who proved themselves equal to the mighty days, . . . praise the God of our fathers that the ignoble counsels of peace were rejected; that the suffering and loss, the blackness of sorrow and despair, were unflinchingly faced, and the years of strife endured; for in the end the slave was freed, the Union restored, and the mighty American republic placed once more as a helmeted queen among nations.[36]

Certainly no single speech can fully represent the complexity of Roosevelt's political career. But it is important to remember that "The Strenuous Life" resonated so clearly with the public of Roosevelt's era that its title was adapted to refer to the entire "Strenuous Age" of which Roosevelt and his contemporaries were a part. Moreover, even if the speech does not cover everything that Roosevelt was as a person and politician, it clearly demonstrates his belief in the frontier ideals of Turner, Remington, and Wister and his determination to integrate that belief into public discourse.

A closer examination of "The Strenuous Life" demonstrates Roosevelt's similarities to his famous contemporaries. Men are at the center of the text, in both its literal incarnation and larger implications. According to Roosevelt, men fight and kill, thus creating history proper (where "history" denotes a space both as narrow and as expansive as the battlefields on which personal virtue is tested and, accordingly, national regimes rise or fall). The mission and resolve of the individual are synonymous with those of the regime—"As it is with the individual, so it is with the nation"—signifying a symbiotic relationship where values are not imparted from one agency to the other, but are largely intuited and manifest to both sides. Accordingly, when Roosevelt asks his rhetorical question about who would teach a boy to value "peace," he genuinely expects an answer of "no one." Peace is a woman's virtue. And women, by implication, are consigned to the home, participants in history only insofar as they are affected by the interminable battles that men wage.[37] One of the interesting (and ironic) turns in the speech is the way that Roosevelt characterizes the violence deployed by men as guaranteeing the freedoms which, in turn, allow for the home's continued security. He paradoxically suggests that his denigration of "women's" values—specifically, his ideas that peace equals weakness, that the rightness of one's beliefs can be decided only through physical combat—is nonetheless the only stance allowing for "the home" (as the locus of women's culture) to continue to exist. As with Wister's Virginian, then, he manages to present his views of necessary violence and the strenuous life as, if not somehow sympathetic, at least not completely antithetical to women's lives and goals.

Beyond gender issues, however, the most important aspect of the speech may be the way that it presents violence not only as a means to glorious victory but also as a form of *duty* in which socially conscientious men must engage on a regular basis. Violence is work—*the* peculiar work of mankind. It defines humans as a race, or for those groups who deploy it in expert fashion, a master race. In this fashion, violence becomes an end in itself rather than simply a means to an end. Certainly Roosevelt's celebration of Civil War victories suggests that violence is usually directed toward some final outcome, but that outcome is largely incidental to merely participating in a life of toil, strife, and physical struggle—implying that when an individual or nation readily engages in such a life, triumph follows naturally.[38] The speech values process over product—or, put somewhat differently, recognizes the ongoing necessity of physical confrontation as a "product" in itself. The emphasis, to oversimplify slightly, is on violence for violence's sake, where the "ultimate triumph" is not a tangible or quantifiable worldly goal so much as a rugged existence that implicitly ensures the attainment of whatever personal or national goals may develop.

This position is very similar to Remington's and Wister's belief that the frontier West made men strong because of the survivalist lifestyle in which they were forced to participate. Importantly, Remington and Wister were inscribing that lifestyle within literary and artistic works, works which were an elegy for the passing of the Western landscape as much as a celebration of the values it could continue to inspire. If Wister and especially Remington valorized a system of "violence for violence's sake," it was not without some tacit admission that the most suitable place to conduct such a life was rapidly disappearing, if not already gone, and that in some respects the most they could accomplish was to "replicate" the values of this bygone age in art.

Roosevelt, unlike his contemporaries, sought to perpetuate the "frontier" lifestyle in literal fashion by trying to navigate the complexities of urban-industrial society in ways that Remington and Wister largely avoided. By recognizing the external world as a metaphor for a landscape of human values, Roosevelt was able to advocate a "Western" code of conduct without requiring unmitigated access to the frontier landscape itself. Moreover, where Remington and Wister tended to view the "cowboy" type (despite its different meaning to each man) as the solitary locus of masculine virtue, Roosevelt understood that the values figured in Western icons had always been representatives of similar traits in the general public. While the cowboy was a potent symbol, he was not the only incarnation of the masculine ideal toward which Americans could strive. Accordingly, Roosevelt preached an overall belief system based on frontier precepts in which the cowboy image played an important, but hardly exclusive, role. Roosevelt's design, as the above speech demonstrates, was to conflate frontier codes of conduct with a specifically American style of comportment, where the guiding dynamic of society lay in the ability of the individual man to rise or fall on his own merits, and where the most sacred virtue was his ability to shoot straight, in both an actual and a rhetorical sense.

The methods by which Roosevelt applied these principles in public life have struck some later critics as paradoxical, indicative of a misguided attempt to fuse a simple (if imagined) past with a complex present reality and, by extension, indicative of the failed nature of the frontier/western myth generally.[39] And it is true that Roosevelt's stances often contradicted one another. He relied heavily on corporations to guarantee America's military might, yet, at the same time, depicted himself as a friend of the lower class, spearheaded the regulation of numerous industries, and railroaded many laws protecting the rights of workers through Congress.[40] Also, despite his reliance on the American industrial complex, he was fully committed to nature-conservation efforts, doubling the amount of federally protected lands during his tenure as president. Perhaps understandably—yet suggesting a conundrum that impinged upon many of his initiatives—he sought to preserve what he could of America's Old Empire even as he busily engaged in forging its new one.

Most importantly, though, Roosevelt could never resolve his own feelings on race. Like Remington and Wister, he believed in the supremacy of the Anglo-Saxon and violently opposed anyone who seemed to stand in the path of that race's progress. Of Native Americans he wrote,

> It was wholly impossible to avoid conflicts with the weaker race, unless we were willing to see the American continent fall into the hands of some other strong power; and even had we adopted such a ludicrous policy, the Indians themselves would have made war upon us. It cannot be too often insisted that they did not own the land; or, at least, that their ownership was merely such as that claimed often by our own white hunters.[41]

Moreover, he made frequent reference to African Americans as "the backward race" and, in later life, developed a theory of "race decadence," in which he implied that miscegenation was causing the devolution of the American spirit. Nevertheless, his strong commitment to individualism and to the idea that all people should rise and fall on their own merits made it difficult for him to dismiss other races entirely. Albeit without some of the energy he devoted to other causes, he did advocate equality of opportunity and education for minorities in an era when "Progressive reforms . . . remained generally innocent of ideas encouraging racial equality or racial justice."[42] Perhaps in a grand cultural scheme, Roosevelt's political inability to handle the complex issues of race and ethnicity in turn-of-the-century America attests most thoroughly to the inefficacy of his Western doctrine as a blueprint for national development. Most scholars see him, at best, as an ambivalent figure in American "race" history,[43] whose aggressive foreign policy derived from his contempt for the non-Anglos whom he confronted. But even when he was preaching a doctrine of "race decadence," Roosevelt still proclaimed that "I, for one, would heartily throw in my fate with the men of alien stock who were true to the old American principles rather than with the men of the old American stock who were traitors to the old American principles."[44] Finally Roosevelt's stance on race seems to approximate both the best and the worst impulses of his age, a combination that speaks not to the immorality of his position as much as to the inherent contradictions of both frontier doctrine and official government policy that he could never resolve.

It is impossible to say exactly how Roosevelt should be remembered in American history, not just in terms of his domestic policies but in terms of foreign policy as well. In his eyes, the global destiny of the United States was manifest in the same way that Westward expansion had been manifest to the early settlers, yet even as his strong-arm style of diplomacy asserted American dominance around the globe, his attitudes toward Germany and Japan can be seen as a direct cause of American involvement in the two world wars and an indirect influence on certain kinds of gunboat diplomacy that exist even today.[45] Regardless of his larger historical legacy, however, Roosevelt gave to western mythology a literal enactment of a hero whom his artist friends could only imagine. An academic who became a voluntary horse soldier almost two decades after his first book was published, a moderate in domestic affairs yet a pathological hawk in foreign matters, Roosevelt represented the blend of Western ruggedness and Eastern intellect self-consciously desired by Wister and grudgingly accepted by Remington. Whatever its successes or failures, his political career, which spanned over three decades, forever engrained in the public mindset the fundamental relation of frontier characteristics to the perpetuation of a distinctly American way of life.

The West as Text

Just as Roosevelt's life cannot be completely defined by his feelings about the West, neither can the popularity of the West around 1900 be attributed solely to the efforts of the four men described above. Later critics have noted the way that America was ripe for a change at the turn of the century, and the western ethos—in books, film, and politics—offered audiences another way of seeing themselves, an alternative to the everyday fashion in which they had previously lived their lives. Certainly multitudes of people were involved in the cultural shift that elevated the western to iconic status.[46] But if nothing else, Turner, Remington, Wister, and Roosevelt were near-perfect exemplars of frontier idealism, and they distilled long-standing ideas about the frontier into philosophies of art, politics, history, and human relations that were simple, pragmatic, highly intuited, and readily available to both popular and intellectual audiences. Their influence over literature is profound, largely because the ideals and rhetorical strategies that they espoused came to dominate writing about the West. Even today, literary critics define the popular western according to motifs that crystallized in the Progressive era. While no rubrics are perfect, these motifs fall primarily into three conceptual categories: the idea of civilization versus savagery, the idea of silence, and the idea of right versus wrong.

Civilization versus Savagery

The notion of a contest between civilization and savagery is perhaps the most fundamental precept of the popular western. John Cawelti, the leading scholar in the study of the popular western, puts it this way: "Westerns must have a certain kind of setting, a particular cast of characters, and follow a limited number of lines of action. A Western that does not take place in the West, near the frontier, at a point in history when social order and anarchy are in tension, and that does not involve some form of pursuit, is simply not a Western."[47] Elaborating on this point, Cawelti contends that the western has to take place not only in the West but also in a location where the boundaries of civilization and savagery are starkly clear, where the fledgling town or settlement is juxtaposed against a barren, unsettled, often unforgiving landscape which is home to the enemies of civilization: bandits, desperadoes, Indians, even nature itself. The core characters of a western are themselves as stark and clearly delineated as the setting. They include "the townspeople or agents of civilization, the savages or outlaws who threaten this first group, and the heroes [far and away the most important characters] who . . . possess many qualities and skills of the savages but are fundamentally committed to the townspeople" (58).

The idea of a semisavage hero fighting for civilization is hardly peculiar to the twentieth century. As Cawelti notes, this protagonist featured in each of Cooper's Leatherstocking novels, where Natty Bumppo battles Indian foes despite his misgivings about the rapacious impulses of pioneers and his inability to submit completely to the institutions that they represent: home, religion, law. Cooper's solution to this problem is to have Natty push progressively west; having settled one frontier, he moves on to the next, where his half-white/half-Indian personality can find legitimate expression. In 1902, with no more frontier to resort to, Wister and Remington ended the hero's quandary with two novels published that same year. Wister's *The Virginian* unites the hero to civilization with his marriage to Molly Wood, a union that ends the hero's tenure as a gunslinging cowboy. Remington's *John Ermine of the Yellowstone* takes the opposite route: after a white man raised by Indians saves a U.S. cavalry post from the Sioux, he attempts to court a white woman, wounds her white suitor during a fight, and is eventually killed by the same cavalry he had sworn to protect.[48]

Whatever its resolution, though, the fact of conflict underscores the western plot. And as I suggested earlier, since civilization always triumphs in this conflict, violence in the western is not so much a means to an end as the end itself. This idea predates the eras of both the Progressives and Cooper, having its origins in the way that the first European settlers in America viewed the colonizing project. For those pioneers, the new continent required "regeneration through violence," an ironic notion in which martial conquest of the wilderness somehow returned people to prelapsarian grace.[49] In this scheme, the "garden" could only be claimed through violent confrontation with the "savage" enemy, where destruction of that enemy was a precondition of salvation in both material and spiritual senses. The wilderness, much as it was for the Israelites, became the test that early pioneers had to endure in order to assume the promised land of America and the mantle of God's grace.[50]

By the founding of the Republic, American intellectuals had largely dismissed the idea of the continent as a New World garden deeded to them by heavenly design. But the spiritual importance of nature remained a large part of the rhetoric surrounding political initiatives for how American land should be used. Franklin and Jefferson, among many others, strongly believed that America's economy should have an agrarian base and even that agriculture offered its practitioners a kind of spiritual invigoration.[51] Early on, then, there was not only an economic but also a philosophical mandate for settling the frontier and encouraging citizens to set up farms there. Even the nation's foremost intellectuals—the Transcendentalists among them—recognized nature's (if not agriculture's) importance and suggested that a close association with the landscape helped to offer Americans their distinctive character. Thus Turner, writing in 1893, did not so much invent the idea of the frontier's redemptive power as capitalize on ideas that had circulated in American letters for some time. Using these ideas, he created a demographic history of the nation that was also the story of the rise of agrarian virtues and a "true" brand of democracy evolving as the country moved westward. Then, aided by the frontier's literal close, he reinvoked the myth of the garden, gave it an economic superstructure, and presented it as matter of fact.

But Turner's Thesis provided no palpable goal for its adherents; there was no more land to be won. Thus his idea became to valorize the process by which the frontier had been settled, and if in his contemporaries' world this valorization assumed a specific racial tint (using the western to demonstrate Anglo-America's ongoing greatness), the issue for later writers was far simpler. Often, these writers did not even use Indians in their stories. The battle was between two white characters: a hero and a villain. While the criteria for each character changed from text to text, the drama in which they were involved remained the same. Lacking much philosophical subtext, the idea of violence for violence's sake became even more important. Having absorbed the notion that savage conflict was necessary for "progress," writers of westerns got so caught up in the idea of progress as unmitigated movement that they often failed to provide justification for the hero's actions beyond the stock elements of the drama itself.

27

The "Origin" of the Popular Western and Some Themes

Accordingly, the western hero became a man particularly adept at the deployment of violence, even if, as was often the case, he could never completely articulate his reasons for defending or opposing the people he did. Wister's Virginian, for instance, kills Trampas to ensure both order and a space in which he can raise a family with Molly Wood, even though Molly time and again tells him that such violence is antithetical to the cause he purports to defend. In reality, the Virginian has to shoot Trampas not to defend any particular position but to consummate the "hard life" he has chosen for himself. His commitment to violence is his commitment to the land, to his race, to the defense of his somewhat "misguided" woman, and to order. It is testament to his readiness for possibly similar future action, to his determination to lead the strenuous existence that will keep him strong. His killing of Trampas is thus a defense of everything for which he stands and of nothing, a largely symbolic gesture designed to play into whatever expectations his audience might have of him.

For, ultimately, all that his audience expects is violence. Whether the western hero kills in the name of race, or masculinity, or class, or nationality, it is the deep sense of wanting to lash out, to strike back, in a sudden and often uncalculated gesture of righteous anger, that attracts adherents to his cause. Per this deployment, violence becomes the fact of doing rather than being done to, the urgency of taking a stand, the idea that "though I may die here, I will at least be noticed and heard." As such, western violence at once represents a personal ontological proposition and an extrapolation into that proposition's universal significance, where the use of a gun fundamentally asserts individual existence and identity even as it offers a Darwinist "survival of the fittest" axiom to govern life. Without his guns, the western hero is not a hero, perhaps not even a man. In Jack Schaefer's *Shane,* the title character cannot fulfill his destiny to protect the Starrett farm until he straps back on his pistol. In Zane Grey's *Riders of the Purple Sage,* Jane Withersteen, despite her disapproval of the gunfighter's lifestyle, must return Lassiter's guns to him because he seems incomplete without them. To say that the gun's absence represents the hero's emasculation is not only, at this late date, a critical commonplace but also, when speaking of the western, a bit of an understatement. The hero's guns are more than a sign of his masculinity; insofar as he literally cannot exist without them, they are the sum of his humanity and, judging from the close association of western hero and national culture, a large portion of American identity as well. The simultaneously exhilarating and horrifying prospect of violence in the popular western is the way that life, in all of its complexity, boils down to a showdown in the street, the split-second flash of a pistol out of a holster, the death which ensues. At one end, ultimate triumph; at the other, ultimate loss. Whether the hero's life is proven by his willingness to risk death or his willingness to take another life is beside the point. What does matter is how the western strips ideological debate and rational discourse down to men with guns, and then strips those men down to the highly formalized, vicious confrontation—the gunfight, the pitched battle, and so on—in which they participate.[52] Violence may occasionally subside in the western tableau, and the fact that the western promises a society beyond the genre's characteristic savagery suggests its intended commitment to a peaceful world. But by the same token, the western never lets us forget the brutal spark from which that latter world issues, the moment of creation born out of destruction—the single small bullet piercing the villain's heart from which civilization, and often a very specific version thereof, can proceed.

Silence

Violence in the western is perhaps most important for its simplicity, reducing the complex dynamics of human intercourse to the either/or proposition—life or death—of the gunfight. Because the hero's actions seek to eliminate complexity, it stands to reason that he cannot spend too much time consciously deliberating those actions. As a result, the western hero after 1900 becomes a man of few words. The change is both pronounced and deliberate. In the Leatherstocking Tales, Natty Bumppo regularly engages in lengthy speeches intended to justify his chosen course of action. Cooper can get away with such moments because, for Natty, the frontier debate is rather simple, a contest between a "savage" existence—desirable because of its lack of social restraints—and a "civilized" lifestyle—a locus of material and spiritual progress. The debate is largely diametric, with the longed-for savagery always giving way to the more moral civilized course. The western after 1900, however, has to deal not only with this civilization/savagery split, but also with the complexities of turn-of-the-century urban-industrial society, the lack of an actual frontier, the presence of a variety of races and ethnicities within American culture, and a clearly defined version of "women's culture."[53] Thus the hero responds by not responding, instead letting his actions speak for him, implicitly afraid that he will not be able to justify himself in language or, worse yet, that his words will be misappropriated and used against him if he chooses to speak.

In the western, the hero's actions are their own justification. His deeper reasons, such as they might be, are largely intuited, designed to allow audience members to come away from the text with often vastly divergent, yet equally potent, senses of the hero's significance.[54] When a hero must explain his deeds, his specific intentions become clearer and less palatable to some audience members. As such, his "mythic" significance— or ability to appeal to many readers due to the philosophical ambiguity of his actions—breaks down. Granted, the uncertain properties of interpretation will always ensure the ability of some readers to glean whatever they want from a given text, but in the case of the western, the object is for *all* readers to come away with what they want. Language complicates this process, for at one level it forces characters to defend their actions in specific terms, and at another level the simple addition of words, of signs, compounds the number of mythic significations that readers must navigate and interpret. More words make it harder for readers to assume the easy, manifest, and self-evident directives that the western is supposed to be about. The ultimate fear in the western is that a hero will slip and say something that he is not supposed to, something completely antithetical to the beliefs of his audience. Language, then, is what truly scares him, for though a bullet may physically stop him, his myth can be undone only by words.

This skepticism toward language is poignantly rendered in *The Virginian* during the scenes surrounding the Virginian's lynching of several supposed cattle rustlers. Before the hero departs on his mission, he confronts Molly Wood, who expresses reservations about what they both suspect he is preparing to do.

On the day that the Virginian parted with Molly, besides the weight of farewell which lay heavy on his heart, his thoughts were also grave with news. The cattle thieves had grown more audacious. Horses and cattle both were being missed, and each man began almost to doubt his neighbor.

"Steps will have to be taken by somebody, I reckon," said the lover.

"By you?" she asked quickly.

"Most likely I'll get mixed up with it."

"What will you have to do?"

"Can't say. I'll tell yu' when I come back."

"Oh, I hope—please don't have anything awful to tell."[55]

A man's gotta do what a man's gotta do, the Virginian implies, and though Molly is horrified when she learns of his involvement in the lynching, she never speaks to him about it again, except to agree when several chapters later he sternly reiterates that he only did "what he had to." However she rationalizes it (the reader is never privy to her logic), Molly somehow comes to terms with the event and even tentatively condones the Virginian's actions. In the same sense, the reader is supposed to make a correspondent connection, accepting as justification for the lynching the Virginian's simple yet oft-invoked pretext of doing what one must.

That the Virginian directs his reticence toward Molly is of paramount importance. Jane Tompkins has noted how the western arrays itself almost point-for-point in opposition to the values of women's novels of the nineteenth century, where speech often involves a confession or outpouring of emotion. For the western hero, Tompkins argues, to speak is to admit pain, to let out feelings that he is not supposed to have, and to show weakness—hence to admit the power attendant upon exploring one's own soul, grieving, and commiserating. Speech, especially intimate conversation, affirms the importance of the domestic order and of stereotypically female spheres of influence. Even in a physical sense, Tompkins argues, words "womanize" the western hero, for they force him to open his mouth and leave himself vulnerable to penetration (which is the one fate—in the form of a bullet—that he is ultimately trying to avoid). Bullets have all kinds of figurative and Freudian counterparts, but Tompkins is at least partly correct when she contends that the hero is the character who is supposed to "penetrate," while avoiding that penetration himself. In the western, language can get a man killed or, worse yet, emasculated. It is simply the one enemy he must avoid.

Right versus Wrong

The idea of "right versus wrong" is perhaps the most obvious in all of popular western literature, yet one that receives surprisingly little attention. If the western's hero acts largely without having to think, it stands to reason that he is acting from an automatic set of moral precepts, even if those precepts change from text to text. Rhetorical strategies aside, people follow the hero of the western because of their implicit belief that he will "do the right thing." He may not act in perfect accordance with Judeo-Christian doctrine, for example, but then again he does not live in a perfect world. In fact, in a world that finds itself in constant flux (as the frontier necessarily is), the hero's consistency and honesty are prized traits. People follow him because, despite his imperfections, he represents a more direct and even-handed negotiation of the complex moral universe than any of his peers.

This is what David B. Davis means when he writes, "Above all, the cowboy is a 'good Joe.'"[56] But "good" may be the wrong word. In *The Virginian,* for example, the hero's participation in a lynching and a shootout, while morally questionable, results in changes that can be considered positive in several ways. Lawlessness is defeated, the valley is opened up for commerce and industry, Wyoming becomes a state (a part of the civilized world), and the Virginian and Molly live happily ever after in their new roles as parents and Western entrepreneurs. Whether virtue is satisfied at every point along the way or not, the ending suggests that the characters settled upon the best possible negotiation, sacrificing certain moral tenets for others and engaging in the kind of ethical give-and-take common to daily existence. Accordingly, I would argue that the real contest in the western is not between the pure concepts of good and evil, as is popularly asserted, but between right and wrong, a subtly different concept that balances ethics against practical and political considerations.

Wister's narrator implies this much when he writes, "Many an act that man does is right or wrong according to the time and place which form, so to speak, its context; strip it of its particular circumstances, and you tear away its meaning." Where good and evil are absolute concepts, that is, right and wrong are more situation-based and negotiable. Most characters view the Virginian's lynching of rustlers as right not so much because it is morally good, but because it appears to be the most efficient method by which Wyoming can develop into a viable economic and orderly cultural space. And in this regard, the novel is highly reflective of Western history in general, where the settlement of the frontier was never exactly a moral proposition. Though ethics were always implicit in American ideas of government, their presence was never allowed to infringe upon certain other "rights": the right to property, for example, or the pursuit of happiness. Even the notion of absolute morality begs the question: whose absolutes? whose cultural tradition? How do you balance, as in the white desire for territorial expansion and Native opposition, two ideas of "pursuit of happiness" that fundamentally conflict with one another? The answer, quite simply, is to fall back on political directive and, just as often, arbitrary standards of difference: race, class, nationality. More often than not, the plot of the popular western pits the land "rights" of white settlers against the "wrongs" being committed against them by Natives, Mexicans, big business, religious "intolerants," or outright "villains." The reader is asked to choose, then, not so much between moral antitheses as between ideological antagonists, with all the political, economic, and cultural baggage that such arguments entail. The hero of the western is not a moral archetype through and through. Rather, he is a figure who most perfectly embodies the blend of moral and practical desires espoused by the culture that gave him rise. He does not question his own actions because to do so would be to upset the delicate balance of ideas which he represents. He merely acts and, in acting, steers us on the "right" course, no matter how our purely moral sensibilities—when we actually stop to reflect on them—might object.

★

The western focus on violence, its imperative toward silence, and its recognition of conditional morality all represent ways of coming to terms with what, especially around 1900, must have seemed like an incredibly confusing world. The first two ideas respond to this complexity by ignoring it, choosing instead to boil human interaction down to a physical confrontation in which action, not language, does the talking. The last idea, however, seems to be a mitigation of the first two, a recognition that circumstances are never quite as pat as a diametric world-view would like to make them. As I embark on the textual-study portion of this book, I would like to focus on this last quality. While the preceding history was designed to familiarize readers with the characteristics of popular western writing, I would like to return to the notion that no single book—at least none that I know—embodies all of these qualities perfectly. As soon as one character in a novel lays out what seems like an unshakable world-view, another character comes along to challenge it. Like the western hero, novels navigate a constantly shifting ideological spectrum on which they rarely fall with absolute precision. Issues like race, gender, class, and ethnicity provide interesting lenses through which we can understand these texts, but there is no final criterion to decide how a book should be labeled or even understood.

My project, once again, is to demonstrate that there are a number of books read in concert and contrast with the standards of the popular western whose final identity may be less certain than critics have previously thought. The impetus behind this effort is to recognize that Western literature is not two starkly dichotomous camps of texts but instead a continuous range of writing united by its preoccupation with a geographic space and certain cultural tenets, regardless of how these variously play out. Needless to say, I am not defending the racism or sexism inherent in some of these novels. Rather, I am trying to shake the certainty—perhaps even sanctimony—of readers who believe that they can distinguish between books alternately engaged in "proper" or "improper" cultural discourse. While certain strands of popular writing may lend themselves to singular readings, the typical novel of the West encompasses many points of view; though in different measure, certainly, and sometimes against an author's wishes, multiple perspectives remain. As tempting as it may be to turn the interpretive act into a political or cultural litmus test, the binary oppositions arising from such attempts are intellectually finite, even self-defeating. Instead, by focusing on moments of cultural flux in novels, by noting the multiple oppositions (rather than *the one* overarching dichotomy) created by such moments, and by continuing to expand our sense of the many voices born of such oppositions, we create a full and multifarious version of Western cultural history—one that balances the many impulses of the field and, even if inadvertently, advances the democratic proposition of polyphony rhetorically championed by so many of us.

Hobomok

*A Brief Case Study
from the Beginning
of the Genre*

The canon of frontier fiction has expanded dramatically in the last
thirty years, owing in large measure to literary scholars who doggedly re-
covered forgotten texts (often authored by women and nonwhites) from
the crevices of history's subbasement. Those efforts, over time, have proven
nothing short of revolutionary. Where earlier literary histories never
thought to question the supreme role of James Fenimore Cooper in defining the frontier novel, more recent studies have pointed to a variety of
narratives whose popularity rivaled Cooper's tales in their day, despite
markedly different cultural and political overtones. Writers like Lydia
Maria Child, Catharine Sedgwick, Caroline Kirkland, and Ann S. Stephens
offered ideological counterpoints to versions of the American West (both
the landscape and its inhabitants) found in Cooper, Francis Parkman, and
many of the early dime novelists. In fact, while it would be too reductive

to say that what these authors provided was a woman's point of view, there is no denying that their fiction derived much of its power from a sympathetic and complex depiction of women's lives—a depiction that, arguably, led to more sympathetic portraits of other marginalized groups, Indians especially.

The existence of these narratives is crucial to one argument of *The Word Rides Again:* namely, that voices "opposed" to white male fictions of the frontier (so-called "traditional" fictions) have existed since the beginning of the genre and have, at least in earlier decades, enjoyed a cultural value roughly equivalent to that of their traditional counterparts. Given their recent recovery, such narratives seem most useful as a response to the hegemony of traditional frontier narratives, and that approach was indeed the one adopted by the majority of scholars writing shortly after the latter-day publication of works like Child's *Hobomok* (1824), Sedgwick's *Hope Leslie* (1827), Kirkland's *A New Home, Who'll Follow?* (1839), and Stephens's *Malaeska* (1860). As Judith Fetterley puts it, these initial readings created a "hagiography characteristic of the first phase of recovery, a hagiography directly proportional to the misogyny informing previous treatments of these writers and texts."[1] Early interpretations, in other words, were confrontational and often righteous, designed to portray women's writing as more complex and introspective than men's—more liberal regarding not only predictably feminist issues like the cultural role of women but also class and race-based issues like worker's rights, abolition, and Indian policy. The readily apparent argument was that, victims of oppression themselves, women novelists demonstrated an automatic sympathy for those people who likewise fell outside a mainstream cultural and political discourse that was defined largely as white, male, and upperclass. Often such interpretations involved the dual reading of "a dominant text and a subtext" (Fetterley, 493), which claimed that, despite women novelists' apparent support of the dominant culture, their work produced an encoded and complex undercurrent emphatically resistant to its more overt ideological posture. The frequent result, in critical terms, was the extreme partition of men's and women's cultural worlds (the classic "separate spheres" model), contrasting the conservative sexism, racism, and economic elitism of many male writers against the more embracing liberalism of the stereotypical nineteenth-century woman of letters.

The problem with this model, however, was the way it tended to idealize women's narratives, overlooking authorial stances that seemed blatantly complicit with the dominant "male" culture, ignoring interpretive problems in order to preserve an academic paradigm that insisted on bipolarism as a matter of principle. In response, the second wave of critics to address these women novelists often swung the pendulum back in the other direction, implicating "these writers and their texts in a variety of nineteenth-century racist, classist, and imperialist projects" (Fetterley, 492). Such divisions did not merely involve separate critical camps; per the evolution of critical responses, individual scholars were sometimes compelled to alter their own stances over time. Readings of *Hobomok* provide a good example. In her 1986 introduction to Child's novel, and even though she admits Child's relatively low "level of political consciousness on the Indian question," Carolyn Karcher still credits the book with "transmut[ing] the errand of conquering or converting the Indian into an errand of embracing his ways."[2] In her 1994 "cultural biography" of Child, however, Karcher is a bit more bleak:

> In short, despite its insights into the connections between male dominance and white supremacy, and despite its daring revisions of patriarchal script, Child's response to the call for an authentic national literature does not succeed in resolving the central contradictions of the American historical novel, nor those of American history itself: that white Americans win their political freedom at the expense of the Indians they exterminate and the Africans they enslave, and that they achieve their cultural independence by expropriating the cultures of the peoples they have systematically debased, devalorized, and deprived of an independent identity.[3]

In charting such shifts, Fetterley and others have warned against readings that "produce a false sense of coherence and . . . rationalize too readily what are clearly incompatible stories" (493), offering instead an interpretive model that embraces "paradox" as a means of probing those ideological systems which purport—like the white-male version of the frontier myth—to be unified and complete. This approach would seem to rely, at least in part, on the Bakhtinian notions of polyphony that I raised in the preface; given the complex interplay of voices which novels cannot avoid, it seems unlikely that any narrative could achieve the high degree of "coherence" required by separate spheres arguments. Such literary theory can be reduced, however, to a far simpler and seemingly obvious proposition: just because a book takes an apparently liberal stance on one issue (women, Indians, the environment, and so forth), it will not necessarily take liberal stances on every issue that it touches. This premise brings readers back to the highly individuated task of reading books one at a time; focusing on the fragile slate of cultural forces each attempts to balance; and recognizing that, however compassionate an author may be, narrative (and real-world) dynamics sometimes require subordinating one liberal impulse to another. For frontier fiction overall, the implications of this brand of reading are profound. Each text becomes a site of cultural conflict mediated by the various voices within the narrative itself; books do not possess liberal or conservative identities per se but handle the negotiation of specific cultural crises in (in)congruous fashion. In this scheme, it becomes possible to talk about the similar way that two novels deal with race, gender, or class without having to worry about the cultural categories into which the books fit—indeed, without having to pass judgment on the "final" status of a book or author at all. Paradox and internal dialogue, then, are not just features of women's frontier narratives (carving out an identity over and against the expectations of masculine ideologies) but of frontier narratives generally (carving out an identity amid the myriad cultural forces that interact and interweave to form any novel). Their presence at the beginning of the frontier narrative tradition—in writers like Child, Sedgwick, and Cooper especially—only highlights the importance of using them as a critical model that can be applied to subsequent texts, to provide a more unified version of frontier literary history than do oppositional models predicated on contemporary conflicts.

A Case in Point

Per Karcher's commentary, Child's *Hobomok* provides a useful example of why frontier narratives should be dealt with on a case-by-case basis, with particular skepticism directed toward readings that frame any text in a perfectly conservative or liberal light. Superficially, the novel promises to undo more simplistic depictions of "minority" characters— Indians and women chief among them—featured in earlier frontier literature. Set in colonial Salem in the middle 1600s, the novel's plot revolves around the relationship of Mary Conant, the daughter of a devout Puritan, and Hobomok, a local Indian chief. Hobomok has become a particular friend of the English settlers, going so far as to quash an Indian ambush led by his enemy, Corbitant, and to deliver the rebel sachems into English custody. He falls in love with Mary, who agrees to marry him only after her beloved, the Episcopalian Charles Brown, is banished from Salem and believed killed in a shipwreck (in fact, Brown has been taken captive by another Indian tribe). Brown returns three years later, at which point Hobomok agrees to divorce Mary—whose heart, he suspects, has always belonged to Brown. Before any of the white characters can stop him, the Indian retreats into the western wilderness to live out his days, with Brown agreeing to raise Hobomok and Mary's son as his own.

Hobomok's marriage to Mary, as well as his fathering her child, represents the book's most radical critique of a traditional frontier ideology, whose racism would have prevented such a match. Hobomok, the book notes, is an anomaly, and his union with Mary is made possible in part by his staunch defense of English civilization in the face of Corbitant, among others. Several English characters remark on his noble qualities, summarized by Mary's friend, Sally Oldham, who describes him as "the best Indian I ever knew" and claims that his marriage makes him seem "almost like an Englishman" (137). Hobomok, then, is not emblematic of his race but suggestive of its potential, a cross-cultural figure blending the best of English and Indian worlds. The rhetoric of the novel, moreover, often rises above the traditional vocabularies surrounding the "noble savage," evidenced in Sally's equation of Hobomok with an Englishman, a statement that starts to break down the bipolar assignment of cultural privilege and intellectual superiority along racial lines. Hobomok even acts as the standard-bearer of faith at times, his mutual commitment to the ideas of a Good Spirit and a Christian God often astonishing the Englishmen. "It is a shame on us," observes Mr. Conant early in the novel, "that an Indian must teach us who is 'our shield and our buckler'" (37).

Hobomok's position between cultures makes him more than a figure of compromise. In his rhetorical fealty to Indian ideals and his willingness to use violence to defend his beliefs, coupled with his commitment to defend the English settlements, he becomes an oblique version of the traditional frontier hero. His own racial identity does not undermine that position so much as expand the possibilities of who can occupy the hero's role. Where Cooper suggests through Natty Bumppo that the hero should be white, Child undercuts that notion with an Indian protagonist whose values—perhaps more than Natty's—bring him firmly into line with the most moral of the English settlers he seeks to protect. The commentary seems as clear as it is revolutionary: if an Indian can be a frontier hero (the most emblematically American of all cultural identities), then there is practically no limit to the possible benefits of cross-racial intercourse for all sides involved.

Child obviously intended to respond to Cooper when she sat down to write *Hobomok*. The opening chapter, set in 1823, depicts an imaginary male author introducing the novel to a friend, who lightheartedly con-

trasts it to Cooper's novels (and to the novels of Cooper's arguable progenitor, Sir Walter Scott).

> "A novel!" quoth I—"when Waverly is galloping over hill and dale, faster
> and more successful than Alexander's conquering sword? Even Ameri-
> can ground is occupied. 'The Spy' is lurking in every closet,—the mind is
> every where supplied with 'Pioneers' on the land, and is soon likely to be
> with 'Pilots' on the deep." (3)

Child's fictional author concedes Cooper's popularity, but just as quickly
makes an appeal for "his" book on the basis of factual accuracy. Eschew-
ing Cooper's "romantic coloring" and "rich imagination," *Hobomok*
promises to be a true "New England history," an end that is facilitated by
the friend's immediate offer of "as many old, historical pamphlets as possible" on which the action might be based. "Barren and uninteresting"
though it may be, the first chapter claims, the novel offers a more literal
rendition of American history than the fanciful creations of Cooper. And
this literal rendition provides a foundation for the larger cultural "truths"
regarding gender and racial equality that the novel is designed to express.
Hobomok's role as the novel's single frontier hero becomes even more
profound in this context. As the principal "heroic" representative of this
more truthful past, he not only affirms the Native American position at
the center of frontier discourse but also undoes much of the real-world
authority afforded to Cooper's more spurious champion, Natty
Bumppo.[4]

If the miscegenation and cultural role-reversal work to Hobomok's
advantage in some respects, though, they also have an insidious underside
embedded not so much in the story that is told but in the various untold
stories whose dynamics the novel seeks to obscure. To take these items
one at a time, while Hobomok's marriage seems to posit him as a reason-
able mate for a white woman, much of the novel undercuts that suitabil-
ity. Mary, for instance, agrees to wed Hobomok only after she believes
Brown to be dead, and the book repeatedly implies that her grief, rather
than love, is responsible for her quick assent to the match. Consider, for
instance, her attitude immediately prior to Hobomok's proposal:

> There was a chaos in Mary's mind;—a dim twilight, which had at first
> made all objects shadowy, and which was rapidly darkening into misery, al-
> most insensible of its source. The sudden stroke which had dashed from her

lips the long promised cup of joy, had almost hurled reason from his throne. What now had life to offer? If she went to England, those for whom she most wished to return, were dead. If she remained in America, what communion could she have with those around her? Even Hobomok, whose language was brief, figurative, and poetic, and whose nature was unwarped by the artifices of civilized life, was far preferable to them. She remembered the idolatry he had always paid her, and in the desolation of the moment, she felt as if he was the only being in the wide world who was left to love her. (121)

The "desolation of the moment," in other words, affects Mary's judgment, "hurl[ing] reason from his throne." And it is not only in "the moment" that the novel suggests her judgment was impaired. Well after the wedding, Mr. Skelton can report to Mary's father Collier's suspicion that Mary was "bereaved of reason" (133), and even the narrator reports that "[f]or several weeks Mary remained in the same stupefied state in which she had been at the time of her marriage" (135). Adding to Mary's heightened emotional state, moreover, is her belief that in marrying Hobomok "I do but submit to my fate" (123), a belief resulting from an incantation that she performed which predicted the Indian as her husband. Her sense of mystical determinism only exacerbates her emotional condition: "A broken and confused mass followed; in which a sense of sudden bereavement, deep and bitter reproaches against her father, and a blind belief in fatality were alone conspicuous" (121). She marries Hobomok, that is, not because she loves him but because she is crazy with grief, mad at her father, and unable to find an alternative.

Beyond the rationalization of the marriage, readers should also remember who most benefits from miscegenation in the novel. Mary, on the one hand, is ultimately able to wed Brown, whose Episcopalianism strikes her father as infinitely more palatable than a cross-racial union. Hobomok, on the other hand, is compelled to retreat westward alone, bereft of a tribal identity, practically admitting that a white man is not only a better match for his wife but a better father for his son as well. Writing in retrospect, some critics argue, Child may have felt she had little option other than to push the Indians into the wilderness (per historical fact), but it should be noted that this same feature is constantly criticized in Cooper's work as a statement of racial supremacy, the tacit belief that Native Americans give way naturally to advancing whites. Subtler still is the contention that, despite Hobomok's expulsion, his son remains behind as a hopeful reminder of the value of white/Indian exchanges. This argument is undone by Mary herself, however, who sees the boy in a less flattering light. When Brown broaches the possibility of their return to England, Mary replies, "I cannot go to England. . . . My boy would disgrace me, and I never will leave him; for love to him is the only way that I can now repay my debt of gratitude" (148). Far from a symbol of unity and redemption, Hobomok's son becomes a "disgrace," a secret to be cloistered away from the civilized world. Even Mary's protestations of love weaken after Brown's return; she likens her maternal duty to the repayment of a debt, a sign that white obligation to the Indians begins and ends with one individual, Hobomok's son.[5]

Not surprisingly, small items in the text foreshadow the ultimate failure of Hobomok's marriage. However domesticated he may be, Child suggests, the Indian retains a savage element encoded in the color of his skin. Several times, the author conspicuously juxtaposes his "love" for the English (including Mary) against his "hatred" for Corbitant, emotions that work in concert to ensure Hobomok's allegiance to Salem but whose contrasting tenor suggests an opposition reminiscent of more traditional civilization/savagery splits. Hobomok's hatred makes him an effective warrior, but at the same time that hatred calls into question his ability to vanquish his "savage" nature completely and become the acceptable husband that Mary deserves. This contrast between Mary's delicate sensibilities and Hobomok's more "brutal" ones recurs in the torch-hunting scene, where the Indians have invited several English along to watch them hunt at night by firelight.

> The arrow of Hobomok was already drawn to the head, when Mary touched his shoulder, as she said, "Don't kill it, Hobomok—don't;" but the weapon was already on the wing, and from his hand it seldom missed its mark. The deer sprung high into the air, its beautiful white breast was displayed for an instant, a faint, mournful sound was heard—and Hobomok stept forward to seize the victim he had wounded. As he brought it up to Mary, the glossy brown of its slender sides was heaving with the last agonies of life, and she turned away from the painful sight. (89)

More than Mary's squeamishness is at play here, for even as the deer literally confirms her horror at Hobomok's ferocity, it more figuratively becomes a version of Mary herself, the "beautiful white breast" pierced in the same way that Mary's chest aches upon consenting to marry. Hobomok becomes an assailant of sorts—of white virtue, of innocence, of virginity—and even though his action is perfectly understandable, it likewise inscribes him as part of a world that must always somehow affront Mary's own. Hands are symbolically loaded in this passage: Hobomok's hand closely identified with the inexorable (and expert) use of violence; Mary's hand unable to sway him from his intended course. In the wedding scene that follows several days later, hands will play an equally important role: the Indian witnesses raise their hands to salute the couple, Hobomok takes Mary's hand to lead her around the wigwam, and they mutually grasp a branch of witch-hazel during the ceremony. But none of these gestures can quite overcome the disjunction signaled in the hunting scene. Even Hobomok's mother recognizes that Mary is "sick" (124) before the wedding, "wounded" like the deer; the Englishwoman succumbs with "the frightful expression of one walking in his sleep" (125), a "victim" of circumstance and of Hobomok's resolve.

In another sense, it should come as no surprise that Hobomok's marriage falters given his position as frontier hero. As with Natty Bumppo, Hobomok is denied a mate because of his allegiance, however suppressed, to a wild way of life. Ironically, what first appears to be Child's radical reinvention of racial roles—Hobomok's installation as the traditionally white hero—becomes her reinscription of traditionally deterministic identities. Hobomok's final flight confirms the incompatibility of white and Native worlds as do Natty's recurrent westward retreats in most of the Leatherstocking Tales. In fact, despite intending her novel as a response to Cooper, Child manages to validate the essentializing vocabularies on which the Leatherstocking Tales depend. Even a noble Indian like Hobomok, the best his race has to offer, cannot purge all of the "savage" impulses that make his entry into civilization impossible. And, lest readers forget, it is often those savage thoughts that dictate his actions. Where Natty Bumppo is moved to defend the civilization that will ultimately destroy him because of his faith that civilization is morally superior, Hobomok's motivation may be far simpler. Early on, the novel notes how in Hobomok's "thoughts were mixed a melancholy presentiment of the destruction of his race, and stern, deep, settled hatred of Corbitant" (33), suggesting that Hobomok battles other Indians less out of love for the English than out of an abiding contempt for his personal nemesis. Confirming this reading, Corbitant ambushes Hobomok one page later—a bitter struggle that would have meant Corbitant's murder had not approaching English voices caused Hobomok to flee before delivering the deathblow. As in other frontier narratives, the model of empire is etched into the personal conflict of two men, both savage, though one serving the needs of white America. Hobomok is only fleetingly aware of the larger implications of his fight (the eventual "destruction" of the Indian), but even when that significance dawns on him, he subordinates it to the "stern, deep, settled hatred" by which he is motivated. His fight with Corbitant becomes the epic imperialist struggle, the inevitability of large-scale violence obscured by the more elemental contest between individuals— single men on whose shoulders, nonetheless, whole cultures rise or fall.

Indeed, Hobomok becomes a problematic character not only because of his ready acceptance of the English but also because of his complete disregard for the feelings of other Indians, including his own tribe. His conflict with Corbitant germinates in the latter's justifiable contempt for the English, even if Corbitant's bellicose posturing is designed to obscure his more rational objections and make him appear simply mean.[6] Corbitant lists his grievances during his first appearance in the book:

> Shame on you, Hobomok! The wolf devours not its own; but Hobomok wears the war-belt of Owanux [Englishmen], and counts his beaver for the white man's squaw. Oh cursed Owanux! The buffalo will die of the bite of a wasp, and no warrior will pluck out his sting. Oh cursed Owanux! And yet Miantonimo buckles on their war belt, and Massasoit says, their pipe smokes well. Look to the east, where the sun rises among the Taratines; to the west, where he sets among the valiant Pequods: then look to the south, among the cowardly Narragansets, and the tribes of Massasoit, thick as the trees of his forests; then look far to the north, where the Great Spirit lifts his hatchet high above the head of the Nipnet! And say, are not the red men like the stars in the sky, or the pebbles in the ocean? But a few sleeps more, let Owanux suck the blood of the Indian, where be the red man then? Look for yesterday's tide, for last year's blossoms, and the rainbow that has hid itself in the clouds! Look for the flame that has died away, for the ice that's melted, and for the snow that lights on the waterfall! Among them you will find the children of the Great Spirit. Yes, they will soon be as an arrow that is lost in its flight, and as the song of a bird flown by. (31)

Perhaps unintentionally, Child strengthens Corbitant's argument by basing it on an appeal to transtribal unity. Astutely, Corbitant has diagnosed the European vocabulary regarding race and recognized the way that it is concerned more with monolithic categories—white, Indian—than with subtle tribal distinctions. Thus, where Hobomok frequently advises the Salem leaders on the local Indian tribes—which are friendly, which are not—Corbitant makes his appeal on the grounds that the English see all

Indians as basically alike and that the settlers, for this simple reason, cannot be trusted indefinitely. His argument gives way in later passages to inarticulate fits of rage, a demonic personality designed to justify Hobomok's ferocious battle with him and subsequent capture of the rebel sachems. But in the single monologue that he is allowed, Corbitant demonstrates a remarkable prescience over the future of Anglo/Indian relations, and the novel makes clear that the other Indians in the uprising "had been wrought upon by [his] eloquence" (41). Writing in the 1820s, Child would have realized how much of Corbitant's predictions had actually come to pass, but if her design was to evoke sympathy for the Indians in her own day, that design was thoroughly undermined by the book's quick reversion to painting Corbitant as a violent savage rather than the savvy politician and smart cultural observer that he may be.

Lora Romero reminds readers how many novels "between 1824 and 1834" adopted an elegiac tone toward the Indians in order to square their observations of imperial practice with "a belief that the rapid decrease in the native population . . . was both spontaneous and ineluctable." As she goes on to write: "The elegiac mode here performs the historical sleight-of-hand crucial to the topos of the doomed aboriginal: it represents the disappearance of the native as not just natural but as having already happened."[7] Hobomok's departure enacts just such a fantasy, his fictional flight in the mid-1600s validating the white presence in Massachusetts in Child's own day. What is most troubling about Hobomok, though, may be his insistence on speaking as an Indian in certain portions of the novel (as when he insists on leaving at the novel's end) but as a "white" person in others (as when he refuses to consider Corbitant's objections to the English). By relying on the dual identity of the frontier hero, but eliding that identity with the doomed "vanishing American," Child manages to create a character whose language conceals any credible version of a native story except for the imperative—and in her eyes incontrovertible—fact of the Indians' westward exodus. In this regard Hobomok might again be read as a sort of tragic hero, a character whose skin color alone (for it's certainly not his belief system at issue) forces him out of white society and into the wilderness. Arguably, Child regrets the lack of alternatives for someone like Hobomok, who clearly deserves better. But one wonders, in the face of such logic, why she did not carve out some fictional space within the English settlement that would have allowed him to stay, validating his role in the new "civilization" and thereby validating the possibility of cross-racial interchange in Child's own day. This wonder only intensifies when one recalls Deborah Gussman's observation that "the historical Hobomok, a Wampanoag chief and ally of the English, eventually converted to Christianity and resided in Plymouth until his death."[8] Child's narrative, then, not only refuses Hobomok a place within civilization but must likewise alter the historical record to accomplish that feat. Whatever her purposes—and most critics see her wanting to return Mary to Puritan society as a more independent woman—Child selects the conclusion that ends worst for the Indians, a voluntary subordination of race to gender issues and, perhaps, an open embrace of the racial credo of the dominant society to which she was in many other ways opposed.

Implications for a Genre

I should note that Karcher and Gussman, though at less length, articulate most of the same racial problems with *Hobomok* that I do. But their purpose, subtly different from mine, is to celebrate the elevation of women in the text, with Child's treatment of the Indians as a side note. This dynamic is especially true of Karcher's work, even the later scholarship, where admissions of problematic racial representations seem largely deferred, downplayed, or reversed outright in order to demonstrate that Child—whatever her faults—was more sinned against than sinning. At some level, of course, I agree with Karcher: given women's position outside the cultural power structures of the time, Child's ability to fashion for her characters new and subversive feminine identities, especially through miscegenation and divorce, moreover in a genre recognized even then as emblematically American and masculine, is nothing short of extraordinary. But in the same breath, I am uncomfortable with any scholarship that seeks to minimize the Indian presence in *Hobomok*. Child uses Hobomok to benefit Mary Conant. Hers is an act of cultural appropriation as complete and one-sided as any in Cooper's novels. To ignore this fact is to endorse a dangerous brand of relativism that hinges almost solely on the personal politics of the critic.

Karcher would no doubt say that I am being too hard on Child. She would rightly point out that Child's feelings about the Indians evolved into a genuine sympathy in her later writing, in particular "An Appeal for the Indians" (1868). But it is important not to read that change in Child's attitude as being too great or revolutionary. Despite her political sense that the Indians had been unfairly handled by frequently brutal government policy, her sympathy did not alter her personal feelings about them or make their culture more attractive to her. As she writes in a May 1868 letter to Charles Sumner:

> I have no romantic feelings about the Indians. On the contrary, I have to struggle with considerable repugnance toward them; and something of the same feeling I have toward all *fighters*. War, even in its best aspects, is a barbarism; and sooner or later, the world will outgrow it. But though my efforts for the Indians are mere duty-work, I do it as earnestly, as I should if they were a people more suited to my tastes. They have been, and are, outrageously wronged and there is abundant proof that they are as capable as other human beings of being developed into noble manhood by just and kindly influences.[9]

The same tone is echoed in a July 1873 letter to Sarah Shaw, which Child penned after a June letter vehemently criticizing President Grant's Indian Policy: "I believe I used some strong language in my last letter. I hope you were not disgusted with it. I have no partiality for the Indians, as a race; but the injustice of our course toward them excites my indignation to an irrepressible degree; and when I see people so entirely indifferent about it, I get furious" (516). With "considerable repugnance" and "no partiality for the Indians, as a race," Child seems motivated by her horror at the government's use of violence as much as by her concern for Natives. Her position is likely more sympathetic than at the time of *Hobomok*'s construction, but there remains an uneasy suggestion that, at base for Child, white/Indian relations are a matter of saving white souls first, with Indians often an afterthought.

Such readings bring Child into line with more traditional frontier writers of her day, Cooper especially. While Cooper demonstrates a profound respect for certain aspects of Indian culture, his audience never doubts where Natty Bumppo's final allegiance lies. The connection of Cooper and Child might be suspect to some readers who, regarding the miscegenation in *Hobomok,* understand most of Cooper's novels to prohibit such relationships at all costs. For example, *The Last of the Mohicans* —that Cooper novel most frequently compared to Child—forbids the fulfillment of the miscegenation plotline by killing off Uncas and Cora, moreover burying them separately. Even so, I would argue that *The Last of the Mohicans* makes more conscious overtures to understanding an Indian way of life—however (un)successful those attempts may be—than *Hobomok*. And clearly, both writers are literary tourists, writing from a sense of the indigene informed as much by their own purposes for that figure as by the reality of that figure's existence. Writing about Cooper and Child as well as Catharine Sedgwick, Domhnall Mitchell has talked about the process, employed by most early frontier writers, of representing Indian characters in a historical landscape:

> This moment of reflection demonstrates what might be termed the conde-scension of retrospect: the writer looks back from the 19th century to the forest as a location for violence in the 17th century and allows for the possi-bility that Indians then might have appreciated nature in the way that New Englanders do in the historical present. The assertion of this quality of ap-preciation in the Native allows the author to imply a level of intercourse be-tween her society and theirs which is not physical but instinctive, and therefore before and beyond any other differences. But what we see hap-pening here is a fictional version of colonization: the forest is a property which once belonged to the Indians, but its ownership is now being negoti-ated and finally appropriated by the white imagination.[10]

For Mitchell, little separates the frontier novels of Cooper, Child, and Sedgwick, despite a preponderance of critical opinion that wishes to read Sedgwick, in particular, as a more enlightened author of Indian charac-ters. In truth, the apparatus for talking about Indians in *Hope Leslie* seems more sophisticated than in works by the other two novelists. Magawisca, the novel's Indian heroine, has no desire to enter white society, under-standing (like a less violent Corbitant) the racial strictures at play in the Anglo world. In addition, the novel takes an arguably kinder view toward miscegenation: mixed-raced lovers are neither separated as in *Hobomok* nor killed outright as in *The Last of the Mohicans* or *The Wept of Wish-ton-Wish* (also by Cooper). But if more racially progressive, *Hope Leslie* still adheres to a cultural essentialism that pushes all of the Indian characters, as well as the white wife of an Indian, into the western wilderness by the story's end, once again inscribing characters along largely racial lines. And if the critical tendency is to read Child and Sedgwick as far less brutal than Cooper, Mitchell is quick to point out that all three novelists still rely on an "equation" where "[i]ntegration is followed by the disappear-ance of the Indian as a separate entity" and "[i]ntercourse leads to the death [including death in exile] of the Native American character" (133).

All this is merely to say that the standards by which we classify novels like *Hobomok, Hope Leslie,* and *The Last of the Mohicans* may not be as readily apparent as some scholars suggest they are. Granted, *Hobomok* and *Hope Leslie* radically redefine American notions of gender roles, but their handling of issues like class or race friction is spotty, regularly leaning toward more traditionally conservative frontier values. Furthermore, the automatic comparison of Child and Sedgwick to *The Last of the Mohicans,* arguably the most "traditional" and masculine of the Leatherstocking Tales, may unfairly pigeonhole the rest of Cooper's work. Within recent Cooper scholarship, only *The Pioneers* approaches the volume of critical response enjoyed by *The Last of the Mohicans*—and even then it is a distant second.[11] Critical tendency has been to read *The Last of the Mohicans* as representative of Cooper's writing, suggesting that racial violence and imperial ambition form the core of his cultural design. Lost in such interpretations, however, is the fact that Cooper, who authored dozens of books, was famous in his day as a historian, satirist, travel writer, and social critic as well as a novelist. His works often lampoon aristocratic pretension and avarice (both at home and in Europe), warn against the excesses of individualism, and lobby for more sensible uses of natural resources and the environment. Even the novels comprising the Leatherstocking Tales cannot be read of an ideological piece. Where Natty Bumppo in *The Last of the Mohicans* is a violent avenger bent on defeating the Hurons, Natty Bumppo in *The Pioneers* resists the restrictive order of white society as embodied by Judge Temple, whose aristocratic elitism and commercial ambition inject a complex class commentary into the more basic opposition of savage and civilized worlds.

★

Finally, serious readers of Child, Cooper, and Sedgwick cannot rely on the easy oppositions that seem to exist between the novelists because —issue to issue, book to book—each author adopts unique progressive stances amid more conventional ones. Despite Child's revision of stereotypical ideas about gender, *Hobomok* still relies on a racial vocabulary that ranks Indians as inferior to whites. Despite Cooper's ongoing class-based resistance to American commercial ventures, *The Last of the Mohicans* employs a violent rhetoric of territorial expansion that vilifies Indians and minimizes the public roles of women. Whatever cultural ends they may or may not accomplish, however, these writers establish that frontier novels have always been a complex site of interchange, negotiation, and value-prioritization—dialogues that occur not only between separate authors, but also between novels by the same author or between different cultural voices located in the same novel. Contemporary scholars occasionally argue that the writers valorized by previous generations of scholars are at fault for our cultural notions of ourselves in the present, a situation arguably remedied by recovering the larger number of neglected books that give us a contrary notion of our historical selves. While such recoveries may problematize our historical self-image, they do not—as Child, Cooper, and Sedgwick prove—supply a bipolar alternative to the "transgressions" of more celebrated works. In fact, if anything, they make studies of the frontier and the West more difficult, compelling critics to account for the myriad of opposed cultural forces implicit in each text and highlighting the sophisticated and multifarious fashion in which cultural identities are constructed. Wistful critics notwithstanding, Child, Cooper, and Sedgwick establish that there is no pure origin of conflict in American culture, arraying the forces of progressivism and conservatism on clearly demarcated sides. It serves as a testament to the longevity and mutability of these problems—race, class, gender, individualism—that almost two hundred years after their expression in the first frontier fictions, American culture (scholarly and otherwise) is only now creating a critical apparatus that can escape the binary oppositions on which these fictions, however falsely, purported to rely.

"She war a woman"

Family Roles,
Gender, and Sexuality
in Bret Harte's
Western Fiction

By almost all accounts, Bret Harte must be considered a progenitor of the popular western in America. Despite the fact that he eschewed the calculated displays of violence central to other frontier texts, Harte's rendition of Western town and mining camp life provided the quintessential backdrop against which the struggle of the frontier hero would take place in many later westerns. Moreover, though his characters are not as stereotypical as certain critics maintain, they are largely foils for the "universal" battle of good and evil that later westerns underscore.[1] In Harte's fiction, questions of morality are usually settled by a contest of souls rather than a showdown in the street, but he ultimately arrives at the same place as other western writers, extolling the triumph of good over evil, maintaining a largely diametric and uncomplicated moral vision of the Western denizens whom he describes. Thus, while differences certainly exist between his stories and those of writers like Cooper or Wister, Harte's early contribution to the development of "some of our most venerable literary stereotypes" cannot be understated.[2] And his name, as one critic from early this century somewhat dramatically affirms, should "be forever associated in the annals of literature with the great foundation of the History of the West."[3]

Yet for all the critical attention that Harte continues to receive, scholars tend to have a difficult time incorporating his fiction into a larger history of popular western writing except through the very generic, and somewhat tenuous, links I have outlined above. This inability stems partly from his defiance of "frontier" convention, both in his liberal attitudes regarding race and in his rejection of earlier "western" literary models. In his newspaper editorials, Harte exhibited a genuine compassion, if not outright respect, for Native, African, and Chinese Americans—once having to flee for his life after writing an editorial that condemned the massacre of sixty Indians by white vigilantes near Eureka, California.[4] And in his fiction, he rejected the tenets of frontier literature as handed down from Cooper, engaging in frequent and incisive parodies of the genre. "Muck-a-Muck" (1867), his most famous send-up of the Leatherstocking Tales, makes Natty Bumppo into "the celebrated Pike Ranger of Donner Lake" who wins the hand of Genevra Tompkins when he kills a grizzly, a California lion, a wild cat, a buffalo, and a Spanish bull with a single shot.[5] Unfortunately, Natty also kills the story's "noble savage," Muck-a-Muck, when he mistakes the hair extensions which the Indian carries for Genevra's scalp. Devastated by his error, Natty calls off the wedding, and Genevra dies "twenty years afterwards, of a broken heart." Donner Lake, echoing the real-life misfortunes of the Donner Party, is deserted, and in an ironic twist, Harte reaffirms the Native position at the center of the narrative when he concludes, "Thus was the death of Muck-a-Muck avenged."

Nonwhite races, however, appear quite infrequently in the stories that truly established Harte's literary fame, those published from 1868 to 1873, including the first significant collection, *The Luck of Roaring Camp and Other Sketches* (1870). Consequently, issues of (non)ethnocentrism alone cannot account for his ambiguous place in the popular western canon. Rather, scholars have pointed to the sentimental excess with which he draws most of his famous characters: tenderhearted miners and prostitutes, pensive gamblers, naïve schoolmarms. The chief contention seems to be that, lacking serious realistic depth, Harte's writing never rises above piously humanist caricature, and, indeed, numerous critics have claimed that he was more of an imitator or parodist than original thinker or social observer.[6] Yet such arguments presuppose that Harte's design was simply to represent the external world, even though his compassionate depiction of other races suggests a very clear attempt to alter the nature of reality as popularly conceived by audiences of his day. Taking this social activism as my cue, I would argue that what critics have labeled sentimental excess is actually Harte's method of exploring certain hegemonic cultural paradigms taken for granted in other western narratives. In particular, the stories published around 1870 seem concerned with the structure of the family, questioning the usefulness of a single patriarchal order in which domestic roles are strictly delineated according to sex. This investigation leads to a critique of gender roles in society at large that, in turn, prompts an examination of sexual identity itself.[7] In his ultimate sympathetic depiction of both homoerotic urges and an explicitly homosexual relationship, Harte not only undermines the western convention of universal heterosexual monogamy, but also radically subverts the supposedly stereotypical characters he creates, stereotypes that both recur throughout his writing and serve as prototypes for much American literature to follow.

Using the western as a window into Harte's reformist sensibilities is particularly appropriate since the western is arguably the most stringent genre in American literature when it comes to delineating family, gender, and sexual roles. Per the tenets outlined in the introduction, this chapter assumes the western to be a place where "men are men, and women are women" and where this supposedly self-evident axiom translates into the nearly inviolate cultural inscription of both sexes. Despite the great deal of "male bonding" which occurs in popular western texts, I will read the genre (on the surface anyway) as an explicitly heterosexual space where men engage together in work, play, and sometimes displays of violence, while women are assigned to the home or the brothel to serve mostly as an outlet for male sexual urges (both reproductive impulse and assertion of masculine potency). Of course, my criteria are somewhat oversimplified, but what is important to bear in mind is the largely absolute dichotomy of gender roles which westerns tend to construct: men work in the mines, drink heavily, and fight off outlaws; women stay at home and tend to the family.[8] Sexual intercourse in the western, if present, always occurs between a man and a woman and is often designed simply to emphasize gender roles, to reiterate who is male, who is female, and how they should act together.[9] Naturally women in the western may vary somewhat, being either virginal schoolmarms or lusty prostitutes, but these incarnations are also highly sexually charged and seem intended to

reaffirm the western male's own (hetero)sexuality. One of the great fears in the western, then, is the breakdown of gender roles that, in turn, might lead to the breakdown of sexual ones. Yet as I argued earlier, this series of breakdowns is exactly what occurs in Harte's fiction, where Harte's early stances on the ambiguous nature of family roles lead to a more pointed attack on the cultural inscription of sexuality itself. Beginning with the well-known "The Luck of Roaring Camp" (August 1868), I will trace this development through several notable stories: "Miggles" (June 1869), "Tennessee's Partner" (October 1869), and finally "The Poet of Sierra Flat" (July 1871). Listed in the chronological order in which they were published, the treatment of these stories should be taken not only as the chosen sequence of this essay but as a fair representation of Harte's own progression of thought on these subjects as well.

"The Luck of Roaring Camp"

In a mining camp in the Sierra Mountains, a baby is born to one Cherokee Sal, "a coarse and, it is to be feared, a very sinful woman"[10] who dies just after giving birth. The men of the camp—there are no other women—must decide what to do with the babe and, after some discussion, settle on adopting and raising the child themselves. Christened Thomas Luck, the baby exerts a civilizing influence over the crew of blackguards and villains, and a newfound prosperity, moral as well as material, descends over Roaring Camp. Triumph gives way to tragedy, however, as a flash flood washes away much of the camp and Thomas Luck drowns despite the mortal efforts of one of the most irascible miners, Kentuck, to save him. The end of the story finds Thomas and Kentuck bound by death, "the strong man . . . clinging to the frail babe as a drowning man is said to cling to a straw" as together they drift "away into the shadowy river that flows forever to the unknown sea" (36).

"The Luck of Roaring Camp" was the first story to firmly establish Harte's fame as a Western writer and remains one of his most well-known and popular even today. It has been read by critics in largely diametric ways. Allen Brown, for instance, sees Thomas Luck as a Christ figure who arrives in Roaring Camp to "save" the community of men from their sinful ways, his death at the story's end symbolic of the sacrifice which, in Christian terms, must be offered to redeem humankind.[11] J. R. Boggan, however, sees Harte's story as an absolute parody of Christian values, notes the irreverence of both the events themselves and the way they are relayed through the narrator, and concludes that "the men of Roaring

Camp are no more regenerated, no more spiritually reborn, than is the Christ child in the person of little Luck."[12] Most likely, the truth lies somewhere between these two readings, for, as Boggan suggests, it is improbable that Harte's penchant for satire would have allowed him to treat the idea of a Second Coming in the Sierras with complete gravity and belief. But by the same token, it is dangerous to assume that Harte's whole intent in "The Luck of Roaring Camp" was to satirize the Christian excess of which he was so frequently accused and from which, throughout his career, he was never quite able to break away. The regeneration experienced by the members of Roaring Camp may not be as absolute or transcendent as Brown claims. But as they band together to become the "parents" of young Thomas Luck, the miners both learn to appreciate that version of family which they struggle to create and receive a kind of spiritual insight to which they have never before been exposed.

To keep for a moment with the religious theme of previous criticisms, I would argue that Thomas Luck should be viewed not as a Christ-figure set down in a world of sin so much as, in good western fashion, an Adamic figure released into the garden of the Sierra foothills, "that air pungent with balsamic odor, that ethereal cordial at once bracing and exhilarating" (29). His "bower" decorated "with flowers, and sweet-smelling shrubs, and generally . . . a cluster of wild honeysuckles, or azaleas, or the painted blossoms of Las Mariposas" (33) strongly echoes not only the literal garden of Genesis but also the bower constructed for Adam and Eve in Milton's Paradise. And like Adam, Thomas is reported to commune with the animals of Eden. As Kentuck once claims, "dern my skin if he wasn't a-talking to a jay bird as was a-sittin' on his lap. There they was, just as free and sociable as anything you please, a-jawin' at each other like two cherrybums" (34). Whether Kentuck's report is exaggerated or not, the image of Thomas's talking to an actual animal suggests his metaphorical role as tamer of Roaring Camp's beasts. Several critics have suggested that Thomas's presence only serves to reaffirm many of those violent and male-centric qualities that typified the camp before his arrival. For example, the gifts which the miners leave by his crib just after his birth—guns, a lady's handkerchief, gold nuggets, cash—all serve to "represent violence, objects of sensual pleasure, or mere monetary booty."[13] Yet as gifts, they are also things that the miners are giving up on Thomas's behalf. Thus if one Freudian reading posits the gifts as a sign of the men's hostile and libidinous ids, then their willingness to part with the possessions suggests a superseding ego-driven desire to suppress their "baser" impulses. To return to a religious reading, even the serpent is subdued when "Kentuck—

who . . . had begun to regard all garments as a second cuticle, which, like a snake's, only sloughed off through decay"—learns to appear before Thomas "every afternoon in a clean shirt and face still shining from his ablutions" (31).

Thomas's identity as Adam may be less important for its overt religious symbolism, however, than for its resonances of frontier tradition, where the fictional hero is understood to be a "new" social and political man struggling to create a version of civilization superior both to European society and to America's own Atlantic Coast out of which the frontier evolved. In traditional frontier literature, the hero is "a man with a gun,"[14] and his method of guiding the nation back into Eden almost always calls for a deployment of violence at which he is particularly skilled. Generally speaking, then, the traditional "Adam" of the frontier is somewhat savage, territorial, and implicitly nationalistic. Harte, however, tropes this version of the rugged frontier pathfinder by making his Adamic protagonist into a defenseless infant and, what's more, by maintaining that the route back into Eden is paved with the codes of sacrifice, kindness, and pacifism which the miners come to adopt. Of course, the traditional western tale hinges on the existence of a frontier in which the hero can operate, and as soon as it is gone, the hero's adventures are either transplanted to the next frontier or ended outright. So, too, with Harte's story, for Thomas can remain a babe only so long, after which he will cease to incorporate the perfect essence of innocence and helplessness required as a foil to the popular western hero's bloodlust and desire for conquest. As a result, the Genesis-like flood must come to destroy Roaring Camp, that Eden which in a world of transgression cannot remain idyllic forever.

Importantly, though, the flood brings with it the implication of rebirth, of a new spring (as when Thomas was born) just beyond the winter snow that causes the river to overflow in the first place. That rebirth does not depend on Thomas's own literal ability to rise from the grave in Christian fashion, as Boggan suggests. Rather, it reflects the internal struggle and conversion that would remain common to Harte's fiction throughout his life, where characters are redeemed not through the unconditional intervention of transcendent grace, but through their own self-exploration and commitment to change.[15] Kentuck may finally be called to his heavenly home by the Luck, but finally it is the realization of an earthly home that "saves" the other residents of Roaring Camp after Thomas's death. For Thomas is not Christ. He does not redeem the former outlaws either through his literal presence or through his final act of so-called sacrifice. Rather, what he offers them may be as simple as an alternative world-view, the possibility of family in more than a physical sense and of nonviolent intercourse even in the ostensibly consummate violent realm of Roaring Camp.[16]

Of course, the problem with viewing Roaring Camp as a version of family is that there are no women in it. Cherokee Sal, like Eve, has fallen victim to "that primal curse . . . which must have made the punishment of the first transgression so dreadful" (23). On the surface, then, Harte's story might appear to perpetuate the archetypically male western fantasy of a female-free space—not only where women aren't, but where they aren't needed either (though in that regard, I would both recall the miners' proposal to bring several families to the camp and suggest that the final flood and Thomas's death thoroughly quash any residual belief in a self-perpetuating male society). A more subversive reading might address the homosocial or even homosexual composition of Roaring Camp, but, again, I think the evidence for such claims is scant or, at best, less abundant than in other Harte tales. Whatever the nature of Roaring Camp before Thomas's arrival, the story proper always remains grounded in the redemptive power of the family, first as it binds the miners to Thomas—as best symbolized by the implicit quality of touch in Kentuck's oft-repeated "He rastled with my finger, . . . the d——d little cuss!" (27)—and later as it binds the miners to one another. The reason there are no women in the camp is not to posit female obsoleteness but, instead, to highlight the contrary. By having no women in camp, the men are forced to assume the stereotypical roles of both father and mother, defender and nurturer, and in so doing, they find their lives made remarkably more complete. Where traditional westerns tend to push stereotypically feminine qualities to the background (indeed, the "home" rarely features in frontier literature),[17] Harte's story plants them firmly at the fore of not only narrative action, but also cultural importance. Ironically what appears to be his slight of women on the surface, much as some of his miners doubt the "general virtue and usefulness" (35) of the opposite sex, becomes his affirmation of not only the importance of feminine qualities in a civilized society but also the necessity of their expression by males. The end result of "The Luck of Roaring Camp," then, is to unfix the cultural ascription of gender traits and duties. Finally, the story implies that society functions best when maternal and paternal qualities are expressed by both sexes in equal measure.

Or at least Harte implies that *men* would do well to explore their more feminine sides. Women specifically are never mentioned. But if the possible value of inverting gender roles is only implied in "The Luck," it is certainly confirmed for both sexes in "Miggles," published nine months later.

The story begins when heavy rains delay a stagecoach driven by Yuba Bill, an itinerant rascal of Harte's fiction, and its passengers are forced to take shelter at Miggles's nearby home. Forcing their way into the house, the passengers discover a paralytic invalid and set to arguing over whether he could be the Miggles of whom they had heard. When the real Miggles arrives moments later, the company is shocked to find that she is a woman. Through the course of a subsequent meal and several conversations, Miggles reveals that she is a former prostitute and that Jim, the invalid, used to be her best customer. Upon Jim's physical deterioration, probably from syphilis, Miggles retired to the country home, spending the "heap of money" he once lavished upon her and a considerable amount of effort caring for him (she refers to him a number of times as her "baby"). The story ends when the passengers push on to town the next day, but not before the Judge, whose generic appellation suggests his authority in such matters, leads the men in a toast, "Well, then, here's to Miggles—GOD BLESS HER!" To which the narrator privately responds, "Perhaps He had. Who knows?"[18]

Where in "The Luck of Roaring Camp" issues of gender and cultural expectation are somewhat subdued, they form the overt and almost complete basis for the narrator's thoughts in "Miggles." Even before the detour to Miggles's residence, he identifies the stagecoach passengers along gender lines, paying careful attention to the company's women.

The French lady on the back seat was asleep too, yet in a half-conscious propriety of attitude, shown even in the disposition of her handkerchief which she held to her forehead and which partially veiled her face. The lady from Virginia City, traveling with her husband, had long since lost all individuality in a wild confusion of ribbons, veils, furs, and shawls. (155)

Hardly an extensive description, these two sentences nonetheless present two stereotypical versions of femininity against which Miggles might later be judged: the French lady as a model of "propriety" and the lady from Virginia City as a model of vanity and extravagance, consumed by her clothes in a literal sense the same way that women overall (hence her loss of "individuality") are supposedly preoccupied with preserving physical beauty. Indeed, the narrator's choice to describe the two women rather than the nine other men on board suggests his notion of a female apartness, the necessity of differentiating the women not only from Miggles later on, but also from the men on the stagecoach before Miggles becomes a factor in the narrative. While his omission of the men cannot be read as a specific delineation of cultural roles according to sex, it can be taken as a mild foregone assumption of masculine identity. Because he believes that readers will automatically understand what men are like, how they look, and how they act (at least to an extent), the narrator sees no need to reiterate such qualities. Both his early descriptions of the party and his various omissions, then, foreground not only the subversion of a stereotypical female/feminine identity which Miggles's appearance will precipitate, but the subversion of his own male/masculine identity as well.

The narrator's internal observations aside, the cultural expectations of the company are expressed more forcefully when the stagecoach arrives at Miggles's residence only to find no one home. Several times the Judge entreats whoever is inside by shouting "Really, my dear sir," and more specifically Yuba Bill bellows, "Come out of that, Miggles, and show yourself! Be a man, Miggles! Don't hide in the dark" (156). The joke, of course, is that the men are the ones really in the dark about Miggles's true identity. And even after her appearance, they remain largely oblivious to the implications that such an identity may have for their own. As the narrator remarks when she enters,

> And this was Miggles! this bright-eyed, full throated young woman, whose wet gown of coarse blue stuff could not hide the beauty of the feminine curves to which it clung; from the chestnut crown of whose head, topped by a man's oilskin sou'wester, to the little feet and ankles, hidden somewhere in the recesses of her boy's brogans, all was grace—this was Miggles, laughing at us, too, in the most airy, frank, offhand manner imaginable. (159)

On the surface, the narrator's description posits Miggles in contradistinction to the two versions of femininity offered earlier. Miggles's beauty is natural and rugged, defying her "gown of coarse blue stuff" in an exact inversion of the way that the Virginia City woman's appearance is totally dependent upon the "ribbons, veils, furs, and shawls" she wears. Moreover, her "airy, frank, offhand manner" stands in stark contrast to the reserved and unflinching (even in sleep) propriety of the French lady. When Miggles darts "a quick, half-defiant glance at the two lady passengers" (159), her challenge is directed not so much toward the literal women as toward the cultural values which they represent. For she realizes that she is an alternative to the feminine norms of so-called civilized society. She is somewhat aggressive, self-made, and self-reliant, and insofar as she makes that identity succeed (after all, *she* is the one offering sustenance to the stagecoach passengers, not the other way around), she more than legitimizes that alternative femininity in both practical and cultural senses.

However, what the narrator's contrast of the three women obscures is the way that Miggles's debunking of her a priori feminine identity opens the possibility of her possessing a masculine identity instead. Indeed, the narrator's overtures to Miggles's beauty and his admiration of her "feminine curves" completely overlook the "man's oilskin sou'wester" (a waterproof hat) and "boy's brogans" (heavy work shoes) in which she is dressed. From top to bottom, in other words, she seems more like a man than a woman—and acts much the same, running two miles in the rain in order to catch up to the stagecoach at the house and, once there, compelling the men into a variety of domestic chores to prepare for dinner. Even dinner itself is further testament to her masculine nature, as the narrator unwittingly notes.

> The meal was a culinary success. But more, it was a social triumph—chiefly, I think, owing to the rare tact of Miggles in guiding the conversation, asking all the questions herself, yet bearing throughout a frankness that rejected the idea of any concealment on her own part, so that we talked of ourselves, of our prospects, of the journey, of the weather, of each other—of everything but our host and hostess. It must be confessed that Miggles's conversation was never elegant, rarely grammatical, and that at times she employed expletives the use of which had generally been yielded to our sex. But they were delivered with such a lighting up of teeth and eyes . . . that it seemed to clear the moral atmosphere. (160–61)

Importantly, not only does Miggles seem more and more like a man as the story progresses, but the stagecoach passengers seem more and more like women, growing absolutely chatty under Miggles's guidance, their masculine sensibilities pricked only when their hostess refuses to "yield" the supposed male prerogative of cursing. Despite the narrator's ongoing insistence on specific cultural roles for the sexes, the gender inversion reaches full pitch several pages later, after the men and women have parted company to go to bed. As the narrator reports,

> Our sex—by which, my dear sir, I allude of course to the stronger portion of humanity—has been generally relieved from the imputation of gossip. Yet I am constrained to say that hardly had the door closed on Miggles than we crowded together, whispering, snickering, smiling, and exchanging suspicions, surmises, and a thousand speculations in regard to our pretty hostess and her singular companion. (162)

The narrator's defense of his specific version of masculinity grows more adamant as he senses his assumptions collapsing, almost as though he believes if he speaks loudly enough he can negate the ramifications of Miggles's presence and the male response to it. But, of course, it is finally the narrator's own observations which best work to reveal his attitudes as mistaken and even laughable. His inability to make his "feminine" performance conform to the masculine rhetoric he employs more than highlights the potential viability of the alternative gender and cultural paradigms represented by Miggles and the inadequacy of the absolute distinctions on which his own system relies.[19]

Simply put, Miggles "out-mans" the men of the story and is even presented as a version of the traditional and consummately masculine frontier hero. A knock on the door during dinner reveals a half-grown grizzly named Joaquin, whom Miggles refers to as her "watchdog." Half seriously, she tells the men "you were in big luck that Joaquin wasn't hanging round when you dropped in tonight" and later explains that "he trots round with me nights like as if he was a man" (161). By taming Nature in the form of Joaquin (moreover, without firing a shot), Miggles proves herself as rugged and resourceful a frontier figure as any created by Cooper. She has, after a fashion, even "conquered" the neighboring Indians, who "do odd jobs" (163) for her when she is in need. Although the Judge immediately makes a comparison to "Una and her lion" (161), Miggles is not a version of those frontier Amazons featured in dime-novel fiction who, in most respects, might as well have been men.[20] The triumph of her performance is that she is able to balance the masculine and feminine aspects of her personality so that she *does* come off as more than Buffalo Bill in drag. Indeed, her implied conquest of the frontier is both more peaceful and more effective—in a phrase, more feminine—than any man's, and as with the citizens of Roaring Camp, everything about her, right down to her furniture which is alternately "covered with gay calico or the skin of some animal" (160), suggests Harte's conviction that men and women both need to express masculine and feminine traits.[21] The final point of gender inversion in the story, then, has to do with the "perfect sexual equality" (161) which the narrator understands Miggles to underwrite, "perfect" because equality is so absolute in her home and because that home functions so well under equality's influence.

Again like Roaring Camp, the home itself is presented in a less than traditional guise in accordance with the change in gender roles. Jim, after all, is nothing but a former client, a john, and Miggles makes it quite clear to the company from the outset that he is neither brother, father, nor husband to her. Yet that lack of a traditional tie does not decrease her devotion to Jim, as the company first suspects, and in some ways may very well *increase* it. As she tells the men after dinner, "And then, too, if we were man and wife now, we'd both know that I was *bound* to do what I do now of my own accord" (164). Jim and Miggles's relationship is based on mutual affection, not on the notion of obedience built into a marriage vow. Granted, in her ministrations, Miggles becomes the stereotypical whore with a heart of gold, and there is no little truth to the assertion that Jim's complete unresponsiveness prevents the reader from seeing how the two of them would interact under more "normal" circumstances (indeed, would the relationship still seem so idyllic if Jim were yet just another horny cowboy fresh off the range?). Nonetheless, Harte does offer a more traditional marriage in the figure of the Virginia City lady and her husband, who do not say a word to each other the entire story and "look away" whenever their eyes meet. Given the alternative, even the relations of Miggles and Jim before Jim's deterioration might be read as more positive, or at least more honest, than the forced devotion and subsequent reticence of other couples.[22]

And in the end, Miggles's relationship to Jim can be read in a variety of ways. In her role as comforter, she becomes a mother (again, she refers to Jim repeatedly as her "baby"); as provider and protector, she is a father or husband; as former lover, she is a wife (though even this identification is continually troped, for in washing Jim's feet at the end of the story, she reiterates her role as prostitute, only this time as the redeemed Mary Magdalene). Moreover, as if things weren't complicated enough, Miggles's unwavering attendance upon the "solitary" and "helpless" Jim itself recalls the failure of Roaring Camp to minister to that other Harte prostitute, Cherokee Sal, who dies in an environment of "isolation" and "loneliness." Just as Jim becomes a version of Sal, then, Miggles becomes an ironic inversion of Stumpy and Kentuck and the rest, men who are themselves partly inverted when they take on the maternal duty of caring for Thomas Luck. In short, the story does not simply alter traditional family structures and gender expectations but explodes them completely, and once again it is the characters doing the most demolition who are treated with the greatest sympathy. Even the men from the stagecoach ultimately recognize the value of Miggles's lifestyle. Not only do they call on God to bless her at story's end but also, in the narrator's final assertion, admit that He probably already has.

"Tennessee's Partner"

Unlike "Miggles," "Tennessee's Partner" on the surface may not seem like a narrative reifying alternative family structures, beginning as it does with the arrest of a notorious highwayman, Tennessee, who is brought to trial before a kangaroo court in the town of Sandy Bar. During the proceedings, Tennessee's former mining partner (never identified by name) arrives and attempts to bribe the court into setting the accused free. The gesture is made with such seeming naïveté and innocence that the court overlooks it and listens patiently as the partner tells of how he and Tennessee lived together even after the partner married and brought his wife home, how Tennessee ran off with the partner's wife, and how the partner welcomed Tennessee back into his house after the wife deserted Tennessee as well. The partner appears as the epitome of Christian mercy and forgiveness, a quality that the court does not share when it sentences Tennessee to hang. After the execution, though, the partner takes Tennessee's body to bury beside his home, an action that shames many of the residents of Sandy Bar into also attending the makeshift service. Following a brief eulogy, the partner insists on burying Tennessee by himself. And at the end of the story, when the partner lies dying, he cries out, "Thar! I told you so!—thar he is—coming this way, too—all by himself, sober, and his face a-shining. Tennessee! Pardner!" To which the narrator concludes, "And so they met."[23]

Linda Burton provides one of the more provocative readings of this story when she considers "the possibly homosexual relationship between Tennessee and his partner."[24] Burton points to the admittedly circumstantial evidence of how the partner refuses to fight Tennessee even after the latter has stolen his wife, and how the partner and Tennessee "live together not only before and after the previously mentioned marriage but also *during* the marriage."[25] Such accommodations, she suggests, make the partner's matrimony a cover for the latent homosexual desire felt by the men, who both attempt to assert their heterosexuality through a relationship with the same woman and who both, after failing, return to a mutually satisfactory domestic partnership with one another. This arrangement is so strong, in fact, that it becomes a kind of marriage unto itself, signified in the partner's taking of Tennessee's name (he is, after all, never identified by other than "Tennessee's partner"). And equally important is the kind of "wifely" devotion which the partner showers on Tennessee, first by offering to give up all his worldly possessions at the trial so that Tennessee might go free, and later by admitting during the eulogy that

> It ain't the first time that I've packed him home on my back, as you see'd me now. It ain't the first time that I brought him to this yer cabin when he couldn't help himself; it ain't the first time that Jinny and I have waited for him on yon hill, and picked him up and so fetched him home, when he couldn't speak and didn't know me. (48)

Furthermore, the rapid deterioration of the previously strong and healthy partner after Tennessee's death suggests that he is pining for a lost love, a love reiterated in his final words when he apparently rejoices at being reunited with Tennessee in Heaven.

Most critics have disagreed with Burton's assessment of the men's relationship, exemplified by Gary Scharnhorst's summary dismissal of it as "not very convincing."[26] Instead, Scharnhorst favors the kind of ironic reading offered by William F. Conner, who claims that the partner intends all along to see Tennessee hang and that "Far from simple, pathetic, and deeply loyal, Tennessee's deadpan partner is complex, clever, and hard-boiled in his dogged individualism and firm sense of frontier justice."[27] According to Conner, Harte intended to trope the expectations of his predominantly sentimental audience first by having Tennessee die, and second by slowly revealing the partner as a man out for vengeance rather than a stereotypically sentimental advocate of mercy. After all, the partner's testimony at the trial only damns Tennessee (seemingly by accident) as does the attempt at bribery, and after Tennessee's death, the partner hauls him to an "unpicturesque" spot and insists on burying him personally as if to complete the act of execution itself. The brief eulogy which enumerates the many favors the partner has done Tennessee is intended to highlight the severity of Tennessee's betrayal, and the partner's rapid demise after the burial is the consequence of his losing an object of revenge rather than an object of love. Even after the funeral, the retiring men of Sandy Bar cannot read the emotion in the partner's face when, at a distance, they look back to see him seated, perhaps crying, perhaps laughing, on the newly filled grave. The effect of Conner's ironic reading is twofold. First, it re-masculates the partner by making him the architect of Tennessee's downfall, an act of repayment for the symbolic emasculation which he suffered when Tennessee ran off with his wife. And second, in a larger sense, it makes the partner the pivotal character in the archetypal revenge plot of traditional frontier fiction, where characters assert their masculinity through calculated displays of violence and where the successful deployment of such violence signifies all other kinds of male, including sexual, potency. Tennessee's partner, then, is transmuted from the sentimental milquetoast that he superficially appears to be into a subtle, if idiosyncratic, version of the frontier hero, ready to take justice into his own hands through whatever means are available.

The fundamental problem with this argument, of course, is that it seems to fly in the face of the bulk of Harte's other fiction. In broadest terms, Harte would continue to produce blatantly "sentimental" narratives for the rest of his life, well after the popularity of such narratives had waned, threatening to leave him penniless. It hardly seems likely that a man stuck in such a productive rut would produce the very conscious, subtle tropes of both literary convention and his own fiction with which Conner credits him. More narrowly, even the stories Harte wrote around the time of "Tennessee's Partner" do not seem to exhibit the philosophical or cultural proclivities that Conner elaborates. Rather, as I have argued, the other tales that made up the 1870 volume of *The Luck of Roaring Camp and Other Sketches,* the title story and "Miggles" among them, tended to subvert the increasingly violent tendencies or strict gender conventions of popular frontier literature. Admittedly, Conner aptly notes that traditional readings of the partner make him into a model of sentimental excess, and it could be argued that the damning result of the partner's attempt to free Tennessee represents Harte's own conscious or subconscious recognition of the limited efficacy of sentimental ideals. But to make the jump from that mild assertion of doubt to a view of the partner as a symbol or even advocate of rugged "frontier justice" hardly seems justified given the context of Harte's other writing. Instead, if "Tennessee's Partner" intentionally challenges any literary convention, it is most likely that of the formula western narrative. In one of the story's more climactic moments, when Tennessee returns to Sandy Bar after stealing the partner's wife only to be forgiven and received back into the partner's home, the "boys who had gathered in the canyon to see the

shooting were naturally indignant" (39). Like the boys, the readers' anticipation of violent confrontation, of a shoot-out, is what the story refuses
to satisfy. When Conner cites Harte's self-avowed practice of using "sentimentality to mock conventional morality,"[28] what he disregards is the
way that conventional morality at the time of the story's publication
would have tolerated, even demanded, the partner's challenging Tennessee to a duel. The fact that the partner refuses such an imperative sets
him apart not only from the citizens of Sandy Bar who later carry out "the
weak and foolish deed" (45) of lynching, but also from the growing mass
of dime-novel adherents who would have expected no less.

Of course, such a reading firmly reinscribes "Tennessee's Partner" as a
tale of "brotherly love," which is the traditional approach critics have
taken toward it.[29] But having acknowledged this, I would like to return to
Burton's assessment of the homosexual (or at least homosocial) aspects of
the text, for it seems to me that the brotherly love interpretation and a
more subversive homoerotic reading are not mutually exclusive and may
very well be part of the continuum from domestic to gender to sexual issues which I am claiming that Harte's fiction charts. The central question
behind such an approach involves the curious way that Tennessee continues to live in the partner's home even after the partner returns with his
new bride. Of course, the men's cohabitation before marriage can be explained as a feature of their business partnership, and accepting Conner's
reading momentarily, the cohabitation after the wife's final departure
might be the partner's way of both biding his time and plotting his revenge. But what Conner cannot explain is the abnormal domestic
arrangement that results from the two men living together *during* the
partner's marriage, before the cardinal sin of wife-stealing takes place. The
western, as a genre, is very guarded about relationships between men and
women, and marriage especially is an inviolable institution. Couples are
strictly monogamous, and marriage itself erects a kind of partition between the couple and the rest of the world.[30] To have even the implication
of infidelity, let alone a homosexual affair or a *ménage à trois,* is patently
verboten. Yet that is the situation confronting us in the partner's home.
Granted, Burton's assumption of homosexual activity is based largely on
innuendo, but at least the presence of Tennessee in the partner's house
suggests a kind of sexual tension uncommon to popular western literature, and the partner's welcoming Tennessee back after the wife's final departure can certainly imply that the real tension has always existed
between the two men rather than between the men and the woman.

Again, with Harte's reputation as moralist, one cannot expect him to place all his cards on the table if he is, in fact, talking about a relationship between the two men which extends deeper than friendship. But certainly he stacks the deck in that direction by making Tennessee a seemingly inextricable feature of the partner's life, and vice versa. The two men are friends, business associates, cohabitors and, in that sense, domestic as well as economic partners. They represent an insular community of men surrounded by a larger all-male community—the only woman in the story is the unnamed wife. And they even have a physical connection in that they share the same woman, perhaps in the same time period. Given these extreme homosocial complexities (complexities inordinate even for the popular western), is it so absurd to assume that a certain, perhaps profound, homosexual tension also exists between the men?[31] Granted, especially with the western, the jump to assuming a homosexual relationship is a precarious one to make, for the western adheres to a pattern of fixing cultural power in the hands of the gunslinger, who is, among other things, always white and heterosexual. Beyond the text itself, on a cultural level, the drive of the western is much the same as in the text, to offer power to a white heterosexual male audience who, as surrogates for the western hero, can maintain an a priori claim to an identity suitable for the retention and exercise of social and political power. In this sense, the "suppression of the homosexual component of human sexuality, and by corollary, the oppression of homosexuals, is . . . a product of the same system whose rules and relations oppress women," for both women and homosexuals offer a potentially subversive converse to the images of white male heterosexual superiority propagated on both explicit political and implicit cultural levels in America.[32] In fact, homophobia is so implicit in western narratives that the subject is rarely, if ever, consciously broached. Where women must be dealt with, homosexuality is more readily concealed, at least on the surface. Thus the western deals with gay issues in the same way it deals with many issues of more than marginal complexity, by refusing to deal with them, instead continually reinscribing white male heterosexuality at the core both of the genre and of cultural, moral, and political progress.

Yet given these conventions, I would again stress that Harte's central literary project was to debunk the traditional western and to break down cultural inscriptions according to race, class, and gender, among others. Undeniably, he valorizes feminine sensibilities in a way that most other westerns would automatically refuse. Could he, then, have made the connection between women's and homosexual issues, between gender and sexuality? And by extension, could he have consciously or subconsciously recognized how both issues related to the western's unflinching articulation of specific gender identities and cultural roles? Regardless of one's answer, the fact that these questions can even be asked points to the very progressive social philosophy which Harte's work underwrites and, given his record on ostensibly sacrosanct cultural conventions, suggests that potential treatment of homosexuality in "Tennessee's Partner" cannot be easily dismissed as "unconvincing." Harte's philosophical progression outlined in this chapter—treating men as women and women as men, privileging nontraditional over traditional domestic orders—moves him more than gradually toward a conflation of masculine and feminine identity. His arguments explode all but the most basic correlations (for example, childbirth) of cultural function to sexed bodies. Given the circumstances, it is hardly unreasonable to entertain ideas about what seems a rather small leap from Harte's tolerant approach to gender performance in the world at large to possibly similar attitudes regarding sexual performance in the privacy of one's own bedroom.

"The Poet of Sierra Flat"

Of course, if Harte is really constructing a sort of cultural progression in the works I have outlined, then the next obvious step would be to move from the depiction of a largely implied and latent homosexual relationship in "Tennessee's Partner" to the depiction of blatantly enacted homoerotic urges—which is exactly what happens in "The Poet of Sierra Flat."

The story begins in the office of the "Sierra Flat Record" when Mr. Morgan McCorkle, "a well-known citizen," introduces the newspaper editor to the "born poet" of the story's title, Milton Chubbuck. "Knowed him for fower year,—since he war a boy," claims McCorkle. "Allers the same, bless you! Can jerk a rhyme as easy as turnin' jack. Never had any eddication; lived out in Missooray all his life. But he's chock full o' poetry" (108). Somewhat skeptical of Sierra Flat's poetic tastes, the editor nonetheless agrees to run Chubbuck's verse when McCorkle offers to pay for its publication at the standard advertisement rate. "The effect of [Chubbuck's first] poem on Sierra Flat was remarkable and unprecedented. The absolute vileness of its doggerel, the gratuitous imbecility of its thought, and above all the crowning audacity of the fact that it was the work of a citizen and published in the county paper, brought it instantly into popularity" (111). Soon Chubbuck is pronounced the regional poet laureate, and his fame soars. Even one of the most disreputable citizens of

Sierra Flat, Boston, manages to acquire "letters of congratulations from H. W. Longfellow, Tennyson, and Browning to Mr. Chubbuck" and obligingly consents "to dictate the replies" (112).

Chubbuck's notoriety established, the story's second half seems to take off on a tangent prompted by the arrival in Sierra Flat of the California Pet, a dance hall performer whose "specialty lay in the personation of youthful masculine character," who "as a *gamin* of the street . . . was irresistible" and "as a Negro-dancer . . . carried the honest miner's heart by storm" (113). The Poet of Sierra Flat is likewise smitten and attends all of the California Pet's performances. Perhaps out of jealousy, though, Boston—the practical joker from earlier—hatches a plan to embarrass the poet in front of the object of his desire. He arranges for Chubbuck to read a poem before the Pet's final performance, during which the men of Sierra Flat will heckle him and ultimately ride him out of town on a rail. When the appointed night arrives, however, Chubbuck gets such bad stage fright that, when Boston jumps onto the stage to collar him, the sympathetic Pet races from behind the curtain dressed as a sailor, kicks Boston into the orchestra pit, and announces in wonderful western fashion, "Wot are you goin' to hit a man fur when he's down, s-a-a-y?" (117). The curtain falls, and the Pet turns to Chubbuck (who has fainted), tears open his shirt to give him air, then starts to laugh hysterically. And to make sure all of his audience gets the joke, Harte shifts the scene quickly to the "Sierra Flat Record" a month later, where Morgan McCorkle, holding a letter from Chubbuck, announces of the poet after a certain amount of hedging, "She war a woman."

For most critics, "The Poet of Sierra Flat" simply represents Harte's send-up of the kind of doggerel that was being written and celebrated by Californians in the 1860s and '70s. Harte himself once accepted the unfortunate responsibility of editing a volume of California poetry and was chagrined to realize that his name would be associated with some very bad verse. Even more discouraging, however, was the public outcry that occurred when he actually did make several editorial decisions and rejected a number of submissions. As Patrick D. Morrow notes, "Judging from the violent disapproval of the volume by virtually every northern California and Nevada newspaper, what the public wanted was an all-inclusive anthology that would print every local versifier's work regardless of merit, making the volume a showcase for every California town's 'cultural' products."[33] The satire in "The Poet of Sierra Flat," then, is on the surface directed most strongly at those individuals like Morgan McCorkle, who are so wrapped up in the self-importance of their specific cultural vision that they cannot see how this preoccupation makes them into ignorant regionalists of the worst kind, both geographically and culturally.

Clearly, however, this satiric reading cannot account for the gender issues raised by the arrival of the California Pet, and I would argue that the second part of the story is designed, as much as anything, to offer a version of American culture radically different from and more expansive than the obviously limited version satirized in the figure of McCorkle. Indisputably Chubbuck and the Pet do more to explode conventional notions of gender than have any Harte characters thus far—the Pet especially, because her fame stems from her express ability to play a man, often better than the men themselves. This performance is substantiated by her very real outmuscling of Boston at the story's end and is followed, for added emphasis, by her delivery of a quintessentially macho western line. Even Chubbuck turns gender expectation on its head in "his" role as local poet. Throughout the story he is classed with such "celestials" as Poe, Longfellow, Browning, Tennyson, and John Milton, a pedigree that in the mind of Sierra Flat serves to distinguish poetry as a strictly male domain. This claim is reiterated repeatedly by McCorkle, who always attaches an assertion of Chubbuck's "male-ness" to his praise for the "young man's" literary ability. In fact, when McCorkle returns to the Sierra Flat Record at the story's end, he makes such a production of noting how "wrong" he was that one cannot help but feel he is talking about Milton Chubbuck's poetic greatness as much as the poet's gender. Of course, Chubbuck is a horrible writer, but McCorkle's assessment is based on his newly acquired knowledge that his protégé was a woman and not a man. Perhaps because he is so finely aware of the way that Chubbuck and the Pet's performances jeopardize his limited view of culture and gender, McCorkle struggles until the bitter end to demean Chubbuck and legitimize himself, when he must blurt out the unthinkable truth (at least to him) that the poet "war a woman."

Like "Miggles," then, "The Poet of Sierra Flat" succeeds in inverting gender roles and offering a credible, positive version of society based on that dynamic. But such inversion is not all "The Poet of Sierra Flat" is doing, for where Miggles adopts her masculine appearance and persona somewhat out of necessity, Chubbuck and the Pet are both voluntary cross-dressers, both involved in a rather convincing (if complex sexually signifying) drama of "playing men." The necessary question, then, is how do we read this mid-nineteenth-century, ostensibly western, story in which there are two female cross-dressers, at least one (the Pet) whose cross-dressing and masculine signification serve only to eroticize her further to both male and female contingents in the text? And, moreover, how do we deal with the expression of desire, if not the strong imputation of a physical relationship by story's end, between the two women? Beginning with the male perspective in Sierra Flat, it seems fair to assume that the men's desire for the Pet in her role as male impersonator stems from the same kind of suppressed homoerotic impulses that feature in "Tennessee's Partner." While the men know that the Pet is female—and it is important to remember Shirley Neuman's caveat that a woman's assumption of masculinity "signifies differently from the masculinely inscribed male's body"[34]—their delight in her specifically masculine performance suggests a transference of homoerotic desire. Because the Pet is a woman dressed as a man, in other words, their witnessing of her performance provides an outlet for homosexual impulses masquerading as, or even combined with, heterosexual urges. Thus the entire continuum of male sexuality as suggested by Sedgwick, from "brotherly love" to homoerotic longing,[35] can be implicitly satisfied (sublimated) without threatening the town's explicit male heterosexual order.

Explanations may be far simpler regarding the relationship of Chubbuck and the Pet, for everyone in Sierra Flat, almost immediately after the Pet's arrival, recognizes Chubbuck's desire for her. Of course, the gender dynamics of the case are somewhat confusing, as the first meeting between poet and actress suggests:

> The interview between Mr. Chubbuck and the "California Pet" took place in a private room of the Union Hotel; propriety being respected by the presence of that arch-humorist, "Boston." . . . However reticent Mr. Chubbuck might have been in the presence of his own sex, toward the fairer portion of humanity he was, like most poets, exceedingly voluble. Accustomed as the "California Pet" had been to excessive compliment, she was fairly embarrassed by the extravagant praises of her visitor. Her personation of boy characters, her dancing of the "champion jig," were particularly dwelt upon with fervid but unmistakable admiration. At last, recovering her audacity and emboldened by the presence of "Boston," the "California Pet" electrified her hearers by demanding, half jestingly, half viciously, if it were as a boy or a girl that she was the subject of his flattering admiration. (115)

For the Pet, still in the dark as to Chubbuck's sex, the immediate implication of the meeting is much like that outlined for the men of Sierra Flat in the previous paragraph: she suspects Chubbuck's homoerotic desire for the male characters she portrays. And her impression offers a basis for one of the story's most provocative readings: the potential of a masculinely inscribed homosexual relationship between two women pretending to be men. But whether Chubbuck desires the Pet as man or as woman, the relationship is necessarily homoerotic owing to the biological inscription of both women's bodies. At base, in other words, the story is about woman's desire for woman, despite the complex interplay of gender and sex signification which itself works to confuse and, many times, to conflate heteroerotic and homoerotic impulses.[36] On one level, then, the point of the story is to legitimize the apparent lesbian relationship which the two women enter (or, at least, to legitimize Chubbuck's lesbian urges) in contradistinction to the strict code of heterosexuality rhetorically championed by the men of Sierra Flat and, by extension, the western genre overall. On another level, though, "The Poet of Sierra Flat" is Harte's *pièce-de-résistance* (or perhaps *coup-de-grâce*) exploding of sexuality into an overt cultural chaos that more accurately represents the submerged desires and intentions of the microcosmic Sierra Flat than its adherence to sexual convention would indicate. Desire in the story is homo yet hetero (and often both); disguised yet openly proffered; misrepresented yet implicitly clear to the story's most desirous and desirable characters; repressed, oppressed, deferred, transferred, and finally revealed in a series of revelations which only serve to further confuse the issues with which the men think, by the story's end, they are finally coming to terms. Indeed, the implication of Chubbuck's relationship to the Pet is so explosive that Col. Starbottle can compare it to the "similar case" of a Philadelphia heiress who threw over a prominent Southern member of Congress in order "to consort with a d——d nigger" (118), a state of affairs which in the 1860s would have seemed the height of imprudence, scandal, and even defiance of natural law. As if things weren't confused enough, then, Harte injects into his critique of sexual mores issues of race, class, and geography as well, expanding the tableau of his story (as if there were some doubt about its metaphoric nature) to take in East and West, high society and the "common man," Black and White. And once again, those characters most defiant of cultural convention—the Pet, Chubbuck, the Philadelphia heiress—are regarded with the greatest sympathy and allowed the richest happiness, while those people who cling to obsolete stereotypes—Boston (who retreats to San Francisco shortly after the Pet's departure) and McCorkle—are left only further confounded, ashamed, upset, frightened, and displaced from the empowered arenas of an evolving society.

★

"The Poet of Sierra Flat"—in its sympathetic depiction of a lesbian relationship—closes out the progressive commentary on domesticity, gender, sexuality, and their inextricable connection that Harte began with "The Luck of Roaring Camp." Despite the seemingly intentional frenzy into which American culture is plunged at the end of "The Poet," as well as the radical implications of all the works I have discussed, it is probably dangerous to guess at how much of Harte's rhetoric was wholly conscious or deliberate. Likewise, to draw close connections between his fiction and his personal life is inadvisable simply because he was so careful, as were the compilers of his private papers, not to reveal information which might have been scandalous to himself or his family. While his own married life proved intolerable, and while he did take up residence with a married couple for many years after his separation, the details of these relationships as well as any evidence of "impropriety" are too sketchy to allow much supposition beyond the facts themselves. Rather, his fictions merely seem to extend his otherwise openly tolerant and pacifistic attitudes—attitudes formed partly in response to intolerant Western political ventures and spurious literary renditions of the frontier which themselves pandered to the equally questionable cultural tastes of the East. Harte favored racial tolerance and cooperation; he was largely anti-imperial, and profamily in an embracing and expansive rather than constrictive and exclusionary sense. He was for his day, then, already a radical thinker before setting pen to paper. Writing merely allowed him to extrapolate his liberal stances to what he viewed to be a rational and moral end, with humorous and often insightful results. Questions of intentionality are therefore moot, for whether Harte expressly meant to offer the analyses he did or simply moved with their logical flow, his results offer a version of the West and American society overall vastly divergent from what many of his contemporaries (not to mention future literary historians) would regard as the cultural mainstream and chief moral precepts of the nation. That Harte has been paraded ad nauseam as a consummate representative of that same mainstream, even granting his inability to break with many of the structural formulas he helped to create, speaks volumes about the subtle subversiveness of his intellect and the ambiguous nature of *the one* American cultural center for which he supposedly speaks. In other words, if Harte is a mainstream writer, then his stories must be taken not just as dandy little gems of western lore, but as a radical reinvention of American notions of the mainstream itself and, as far as the western is concerned, a complete (if early) reorientation of those characters, events, and themes that have been accepted as archetypal symbols of both the American frontier and the more enduring American character.

"Don't
forget the
cowboys,
Sandy"

*Mark Twain and the
Western Myth*

It's awfully tempting to read *A Connecticut Yankee in King Arthur's Court* as a version of the popular western. Hank Morgan, the traditional western hero, is poised on the brink between civilization and savagery at a time when those forces are in crucial (and even mythic) conflict. He adopts the trappings of the cowboy, most conspicuously in his six-guns, and is constantly ready to use violence—at which he is particularly adept—to meet his ends. He refers to the residents of Camelot as "Indians" and "savages," which expresses his almost preternatural superiority to them. But at the same time, he longs to fit into Camelot society and even tries to take a "native" wife, who is ultimately denied him in the novel's violent ending.

In the great scheme of the western genre, should it matter that this story takes place at the dawn of British "civilization" rather than on the

American frontier? Or that the "savages" in Hank Morgan's world are knights and not Indians? Or that Hank, in his previous life, was more urban industrialist than child of the wilderness? The answer, needless to say, is yes and no. Clearly *A Connecticut Yankee in King Arthur's Court* cannot be considered a conventional western in the way that a twentieth-century audience understood the genre. But also clearly, the novel explores many of the tensions that would be worked out in later western books and films. Twain's novel was published in 1889, prior to the close of the frontier and the appearance of works by Turner and subsequent novelists designed to elegize the frontier's passing or to codify its virtues in the persons of specific historical and fictional characters. More than a response to popular mythology, *A Connecticut Yankee* anticipates and embraces certain ideals of the formula western, even as it remains skeptical about their literal enactment.

In this sense *A Connecticut Yankee* logically extends Twain's own writing about the West—especially *Roughing It,* where the literal frontier regularly fails to meet the expectations of the tenderfoot narrator, a version of the author himself. In that book, the westward movement ends at the Sandwich Islands with the narrator's half-joking attempt to reclaim his "savage" ancestry by watching scantily clad native women. Unable to find the promised land that he has sought, he has literally reached the point where to travel further west would be to head east, into the Far East of Asia. While the narrator can make light of this development upon his return to New England, the implications for Twain were far more troubling, perhaps reaching their fullest expression in his later work. At the end of *Huck Finn,* for instance, when Huck promises to light out for the Territory, readers should be aware that the West he will find is the same corrupted space that features in both *Roughing It* and Twain's autobiography. Frontier democracy is a myth, Twain's experience tells him, a worthy dream that unfortunately can never be matched by reality.

A Connecticut Yankee extends this sentiment, reviving Twain's romantic desire to find a time and place in which frontier ideals could succeed but coupling that desire with his growing cynicism about the "civilizing" process generally. This contrast is captured in critical responses to the novel, which see Hank either as a representative of Twain's own imperial attitudes or as his satiric attack on the same. Certainly the Boss's success reflects Twain's belief in the possible benefits of technology as well as his skepticism at philosophies hailing the virtues of primitivism. But Hank's failures, which are numerous and ultimately more important than his successes, demonstrate even stronger feelings from their author: profound distrust of individuals claiming social or intellectual privilege, misgivings about the ethics of industrial capitalism, and horror at the indiscriminate violence used against marginalized people (including Indians). To an extent, *A Connecticut Yankee* is Twain's complexly personal attempt to unite his warring impulses about the imperial venture—and it is just as profoundly his failure to do so. The particular genius of the novel is the way that it wants to be a version of the popular frontier story but undercuts itself at every turn, closing with a brand of pathos that also echoes yet undermines other frontier narratives. In constructing the novel, Twain allows the inconsistencies of Hank's positions to unravel to their ultimate end, producing a character that is hero and anti-hero at the same time. The timing of this character is notable. Exploring frontier "values" before they were articulated by their chief proponents, moreover recognizing their flaws, the novel expertly anticipates not only twentieth-century popular westerns but also the subsequent revisionist texts that would challenge the moral primacy of those formula stories.

★

As Jane Gardiner has noted, much criticism of *A Connecticut Yankee* focuses on the unresolvable issue of whether Twain, in creating the apparently self-contradicting personality of Hank Morgan, was "a closet pastoralist or . . . a strict nineteenth-century technological progressive."[1] Her question echoes the sentiment of Henry Nash Smith, who saw Twain as oscillating "between the brave new world of science and technology, and nostalgia for the simple agrarian world that the industrial revolution was destroying before his eyes."[2] The conflict outlined by these two critics is fundamental to American frontier literature, pitting a desire for industrial progress against a largely intuited Romantic belief in the morally redemptive powers of the natural world. Central to this debate is the frontier hero, that character who, at apparent odds with himself, is "fundamentally committed" both to the advance of civilization and to the protection of his own "wild" lifestyle.[3] The latter impulse, as Gardiner and Smith suggest, inscribes the frontier hero firmly as a child of nature—a pioneer, a hunter, a cowboy. And his defense of the wilderness, or at least his nostalgia at its passing, suggests the near incompatibility of pastoral and industrial urges. In the most artful instances, he is a tragic figure compelled to sacrifice part of his identity in order to serve others, just as nature itself is sacrificed in order to allow for the evolution of a capitalist-industrial society.

In many respects, though, it is a mistake to read the frontier hero in this fashion, for in reality, frontier literature—which grew in popularity at staggering rates during Twain's lifetime—invoked a sympathetic, if not symbiotic, relationship between industrial and pastoral social models. In fact, the frontier hero marked the great link between such ideals in that he was the one character capable of using the products of industry, the gun in particular, to convert the savage wilderness into a relatively peaceful garden where pastoral ideals could hold sway. Hank Morgan is not a nineteenth-century philosophical paradox. Rather, his position as foreman at the Colt arms factory places him firmly in line with this version of the arbitrating frontier hero, the industrial muscle behind those men who conquered the American West and made it safe for the yeoman farmers to follow.

Hank is no agrarian, of course, and his determination to metamorphose Arthur's feudal wilderness into a systematized industrial society does not explicitly illustrate his function as champion of both the garden and industrial myths. Yet Hank displays time and again a respect for the natural world, at least in certain incarnations. His very first description of Camelot begins, "It was a soft, reposeful summer landscape, as lovely as a dream, and as lonesome as Sunday. The air was full of the smell of flowers, and the buzzing of insects, and the twittering of birds, and there were no people, no wagons, there was no stir of life, nothing going on."4 Twelve chapters later, this landscape is rendered in greater detail when he sets out on his "adventure" with Sandy.

Straight off, we were in the country. It was most lovely and pleasant in those sylvan solitudes in the early cool morning in the first freshness of autumn. From hilltops we saw fair green valleys lying spread out below, with streams winding through them, and island groves of trees here and there, and huge lonely oaks scattered about and casting black blots of shade; and beyond the valleys we saw the ranges of hills, blue with haze, stretching away in billowy perspective to the horizon, with at wide intervals a dim fleck of white or gray on a wave summit, which we knew was a castle. We crossed broad natural lawns sparkling with dew, and we moved like spirits, the cushioned turf giving out no sound of footfall; we dreamed along through glades in a mist of green light that got its tint from the sundrenched roof of leaves overhead, and by our feet the clearest and coldest of runlets went frisking and gossiping over its reefs and making a sort of whimpering music comfortable to hear; and at times we left the world behind and entered into the solemn great deeps and rich gloom of the forest, where furtive wild things whisked and scurried by and were gone before you could even get your eye on the place where the noise was; and where only the earliest birds were turning out and getting to business with a song here and a quarrel yonder and a mysterious far-off hammering and drumming for worms on a tree trunk away somewhere in the impenetrable remoteness of the woods. (74–75)

Clearly the natural world represents more to Hank than a blank industrial slate on which his capitalist ambitions might be etched. In fact, his descriptions could be considered Romantically excessive—"moving like spirits" through a "dream" landscape. But Hank is no innocent, and if certain observations make him seem like a childlike resident of Paradise (as Sandy is), then his subsequent exercise of technological superiority makes him into a version of the world-wise cowboy using his guns to return the corrupted wilderness to prelapsarian grace. Take, for instance, his actions in the Valley of Holiness. Against a backdrop of what could be any frontier town in America ("distant and isolated" buildings "shrunken to toy constructions in the lonely waste of what seemed a desert—and was"), Hank uses dynamite to restart the miraculous fountain, proclaiming his accomplishment a "miracle" of occult arts. Magic or not, his drawing water from stone suggests his metaphorical connection to Percival, who brings water to a dead land in Arthurian tradition, or even to Moses, and his relation to either of these suggests his larger role as the deliverer who will usher civilization into its promised era of peace and contentment, back into Eden. Despite the overt industrial trappings of his rhetoric, Hank is very much a surrogate of the American frontier champion—connected to the land through his "taming" of it, marked by his repeated pledge to bring order, committed to a destiny which claims to be manifest even as it is somewhat vague and strangely akin to the nineteenth-century colonial models whose shortcomings Hank is trying to mend.

Hank's problem revolves around what Twain might have seen as a peculiarly American naïveté: the ironic notion that democracy breeds leaders who can exert an absolute and perfect moral authority. This idea is central to frontier literature, where heroes are almost divinely selected to lead (without challenge) the democratic society around them. Later, in his seminal western novel *The Virginian,* Owen Wister would differentiate between "the quality and the equality," where the former are men who so embody "American" values—strength, courage, straightforwardness, ingenuity—that they seem supernaturally chosen to govern the latter. It does not take much imagination to see how Wister's scheme of individual merit could easily transform itself into a racist or ethnocentric doctrine; Wister himself felt certain that Anglo-Saxons would occupy the top of the social scale. In similar fashion, Hank sees his moral authority as the superior product of historical evolution, oblivious to the poignant analogues between his own autocratic tendencies and Arthur's system of monarchical control. His imperial impulse evolves from his intensely personal conviction that he is superior to Camelot's finest, making him from the outset little more than an unwitting version of that system he intends to destroy.

Twain was keenly aware of the close parallels between Hank and Arthur, as well as the sociopolitical systems for which both men spoke. Later, in a 1906 essay entitled "We Are Americanizing Europe," he would write,

> For good or for evil we continue to educate Europe. We have held the post of instructor for more than a century and a quarter now. We were not elected to it, we merely took it. We are of the Anglo-Saxon race. At the banquet last winter of that organization which calls itself the Ends of the Earth Club, the chairman, a retired regular army officer of high grade, proclaimed in a loud voice, and with fervency, "We are of the Anglo-Saxon race, and when the Anglo-Saxon wants a thing *he just takes it.*"
>
> . . . We imported our imperialism from monarchical Europe, also our curious notions of patriotism—that is, if we have any principle of patriotism which any person can definitely and intelligibly define. It is but fair then, no doubt, that we should instruct Europe in return for these and the other kinds of instruction which we have received from that source.[5]

Foremost, this passage specifically indicts America's failure to move beyond the violent methods of empire building employed by earlier European nations. But in light of *A Connecticut Yankee*, Twain's criticism assumes an added dimension, recognizing how American imperialism is more of a racial than nationalistic (or patriotic) proposition. Rather than advancing a democratic society, imperialism deposits inordinate power in the hands of a few—per Twain's anecdote, the Anglo-Saxon brethren of the chairman. Indeed, the chairman's words suggest Twain's idea (echoed in Hank) that imperialism proceeds as much from individual megalomania as group prejudice. Notice the way that the chairman's exhortations move from the plural "we" to the singular "he" as he puts forward his martial agenda. As with Hank, the chairman's sense of superiority seems deeply rooted in his sense of personal entitlement, a sense that is enhanced by— but subtly independent from—his Anglo-Saxon identity.

Of course, Hank's brand of colonialism is different from Arthur's in that he purports to bring democracy, and if readers can take him at his word, he at least plans some version of a free state. Richard Slotkin understands Hank's sensibility to be part of "the strong contrasts which Twain offers between Yankee progress and Arthurian 'benightedness.'"

> The Yankee speaks for science against magic, for egalitarian values against the aristocracy of birth, for a merit system of promotions against one based on connections, for an equitable code of laws against law of might, for the sharing of power against the monopolization of force by a privileged class. He is for religious toleration and against cruel and unusual punishments. He founds a patent office to support technological innovation. He is for free trade in commodities and against monopolies of all kinds. He offers England a chance to avoid its medievalism and leap into the light of modern Americanism without the pain of intervening stages.[6]

Slotkin accepts Hank's rhetoric at face value, and even Hank seems to believe that he is working for the good of the people. But it is difficult to buy Hank as the largely benevolent figure described above when most of his efforts, as Slotkin agrees, serve to benefit him personally until they devolve into utter fiasco. Slotkin portrays Hank as a well-intended republican— that is, a man with a democratic plan but little ability to execute it. As such, the critical thrust of Twain's novel shifts from Hank's ideology itself to where its implementation goes astray. To view Hank Morgan as a potential moral and political redeemer, however, is again to read him as a kind of frontier hero newly arrived to eradicate savagery, and it is this identity which calls his (as well as Twain's) purpose in Camelot into question. The paradox of the American frontier hero is that he rhetorically defends democracy when, in reality, both his ideology and his method are highly individualistic, seldom justified in words, and predicated on the axiom not that might *makes* right but that might is almost mystically assigned to that individual most worthy of it. To believe in this hero is to believe in an absolutely romantic version of law and government, as well as in the select few people qualified to enforce it. As a rational progressive, believing above all in those things which he can see and touch, which he can manufacture, Hank is the one person in the text who should question the gunslinger identity, for it flies in the face of both empirical reason and democratic process. Yet with startling and explicit regularity, he identifies himself as just such a figure, the fastest gun into whose hands power has been delivered and who possesses some transcendent right, if not obligation, to use it. Contrary to Slotkin's assertion, Hank favors all kinds of monopolies, cruel and unusual punishments, and laws of might, so long as he is the one to dispense and profit by them, so long as they are committed in democracy's name.

And it is egomania, without a doubt, driving Hank's grasp of his situation. No sooner is he in Camelot than he conceives of a system of practically fascist control. "I would boss the whole country inside of three months," he claims, even as he is being paraded around by Sir Kay and in danger of execution, "for I judged I would have the start of the best-educated man in the kingdom by a matter of thirteen hundred years and upwards" (23–24). Several pages later, before his intended execution, he continues,

> It came into my mind, in the nick of time, how Columbus, or Cortez, or one of those people, played an eclipse as a saving trump once, on some savages, and I saw my chance. I could play it myself, now; and it wouldn't be any plagiarism, either, because I should get it in nearly a thousand years ahead of those parties. (39)

If there is a single guiding principle to the frontier myth in America, it is the idea of regeneration, of being a new people in a new world, starting over without the fallacies of an ancestral culture.[7] In his preparation to "play the eclipse," Hank makes his succinct but incredibly powerful claim to such an Adamic identity. By comparing himself to Columbus, he renders his arrival in Camelot into an act of discovery, positing medieval Britain as his New World in which a truly original Eden can take hold. This assertion signifies doubly, for even as it posits Hank as the chief agent of cultural origination (the inventor of civilization, as it were), it likewise frees him from the bonds of his own discovered or colonized identity. By traveling backward in time thirteen hundred years, he has managed to predate Columbus's New World voyage and, by extension, negated what he sees as the slipshod European influence attendant upon American colonization.[8] He has detached himself from history, as his dismissal of the charge of "plagiarism" suggests. His voyage of discovery and self-creation complete, he can even trump the exploits of Cortez and Columbus by colonizing the Old World in proper New World fashion.

> I saw that I was just another Robinson Crusoe cast away on an uninhabited island, with no society but more or less tame animals, and if I wanted to make life bearable I must do as he did—invent, contrive, create, reorganize things; set brain and hand to work, and keep them busy. (47)

Despite his numerous deprecations of the Church and religion, Hank views his role as closely akin to God's. His business is one of invention—or at least re-invention—of making something out of the void (the "uninhabited island") which confronts him. His reference to the Britons as "animals" suggests his view of them not just as intellectual and moral inferiors, but as servants of the enlightened power that he represents. As he says after his repair of the well in the Valley of Holiness, "When I started to the chapel, the populace uncovered and fell back reverently to make a wide way for me, as if I had been some kind of superior being—which I was" (160).

Appropriately for the founder of history's first newspaper, Hank starts to believe his own press, transforming his feats of technological innovation into "miracles," himself into a deity. After the eclipse, he reasons that "I had done my entire public a kindness in sparing the sun" (53), forgetting that only minutes before he had considered it to be "playing a trick" rather than a genuine expression of his power. An avowed opponent of the Camelot myth, he nonetheless seems comfortable assuming a prominent place within it. Ousting the former champion wizard, Merlin—"the mighty liar and magician" who never ceases to "worketh his one tale" (29)—Hank becomes a version of the same, "happily trapped within his own self-assurance, his own point of view, his own ethnocentrism, as it were."[9] Nor is his lack of introspection purely coincidental. In his unwavering adherence to his self-assigned mission and self-absorbed worldview, Hank tacitly reiterates his guise as western hero, the adamant conviction with which he sets to conquering Camelot serving as that conquest's "manifest" justification. Certainly it stands to reason that if "a man has to do what a man has to do," then a superman can do no less; Hank has simply extended the frontier hero's dictum to its logical extreme. And notably, by merging his vocabularies of science and magic, he accomplishes the same end as American colonials who understood their technological superiority to be a sign of the transcendent "rightness" attendant upon their conquest of the New World.[10]

For the frontier hero, connections between violence and morality are symbiotic: the hero, always on the side of justice and civilization, is also always the fastest draw. One quality does not proceed from the other; rather, they are circular and self-justifying. The hero has power because he is morally qualified to use it, and he is morally qualified because he is the most powerful. Similarly, Hank derives his social power from his prowess with a gun yet sees that prowess as a supernatural sanction of his agenda. Since his skill at invention is far superior to that of his medieval counterparts, he reasons that his moral faculties are equally refined. And in cyclical fashion, it is the push toward democracy born of Hank's moral instincts that keeps him on his industrial toes, inventing more and more items for his own use in Britain, continually one-upping his previous performances in order to maintain his position as leader. Such status forms the fundamental paradox of the novel: Hank kills because he is a moral being, able to decide who in Camelot should live or die, yet finally his ethical authority derives almost solely from his ability to carry out threats of violence. He is a god destined to create—new manufactured goods, new political systems, a new world—yet ironically, given the focus on weapons production in his industrial ventures, his ability to create is validated only by his concomitant ability, indeed his implicit promise, to destroy.[11]

Of course, Hank's willingness to obliterate an existent society in order to erect his new one strongly echoes imperial ventures in the American West, and the time of *A Connecticut Yankee*'s production—roughly 1886 to 1889, late in the era of the Indian wars—suggests that Twain had such comparisons in mind. Despite the fact that Hank is "colonizing" the English, his own race, the forms and strategies he brings to the imperial mission closely parody the ethnocentric thrust of New World conquest. During his quest with Sandy, for instance, he comes across a knight whom he has enlisted to sell the items produced in his factories. The knight wears a sign reading, "*Persimmon's soap—All the Prime-Donne Use It,*" and his role as walking billboard has been read by critics as Twain's satire on the dual ridiculousness of chivalry and American industrialism. The sign, however, also represents Hank's fixation with cleanliness, his desire to wipe away the impurities of medieval culture, beginning at the level of the people themselves. The dilemma of empire becomes a matter of hygiene, and as Hank's imperial delusions become grander, he more consciously tailors his efforts toward the removal of dirt, demonstrated by his plan to send missionaries of civilization out among the populace. "These missionaries," he argues, "would gradually, and without creating suspicion or exciting alarm, introduce a rudimentary cleanliness among the nobility, and from them it would work down to the people, if the priests could be kept quiet" (99). In American frontier terminology, Hank's efforts amount to "cleaning up this here town," but as John Cawelti has noted, such housekeeping often symbolizes the tacit extermination of some racial or cultural Other, usually Indians. By speaking in terms of hygiene, Hank merely domesticates the exigencies of empire, concealing, both from himself and the populace, the inevitable violence that the imperialist must employ.

Twain's interest in Native Americans is not specific to *A Connecticut Yankee* but surfaces in several earlier works, most notably the narrator's encounter with the "Goshoot" Indians halfway through *Roughing It*. Memorable for its echoes of Hank Morgan, the meeting proves a terrible disappointment to the narrator because it undoes, in Slotkin's words, "his expectations . . . of the Noble Red Man."[12]

> The disgust which the Goshoots gave me, a disciple of Cooper and a worshipper of the Red Man—even of the scholarly savages in the "Last of the Mohicans" who are fittingly associated with backwoodsmen who divide each sentence into equal parts: one part critically grammatical, refined and choice of language, and the other part just such an attempt to talk like a hunter or a mountaineer, as a Broadway clerk might after eating an edition of Emerson Bennett's works and studying frontier life at the Bowery Theatre a couple of weeks—I say that the nausea which the Goshoots gave me, an Indian worshipper, set me to examining authorities, to see if perchance I had been over-estimating the Red Man while viewing him through the mellow moonshine of romance. The revelations that came were disenchanting. It was curious to see how quickly the paint and tinsel fell away from him and left him treacherous, filthy, and repulsive—and how quickly the evidences accumulated that whenever one finds an Indian tribe he has only found Goshoots more or less modified by circumstances and surroundings—but Goshoots, after all. They deserve pity, poor creatures, and they can have mine—at this distance. Nearer by, they never get anybody's.[13]

From this passage, Slotkin deduces not only Twain's visceral disgust with the Goshoots but also an anti-Indian stance that paralleled both the rhetoric of contemporary newspapers and the published opinions of none other than George Armstrong Custer. As a result, Slotkin surmises that Twain began *A Connecticut Yankee* almost in favor of Hank's imperial efforts and that it was only in finishing the book, realizing the violent end toward which his protagonist was headed, that he rethought his position on industrialism and expansionism in the American West.[14]

Slotkin is undoubtedly right to see this portrait of the Gosiute as Twain's jab at the cult of the Noble Savage, challenging "the myth of a primitive nobility, of an alternative in man's wilderness condition."[15] What he conveniently omits, however, is the closing sentence of the narrator's encounter with the Gosiute, which comes only one paragraph after the description above. "If we cannot find it in our hearts to give those poor naked creatures our Christian sympathy and compassion," the narrator says, "in God's name let us at least not throw mud at them" (169). This final sentiment somewhat revises the tone of the narrator's description; far from vitriolic, it suggests pity over the Indians' demise and even regret at white involvement in that process. Importantly, the narrator of *Roughing It* can never again see Indians through a romantic lens, but his disappointment stops short of wishing them further harm.[16] Hank's later association of hygiene and empire might represent Twain's own subtle regret at having made similar connections earlier in his career. For though the depiction of the Gosiute as unwashed and impoverished seems at least partly intended to evoke sympathy, it does not take much, as Slotkin demonstrates, to transform that depiction into justification for Hank's policy of racial cleansing. Whatever the extent of Twain's personal sentiment in *A Connecticut Yankee,* the passages from *Roughing It* confirm both his misgivings regarding the "civilized" treatment of Indians and his sense that racism is implicit in the industrial-imperial venture.

What is especially frightening about *A Connecticut Yankee,* though, is how quickly Hank can adapt his imperial vocabulary to new subjects. His comparisons of Indians and Britons pervade the text. Regarding the knights, he concludes that "philosophical bearing is not an outcome of mental training, intellectual fortitude, reasoning; it is mere animal training; they are white Indians" (26). And he makes similar observations after his first meeting with Sandy: "Measured by modern standards, they were merely modified savages, these people. This noble lady showed no impatience to get to breakfast—and that smacks of the savage, too. On their journeys, these Britons were used to long fasts, and knew how to bear them; and also how to freight up against possible fasts before starting, after the style of the Indian and the anaconda" (81). Importantly, the conjunction of "Indian" and "anaconda" reflects Hank's general tendency to conflate words like "savage," "Indian," and "animal" until these identities merge into one another, a dehumanizing process that further removes any moral impediment to his reinventing Camelot. As he tells Sandy, "The fact is, it is just a sort of polished up court of Comanches, and there isn't a squaw in it who doesn't stand ready at the dropping of a hat to desert to the buck with the biggest string of scalps at his belt" (93). This idea becomes frighteningly ironic, though, as the number of scalps following in Hank's own wake continues to mount.

Of course, as with nineteenth-century conceptions of the frontier, Hank's Camelot purports to be a place where an individual can rise on his own merit.[17] And superficially Hank does strive to guarantee personal liberties, both economic and political, from his first moments as Boss.

> That reminds me to remark, in passing, that the very first official thing I did, in my administration—and it was on the very first day of it, too—was to start a patent office; for I knew that a country without a patent office and good patent laws was just a crab, and couldn't travel any way but sideways or backwards. (58)

Despite the individualistic thrust of this move, it cannot be lost on even the most casual observer how instituting a patent office works more to consolidate Hank's own power than to facilitate invention and initiative among the populace. As the man with all the "ideas," he has the most to gain from an official body that will protect them. His overtures to class abolition notwithstanding, Hank's patent office offers Camelot an alternative social hierarchy, pitting a system of industrial "merit" against the "arbitrary" standards of chivalry, monarchy, and peerage. Ideas themselves become the chief currency, dividing "those with" from "those without" perhaps more absolutely than the feudal caste structure. Hank claims that the patent office serves to balance the scales between heretofore privileged and marginalized groups, but his true intent remains his own aggrandizement. The closer he moves to the center of Arthurian power structures (increasingly becoming the Boss he claims to be), the more his rhetoric of individualism merges ironically with dictums of government control, fortifying the power he has won. When he is the outsider battling the entrenched feudal system, that is, he champions individual rights in order to guarantee his own route to power. But when that same feudal structure later challenges Hank's empowered position—asserting, as it were, its right to dissent—Hank simply denies the claims, pretending that the Britons do not fully understand the nature of democracy and that, as with

Native Americans, they must be guided on paths contrary to their wishes "for their own good."[18]

Appropriately, even the items manufactured by Hank exhibit a western flavor. Twice he uses the telephone/telegraph in the Valley of Holiness, first when he orders supplies to repair the Well and later when he discredits an unnamed magician who claims the gift of prophecy. In the latter case, Hank calls back to Camelot to learn Arthur's itinerary, then defies the magician to foresee Arthur's location at the end of several days. The King's destination, of course, is the Valley of Holiness, the magician is mistaken, and he is literally ridden out of town "on a rail" (170) by the monks. Perhaps a fitting punishment, the magician's untimely demise nonetheless confirms the telephone's immediate impact on medieval society. By making Arthur's world smaller, at least in a figurative sense, the telephone signals the death of other kinds of informational exchange. No longer will the falsehoods of the magician or the knights be believed; their exaggerated stories have been undermined by a more credible and immediate source. In this way, the telephone has much the same effect on Camelot as the telegraph had on the American frontier, the wooden poles and wires replacing almost overnight the outdone horse and rider. But as with the American Indians, not everyone in the Boss's world is privy to the telephone's use. The operator in the Valley reminds Hank of this fact when he says, "Ah, ye will remember we move by night, and avoid speech with all. We learn naught but that we get by the telephone from Camelot" (164). Rather than a public service, long-distance communication becomes another one of Hank's imperial mechanisms. Ironically assuming the position occupied by the magician only pages before, Hank will not even risk the possibility of dissent—the operators interact with no one but each other and receive their instructions directly from him.

The idea of information and who controls it—who is the novel's repository of "truth"—arises again with Hank's invention of the newspaper. As usual, Hank is far more concerned with spreading his own message than with offering the Britons a new medium through which to exchange their ideas, a feature demonstrated by his pep talk to the kingdom's first paperboys.

> It is a public journal; I will explain what it is another time. It is not cloth, it is made of paper; sometime I will explain what paper is. The lines on it are reading matter; and not written by hand, but printed; by and by I will explain what printing is. A thousand of these sheets have been made, all exactly like this, in every minute detail—they can't be told apart. (191)

The perfect reproducibility of the paper stands in for the homogenization and acculturation that, despite his rhetorical defense of individuality, form the core of Hank's design in Camelot. Not unlike Arthur, he envisions a world in which the will of the individual and the will of the state are one and the same. Hank's problem, however, is that he refuses to let democracy take its slow course toward this end and so attempts to accelerate the process through political directive disseminated by his newspaper. In his own day, Twain was concerned about this relationship between newspapers and political ambition, as his essay "As Regards Patriotism" makes clear:

> Patriotism is . . . a religion—love of country, worship of country, devotion to the country's flag and honor and welfare.
>
> In absolute monarchies it is furnished from the throne, cut and dried, to the subject; in England and America it is furnished, cut and dried, to the citizen by the politician and the newspaper.[19]

Part of Twain's purpose in *A Connecticut Yankee* may be to indict those tabloids of his own day which, as Slotkin points out, vociferously favored a policy of genocide against Indians and discrimination against other races. But more likely, his attack is made on the grounds of the cultural indoctrination, or "training," which newspapers seem to supply. Later, in "As Regards Patriotism," Twain blames prejudicial reporting for making Americans "glad" to take "any weak nation's country and liberties away from it" (45). Newspaper reporting, he continues, "can turn bad morals to good, good morals to bad; it can destroy principles, it can re-create them; it can debase angels to men and lift men to angelship." Whether he realizes it or not, Hank desires this kind of power.[20] He revels in the absolute control that the paper seems to exert over the Britons. Consider his obtusely maternal reaction watching the people read his first edition: "I knew, then, how a mother feels when women . . . take her new baby . . . and bend their heads over it in a tranced adoration that makes all the rest of the universe vanish out of their consciousness and be as if it were not, for that time" (191–92).

Put otherwise, Hank's goal of national re-creation is absolute, and Twain objects to it on these grounds, appalled by his protagonist's faith in a "training" that will convert the Britons from thinking individuals to automata. Nor can such techniques be read independently of the period of *A Connecticut Yankee*'s production, when similar policies were instituted against Native Americans. From 1886 to 1889, the United States Govern-

ment passed resolutions that required the exclusive use of English in all
Native schools, regulated marriages between white men and Native
women (a policy which has an echo in Hank's relationship to Sandy),
compelled more Natives to attend reservation schools, and enforced standards of "patriotism" among Indian children.[21] Given the echoes of these
policies in *A Connecticut Yankee,* it seems safe to say that—whatever his
feelings about primitivism—Twain had equally grave misgivings about
government conduct toward Indians and other minorities. Much thought
in recent scholarship has been devoted to Hank Morgan's relation to his
real-world nominative forebears, among them J. P. Morgan the banker
and Henry Morgan the pirate. Perhaps it is only a coincidence that in
1889, the year of *A Connecticut Yankee's* publication, the authoritarian
Commissioner of Native Affairs was named Morgan—Thomas J. Morgan
—also.

The patent office, the telephone, and the newspaper circumstantially
connect Hank's imperial methods to those employed during the conquest
of the American West. But it is his invention of weapons—gunpowder,
firearms, bombs—that confirms these echoes. Barely a chapter passes
without Hank's dynamiting something: Merlin's Tower, for example, or
the Well of Holiness. The most poignant explosion, however, may come
while he travels incognito with Arthur, when they are accosted by two
knights. As the knights charge, Hank lobs a grenade in their direction:
"Yes, it was a neat thing, very neat and pretty to see. It resembled a steamboat explosion on the Mississippi; and during the next fifteen minutes we
stood under a steady drizzle of microscopic fragments of knights and
hardware and horseflesh" (199). The description of "a steamboat explosion on the Mississippi" was no doubt a very personal one to Twain,
whose younger brother, Henry, died in just such an accident and for
whose death Twain always retained, whether rightly or not, some sense of
responsibility.[22] Given this circumstance, it is unlikely that the author
could view Morgan's deployment of such violence without some sense of
regret or repugnance. Beyond its personal significance, however, Hank's
action further undermines his rhetoric of assistance and underscores the
self-satisfaction he brings to the act of killing. In the case of the knights,
he claims self-defense; had he not blown them up, they would have certainly run him through. But while such a claim may be true in the immediacy, it conceals the equally central points that Hank knows he is in
little real danger and that the level of force with which he chooses to respond is far more than "defensive." Here Hank assumes the position of
the reluctant gunfighter, that Achilles-like character who rhetorically

wants to avoid confrontation but whose martial skills make it inevitable that he will take the field (or enter the final showdown) and prevail. This persona is a kind of disguise that, by the nineteenth century, was designed to bolster the hero's claims to a superior moral nature; he fought not because he wanted to but because he had to. On the other hand, he rarely operated within the confines of the law, rarely considered alternatives to violent confrontation, and rarely regretted the lethal force that he used. Similarly Hank expresses pride over the knights' deaths, using words like "neat" and "pretty" to describe the effect of his weapons. He may not have been bucking for a fight, but his quick entry into battle confirms his willingness—like the gunfighter—to do what he has to do. Indeed, Hank prefers violent confrontation to rational persuasion; like the frontier hero, his defense of civilization makes him no less ready to meet the savage enemy on the enemy's terms. He only needs enough people to provoke him, so that he can morally justify his destruction of Arthur's realm once and for all.

And of course, he receives this chance when challenged to the final tournament, where he makes the western basis of his imperial design manifestly clear. Choosing a maneuverable Indian pony instead of a charger, Hank waits in authentic cowboy fashion to be "called out" to his showdown, where he will fight whatever knights challenge him "as long as [he] might be willing to respond" (276). First he faces Sir Sagramor, embarrassing the knight in impeccable frontier style.

> I was sitting my horse at ease, and swinging the great loop of my lasso in wide circles about my head; the moment he was under way, I started for him; when the space between us had narrowed to forty feet, I sent the snaky spirals of the rope a-cleaving through the air, then darted aside and faced about and brought my trained animal to a halt with all his feet braced under him for a surge. The next moment the rope sprang taut and yanked Sir Sagramor out of the saddle! Great Scott, but there was a sensation.
>
> Unquestionably, the popular thing in the world is novelty. These people had never seen anything of that cowboy business before, and it carried them clear off their feet with delight. (278)

Even the tournament, designed for entertainment, is raised by Hank to a new level of Buffalo Bill showmanship. Violence becomes performance, all part of the show. By making himself a ringmaster instead of executioner, Hank conceals the horrific aspect of his actions, much as the art and artifice of Twain's day (in the work of Frederic Remington or Buffalo

Bill, for instance) reduced the Western enterprise to a signifying system of active, violent, and supposedly heroic images. When Sagramor rounds for a final pass, the crowd cries out to Hank, "Fly, fly! Save thyself! This is murther!" (281). And it is murder, only not as the crowd suspects.

> I never budged so much as an inch, till that thundering apparition had got within fifteen paces of me; then I snatched a dragoon revolver out of my holster, there was a flash and a roar, and the revolver was back in the holster before anybody could tell what had happened.
>
> Here was a riderless horse plunging by, and yonder lay Sir Sagramor, stone dead. (281)

Sagramor's death is a rallying point for the rest of chivalry, though they remain in the dark as to what magic The Boss employs. He waits ready as they come—the lone frontier hero, the man with no past—and when they draw near, faces them down, both guns blazing.[23]

> In just no time, five hundred knights were scrambling into their saddles, and before you could wink a widely scattering drove were under way and clattering down upon me. I snatched both revolvers from the holsters and began to measure distance and calculate chances.
>
> Bang! One saddle empty. Bang! another one. Bang—bang! and I bagged two. Well it was nip and tuck with us, and I knew it. If I spent the eleventh shot without convincing these people, the twelfth man would kill me, sure.
>
> And so I never did feel so happy as I did when my ninth downed its man and I detected the wavering in the crowd which is premonitory of panic. An instant lost now, could knock out my last chance. But I didn't lose it. I raised both revolvers and pointed them—the halted host stood their ground just about one good square moment, then broke and fled. (282)

Notably the tournament is not an extracultural contest pitting monarchy against democracy, savagery against civilization, but a showdown between warring power interests within the culture itself—the feudalists versus the robber baron. The tournament allows the two fastest gunfighters in town to face each other, with the general citizenry involved only insofar as they wait to see who will "boss" them. Superficially, that final Boss would appear to be Hank Morgan, but Hank's triumph at arms is merely an extension of the several "final victories" over chivalry he has claimed throughout the novel—his destruction of Merlin's tower, his shooting of Sagramor—which have proven not so final at all. In underestimating the knights' resolve and refusing to recognize chivalry's implicit similarities to his own reign of terror, he completes the foundation for the Battle of the Sand Belt, where he must resort to the unadulterated genocide toward which his imperial rhetoric has propelled him.

Importantly the Armageddon of the novel's end destroys both Arthur's old feudal order and Hank's new democratic one. Just as the battle signals the closing down of Camelot, it likewise symbolizes the closing down of the American frontier (as Frederick Jackson Turner would note explicitly only several years after the publication of Twain's novel). It is only slightly amusing, then, that the finale of Hank's frontier is announced by the series of wires that Clarence strings throughout the kingdom, much as barbed wire destroyed the open range. As Clarence tells Hank, "We shan't have to leave our fortress, now, when we want to blow up our civilization" (301). But if Turner's discussion of the passing frontier would be couched in elegiac terms, Twain's assessment—as the reference to blowing up civilization confirms—is more along the lines of good riddance to bad rubbish. Finally, the Battle of the Sand Belt blurs Hank's political objectives, turning his "victory" into a largely meaningless celebration of violence and its efficiency.

Amid this chaos, in fact, all myth seems reduced to its most fundamental level. Arthur's dream of feudal order and Hank's idea of frontier democracy converge as they devolve into the single inarticulate act left to them. Even Merlin notes this close association when he mesmerizes Hank after the battle.

> "Ye were conquerors; ye are conquered! Those others are perishing—you also. Ye shall all die in this place—every one—except *him*. He sleepeth, now—and shall sleep thirteen centuries. I am Merlin!"
>
> Then such a delirium of silly laughter overtook him that he reeled about like a drunken man, and presently fetched up against one of our wires. His mouth is spread open yet; apparently he is still laughing. I suppose the face will retain that petrified laugh until the corpse turns to dust. (318)

Merlin falls prey to his own sense of mythic self-importance, supplying (in his death) one of the most poignant and representative images of the novel. His death brings the novel's various mythic cycles full circle: Hercules, that remnant of classical folklore, cracks Hank Morgan over the head with a crowbar; Hank defeats Merlin by blowing up his tower; Merlin reconquers Hank by sending him back to the century of his origin;

and Hank beats Merlin again, "posthumously" this time, with the electrical wire left at the mouth of the cave. The only myth remaining is the myth of religion, in the form of the Interdict, whose overt forms of violence would eventually force religious refugees to the New World. And in turn, those religious refugees would exercise their own version of true belief, giving rise—in overt ethnocentrism as well as more subtle cultural practices—to the ideology of frontier conquest transported to Camelot by Hank Morgan. Myth is circular here even as it is finite, a quality designed to conflate the novel's various myth-systems and highlight the inexorable self-destruction prefigured in their respective origins.

The novel's ending reaffirms this kind of hopelessness, Hank's death far away from those two people, Sandy and Hello-Central, who he finally realizes are all that matter. Critics have variously noted the inadequacy of this ending, pointing either to the oversentimentalized nature of Hank's dying soliloquy or to his unlikely transportation back to his own time in order to allow his story to end with the same annihilation as other Arthurian narratives. But Hank's downfall may be most important for the way that Twain uses it to revise American frontier conventions. Like other frontier heroes, Hank is denied a mate, losing Sandy after the final violence in Camelot. But unlike other heroes, Hank never completes the frontier's transition from a savage to a civilized space. In the world of frontier literature, these two facts are paradoxical. Being denied a mate is a direct result of the advent of civilization; never wholly removed from the savage world, the hero cannot enter into marriage because it is civilization's most fundamental covenant.

Thus the ending of *A Connecticut Yankee* should be read as an absolute failure of frontier doctrine, writ large in the smashed dream of empire and small in the unfulfilled promise of home and family. Jane Tompkins, in particular, has noted the way that the formula western arranges itself in direct opposition to women's culture, favoring violence over peaceful dialogue and worldly conflict over domestic issues. The irony of the formula western, then, is that its hero purports to guarantee a civilized space but achieves this end through means that are completely antithetical to the values of the culture he seeks to install. Well before the revisionist westerns of the twentieth century, *A Connecticut Yankee* merely followed this irony to its logical conclusion. Finally Hank's dream of old age with Sandy and Hello-Central becomes as untenable as his dream of imperial order. He discovers too late that his destruction of "savagery" signals his own descent into brutality and a repudiation of the peaceful values on which any stable version of "home" might be founded. Richard S. Pressman has argued that Hank "expires in typical sentimental fashion, longing for his lost domestic happiness, in a pastoral utopia, a 'nowhere' that never was."[24] But in the end, Hank has become more than a fallen Adam pining for his lost Eden (and Eve). He is a tragic hero in the truest sense, whose attempts at a benevolent version of empire reveal the vacuity of that dream and ultimately destroy the familial peace that he has believed himself to guarantee all along.

A Man's Role

Literary Influence and The Virginian

No book—at least none that I know—inspires more contrary responses than Owen Wister's *The Virginian* (1902). Where some critics see the book as a complex exploration of the links between violence and masculine identity in American culture, others tend to highlight its sexist elements, its indifference to family concerns, and its conspicuous endorsement of certain brands of brutality. Recent substantial interpretations continue in this vein. On the one hand, Lee Clark Mitchell and Forrest G. Robinson contend that *The Virginian* is simply not as violent as the subsequent popular westerns to which it is compared and that the "novel . . . raised expectations for a genre it did not actually quite define, prompting readers to exceed the text in their own reconstructions."[1] On the other hand, Jane Tompkins argues that the book is a misogynistic diatribe, derived from Wister's own strained relationship with a "domineering" mother and endorsing a world-view in which men "shall be master" of women.[2]

Disparate analyses aside, what really separates Tompkins from Mitchell/Robinson, I would argue, is the way that Tompkins presumes *The Virginian*'s place at the head of the twentieth-century popular western tradition while Mitchell and Robinson question that placement. Though it may seem subtle, the difference lies in the choice of whether to read *The Virginian* forward through the lens of the film, TV, radio, and book westerns that it supposedly inspired, or backward through the lens of literary predecessors from whom Wister synthesized his protagonist. The former approach creates a monolithic view of the book, where the sins of subsequent westerns are already embedded in the words and actions of Wister's hero. The latter approach liberates the novel from such connections and encourages critics to consider its links to other literature both within and beyond the boundaries of frontier fiction.

That second technique seems more complex to me, and while I would never overlook the overt racism, sexism, or ethnocentrism in some scenes, I think it only fair to explore *The Virginian* without the parameters of formula westerns having already determined how the book should be read. By design, Wister's novel extends and responds to a myriad of narratives preceding it, often signifying on those texts in multiple ways. Indeed, critical arguments meant to inscribe *The Virginian* as the progenitor of the twentieth-century western focus almost exclusively on the types of violent male performance that feature in the text. Those readings often ignore the context of such performance, both within the novel (where violence is undermined by a set of not-so-subtle subtexts) and in the line of its literary predecessors (whose simpler acceptance of male violence is regularly called into question by Wister's characters, the hero included). Finally, despite its formula reputation, *The Virginian* demonstrates a propensity to respond to issues of violence with remarkable complexity, and it ends not with a definite endorsement of social roles predicated on race, class, and gender (as some critics claim) but with a series of open-ended questions about cultural authority whose answers, it would seem, continue to be negotiated after the novel's ending.

From Cooper to Wister

Most critics writing about *The Virginian* take for granted a direct line of descent between James Fenimore Cooper and Wister. In fact, the only difference such critics note between these writers is that, where Cooper sees the schism between Western savagery and Eastern civilization as unassailable, Wister manages to unite the two by marrying his hero to Molly Wood. This position has been eloquently summarized by Christine Bold, whose *Selling the Wild West* serves as one of the most authoritative books on the development of the western genre through 1960. As Bold writes:

> By underscoring the contrasts between Eastern woman and Western man, Wister made their marriage that much more dramatic a resolution of their differences. At one level, Wister was simply acting out the conventional wedding which ends the pastoral romance. But he was also doing something important and novel within the development of the Western formula. By resolving the tensions between East and West presented in his love story, he healed one of the divisions exposed by Cooper—the Western hero's unfitness as a mate for the genteel heroine. This problem . . . was largely sidestepped by the dime novelists. They tended to provide Eastern heroes for their cultured heroines and never really foregrounded the love story. So, as many critics have pointed out, Wister was the first to create a Western hero who was handsome and chivalrous enough (partly because of his Southern origins) to marry an educated Easterner. The wedding enacts the first full reconciliation of Eastern civilization and Western wilderness in the popular Western genre. Countless later Westerns imitate the love story in *The Virginian* and repeat its romantic happy ending. The centering of the Western hero and his successful romance with a cultured heroine was Wister's main deviation from the dime novel plot and the major element of what became the new version of the Western formula.[3]

Bold's argument provides one possible lineage for Wister's hero. Certainly Wister was writing out of the same frontier tensions that had influenced Cooper, and there is no denying the sharp contrast between the resolutions of *The Virginian* and each of the Leatherstocking Tales. But by the same token, Bold's reading requires an uninterrupted, sixty-year jump from Cooper to Wister, despite a number of possible antecedents to the Virginian produced in the intervening years. And it also requires that Wister be read in the popular western vein, even when the novel itself provides a literary lineage independent of the frontier genre. Absent the twentieth-century texts that he would help to define, Wister saw himself writing out of several traditions. What follows is an analysis of those traditions and their impact on *The Virginian:* the popular frontier tradition, to be sure, but also the more literary tradition of Western regional writing and even the "high art" traditions of the English Renaissance and Victorian Period.

The Frontier Tradition

While he might have utilized them differently, Wister did not invent most of the "important and novel" plot changes with which Bold credits him. Long before *The Virginian,* members of the San Francisco Circle—Bret Harte and Joaquin Miller especially—were writing fictions in which "Eastern woman and Western man" were forming viable relationships. And even in Wister's own day literary writers—most prominently Stephen Crane—seemed obsessed with the intersection of frontier and domestic cultures, writing works that explored the various possibilities of such interaction. While the parallels between Wister and these predecessors are not exact, their intervening presence after Cooper certainly complicates the notions of cultural milieu and literary history attendant upon readings of *The Virginian*'s place in the frontier tradition.

Foremost, Bret Harte should be read as a precursor to Wister not only because of the Western landscapes dominating his stories, but also because Harte was widely popular in the latter half of the nineteenth century, making it almost certain that Wister was familiar with his work. While Harte's writing never resolved the romance plot as fully as *The Virginian,* many of his stories were preoccupied with love relationships, both traditional and nontraditional. John Seelye suggests that Harte anticipated Wister by developing characters whose rough western exteriors belied an amazing penchant for compassion (for example, the miners who adopt a baby in "The Luck of Roaring Camp" or the crew of blackguards who befriend Tom Simson and his fiancée in "The Outcasts of Poker Flat").[4] But even this assessment ignores the more obvious connection to a battery of Harte stories seeking explicitly to unite Eastern and Western characters. The best-known of these stories, and the most relevant to Wister, is "The Idyl of Red Gulch," in which a drunken Sierra miner named Sandy Morton reforms himself in order to court Miss Mary, a schoolmistress from San Francisco. As with the Virginian, Sandy's initial attempts with Miss Mary are halting and awkward. But he persists in direct gentlemanly fashion until, eventually, the couple find themselves together in the forest, where Miss Mary weaves garlands of flowers with Sandy lying at her feet—an encounter which, while falling short of consummation, does strike Miss Mary as "the shortest day of her weary life."[5]

Despite this union of Western man and Eastern woman, the parallels between Harte and Wister are not exact. For one thing, Sandy is a drunken rascal rather than a frontier hero. Moreover, his relationship with Miss Mary eventually falters when she learns that he has had a child with another woman (a prostitute, no less). But if love does not conquer all in Harte's story, the conditions under which the relationship forms certainly anticipate those of *The Virginian*. Miss Mary is an outsider, a schoolteacher, and a representative of the civilization that will ultimately reach the farthest throws of California, even Red Gulch. Her position causes her to regard the adult population of the town with disdain, such that her love for Sandy can find expression only after she has undergone a profound, if unarticulated, internal conversion. Several times, Harte mentions her initial aloofness: "Miss Mary, being possessed of certain rigid notions of her own, had not, perhaps, properly appreciated the demonstrative gallantry for which the Californian has been so justly celebrated by his brother Californian, and had, as a new-comer, perhaps, fairly earned the reputation of being 'stuck up'" (79). It is this contrary starting position which makes her love for the miner much more profound, just as Sandy's own movement from drunken lout to "natural gentleman" testifies to the conversionary power of their attraction. As with the Virginian and Molly, Sandy and Mary begin in extreme opposition only to gravitate inexplicably toward one another, a convergence which suggests the feasibility of any relationship, even one as dichotomous as East and West. To adopt Bold's language, "By underscoring the contrasts between Eastern woman and Western man, [Harte] made their [union] that much more dramatic a resolution of their differences."

If Harte provided the seed for romantic interaction between East and West, though, it reached fruition in the writing of Joaquin Miller, who borrowed heavily from Harte in order to produce his novel, *First Fam'lies in the Sierras* (1875), later turned into a play, *The Danites of the Sierras* (1881). The action of the novel combines the plots of several Harte stories (including "The Luck of Roaring Camp," "The Idyl of Red Gulch," and "The Poet of Sierra Flat")[6] and revolves around the arrival of two women in a California mining town, one a widowed schoolteacher from the East, the other a woman masquerading as a boy in order to avoid the Danites, or Mormon avengers.[7] As Seelye has noted, the principal action of the novel involves several courtships, chief among them the relationship—as in Harte—between a schoolteacher and a miner named Sandy. But where Harte's Sandy fails to win the hand of his beloved, Miller's Sandy "in the end marries the 'Widow,' as she is called, the first in a string of marriages that signal the final transformation of the camp."[8]

The shift from Harte to Miller should not be underestimated. Where Miss Mary rejects Sandy in "The Idyl of Red Gulch" for his singular indulgence with a prostitute (suggesting that some offenses will always prohibit relationships between Eastern and Western characters), Miller throws up no such impediment to Sandy and the Widow's marriage. Indeed, when the Widow has her first child only nine months after her wedding, she is tended by two prostitutes, whose presence during the consummately intimate and domestic birth-event suggests an elision of public and private spheres uncommon even in Harte, not to mention a shift in the overt cultural mores of the western story. Sandy's marriage clears the way for the rest of the miners to make matches of their own, creating a paradigm in which even the "common" men of the mining camp are able to compete and express their worth. In this sense, *First Fam'lies of the Sierras* employs the rhetoric of not only period sentimental narratives (which held that even ruffians and harlots could be redeemed by the presence of Christian love and grace), but also later formula westerns (whose heavily democratic ethic held that men should be judged not by artificial and class-based moral codes but by the caliber of their actions).

If the novel is democratic on the one hand, though, it is equally clear that Sandy provides the standard by which all other men should be judged, and in this regard Miller most clearly anticipates the development of the Virginian. Miller employs a rhetoric that, even while it celebrates an American notion of inherent equality, recognizes the elevation of a certain few men whose superiority is almost divine in origin.[9] His description of Sandy, which follows at length, sounds strikingly similar to a number of passages from Wister. Just as important is the ensuing comment by the narrator, who provides a philosophical context for Sandy's ascendancy in much the way that Wister's tenderfoot narrator differentiates between "the quality and the equality" in the opening lines of chapter thirteen in *The Virginian:*

> This Sandy never blustered or asserted himself at all. He was born above most men of his class, and he stood at their head boldly without knowing it. Had he been born an Indian he would have been a chief, would have led in battle, and dictated in council, without question or without opposition from any one. Had he been born in the old time of kings, he would have put out his hand, taken a crown, and worn it as a man wears the most fitting garment, by instinct. Sandy was born king of the Forks. He was king already, without knowing it or caring to rule it.

There are people just like that in the world, you know,—great, silent, fearless fellows, or at least there are in the Sierra-world, and they are as good as they are great. They are there, throned there, filling up more of the world than any ten thousand of those feeble things that God sent into the world, in mercy to the poor good men who sit all day silent, and cross-legged, and in nine parts, sewing, on a table. (Miller, 76–77)

Miller phrases this last sentence ambiguously enough to suggest that the "ten thousand" over whom Sandy is elevated includes both men and women, moreover that his deference to marriage elevates that institution even as Sandy's own importance remains independent of such bonds (just as, in marrying, the Virginian reaffirms how much he has been changed by his relationship with Molly even if their union makes him no less a man). Granted, Sandy does not engage in the same kind of violence that the Virginian does, but his relationship to the Widow—his position in the community, his preternatural heroism, and his pursuit and eventual marriage of his beloved—is identical to the scenario put forward in *The Virginian* a quarter-century later.[10]

Western violence, so integral to dime novels, would be added to this plotline in the 1890s by a group of literary writers, Wister among them, concerned with the closing down of the frontier and the integration of frontier types into the evolving civilization. Particularly important in the texts of this period were all of the themes characteristic of later literary western narratives: the opposition of public and private spheres; the domesticating influence of marriage; the imposition of class values symptomatic of urban/urbane America; and the evolving roles of men and women generally. Of these, Stephen Crane's "The Bride Comes to Yellow Sky" (1898) is probably the most remarkable, since it is so clearly concerned with the conventions of formula westerns—the saloon scene, the gunfight, a heroic sheriff—and offers a moral about marriage apparently in line with *The Virginian*. But equally important are the numerous other works—Frank Norris's *McTeague* (1899), for instance, or Jack London's *Martin Eden* (1909)—which suggest that Wister produced *The Virginian* in a climate of legitimate concern over both the final settlement of the frontier and the larger importance of frontier values in the American imagination. Rather than pulp fantasy, such works were using the Western region to interpret and revise the conventions not only of frontier literature but of the national literature as well.

It is in this sense ironic that Crane's "The Bride Comes to Yellow Sky" first appears to be a simple parody of western conventions, in which the outlaw Scratchy Wilson sacrifices his desired gunfight with Jack Potter as a concession to the marshal's new married status. Certainly Crane intended the story to be humorous, even childlike. Jack Potter and his new bride are so naïve that they cannot even order for themselves in the train's dining car, but must be coached uncomfortably through the meal by a porter. The incredulous salesman in the saloon must confirm and reconfirm Scratchy's almost ludicrously bad temperament. And even Scratchy himself is dumbstruck by the bride, his "funnel-shaped tracks in the heavy sand" combining his complete incredulity over Jack Potter's new situation with a simultaneous recognition that his own relationship to Potter has changed forever. In one telling passage, Crane notes how Scratchy's "boots had red tops with gilded imprints, of the kind beloved in winter by little sledding boys on the hillsides of New England."[11] Clearly, even the gunplay in which Potter and Wilson were formerly involved is a boy's game, a competition that is innocent in its own way even as it is rough. Marriage cuts the game short. It is the single irrefutable gesture of adulthood, and it ushers not only the Potters and Scratchy into a newly civilized era, but also the entire town of Yellow Sky and the West as a whole.

A closer reading of the story, however, suggests that "The Bride Comes to Yellow Sky" is not an antithesis of *The Virginian* so much as the same story located in a different place on the timeline. Despite its comic tint, the violence in the story (both actual and implied) is a serious business. The threat posed by Scratchy is so pronounced that the bartender has fortified his bar with metal plating and keeps a loaded Winchester on hand for such a purpose. When the salesman asks if Scratchy would actually kill anyone, he never receives a straight reply, only the bartender's oblique admonition that "He's out to shoot, and he's out for trouble. Don't see any good in experimentin' with him." And when Scratchy finally arrives, he mostly lives up to the town's expectations: his shots into the saloon are recklessly dangerous, and his firing several times at the stray dog seems irrationally cruel. Some critics contend that Crane uses such moments of near-violence to build audience anticipation for the showdown between Scratchy and Potter that never occurs. But the story provides clear evidence that such confrontations are not always harmless; Potter, as the barkeeper notes, "shot Wilson up once,—in the leg." And the potentially grave result of these showdowns is reinforced by the fact that Scratchy is "the last one of the old gang who used to hang out along the river here." Comical though he may be, and emblematic of an obsolete lifestyle, Scratchy remains the final representative of the kind of men who have disappeared from Yellow Sky, likely under the violent conditions that form the unspoken action of the story's past.

This point is remarkable because, in a manner of speaking, it aligns Crane more closely with Wister than more superficial readings would allow. For Crane, Potter's marriage is the final renunciation of very real hostilities, the advent of an adult life in which bullets are replaced by more civilized brands of interaction. In the same way, the Virginian's marriage to Molly Wood signals the hero's renunciation of his old lifestyle—including his killing of Trampas—and his development into "an important man, with a strong grip on many various enterprises."[12] The change is as absolute as it is sudden, and despite the Virginian's post-wedding desire to "become the ground, become the water, become the trees, mix with the whole thing" (385), he accedes to the stronger (if more pedestrian) imperative to be a good husband and father. Granted, the Virginian's change is problematic given the almost four hundred contrary pages that precede his submission to hearth and home. Crane—writing a synopsis of the western narrative, moreover beginning his tale after the wedding rather than long before—does not have to deal with much excess baggage regarding Scratchy's previous contests with Potter (or, for that matter, Potter's previous run-ins with other villains). But in order for Crane's story to be effective, an audience must take for granted the implied violent past of the male characters. They must read, but not too closely, the conventional frontier narrative that tacitly contextualizes the final encounter; otherwise, Potter's insistence that he is unarmed and Scratchy's acquiescence to an unspoken domestic authority have no meaning. In order for civilization's advance to resonate, it must be advancing against something else—in this case, the very real brutality of the waning frontier.

Not every Western fiction at the time viewed the meeting of savage and civilized worlds so optimistically. George McTeague, whose uxoricide confirms the incompatibility of frontier and domestic myths, extends the Westerner's code of violence to one logical conclusion. And Martin Eden, who gives up life as a cowhand and sailor to become a writer, is driven to suicide by his discoveries about urbane civilization: its strong resistance to social mobility, its ethnocentrism, and its genuine distaste for the working class. Norris and London seem to take opposing positions in the frontier debate. While Norris (despite pessimism about urbanization) sees frontier violence as the most immediate threat to domestic contentment, London portrays civilization as a brand of myth that is often just as brutal as the "savagery" it purports to displace. Despite their dichotomous views, though, Norris and London use a similar technique to get their ideas across. Like Crane and Wister, they chart the interchange of cultural spaces through the interchange of specific men and women—McTeague and Trina on the one hand, Martin and Ruth Morse on the other—where, simply put, men symbolize the frontier and women symbolize civilization.

My point here is not to find a causal relationship between Crane, Wister, Norris, and London (though it is likely that the men, publishing in some of the same magazines, were aware of each other's work). Instead I merely submit that Wister, writing alongside literary authors with similar concerns and having inherited a narrative tradition from earlier artists, saw himself as a literary author working through the serious and vexing question of how the frontier had shaped American culture. Despite the temptation to read Wister as simplistic, it is important to recognize that a number of earlier models, Miller especially, provided the kind of apotheosis that features in *The Virginian*. And if Wister's literary contemporaries did not lionize frontier values the same way he did, they at least demonstrated a grudging respect for certain elements of the Virginian's character. Thus Jack Potter and even Martin Eden become versions of the western hero: straightforward, brave, honest, and hardworking, though admittedly naïve. While today Wister cannot be considered completely apart from the twentieth-century genre that he so profoundly impacted, it is only fair that critics should recognize the literary circles to which he aspired, whose concerns he addressed, and whose members (including Henry James) lauded him as one of their own. To read Wister as the father of the popular western, descended from Cooper sixty years earlier, is fair when taking the long view of the genre at the end of the twentieth century. But such readings should always be mindful of the artistic sources on which Wister was drawing as well as the literary community of the day within which he was working.

The Virginian and High Art

That *The Virginian* seeks to be a work of high literature is also made clear by the books that the protagonist receives from Molly Wood. Critics almost uniformly read these works as a dismissal of women and women's lives. The Virginian enjoys the direct physical confrontation of Prince Hal and Harry Hotspur in *Henry IV;* he prefers Mercutio to Romeo because the latter talks too much ("There is beautiful language," he writes to Molly, "but Romeo is no man" [217]); and he dismisses Jane

Austen as "frillery" (250). Some critics even suggest that, like Cooper, much of Wister's fiction is adapted from the male-centered, violent, and "nationalistic" novels of Sir Walter Scott, citing as evidence the Virginian's appreciation of *Kenilworth*. Clearly, Wister is painting a lineage for his book in the preferred library of his protagonist. But it would be a mistake to view the symbolism of that library as one-sided or straightforward. As with Wister's engagement of his own literary peers, *The Virginian*'s echoes of Shakespeare and Scott are complex, and their meanings cut several ways.

Henry IV is a perfect example. On the surface, the Virginian celebrates Hal and Hotspur in equal measure, valorizing not so much either man but the vital contest in which they are involved. This celebration is particularly important given its proximity, late in the novel, to the Virginian's own showdown with Trampas. Shakespeare's "endorsement" of martial conflict echoes the Virginian's own, such that the Virginian can present his actions as a natural expression of manhood, the same kind to which men (even Shakespearean ones) have resorted throughout history. As he puts it to Molly,

> "Shakespeare. *Henry the Fourth*. The British king is fighting, and there is his son the prince. He cert'nly must have been a jim-dandy of a boy if that is all true. Only he would go around town with a mighty triflin' gang. They sported and they held up citizens. And his father hated his travelling [*sic*] with trash like them. It was right natural—the boy and the old man! But the boy showed himself a man too. He killed a big fighter on the other side who was another jim-dandy—and he was sorry for having it to do. . . . I understand most all of that. There was a fat man kept everybody laughing. He was awful natural too; except yu' don't commonly meet 'em so fat. But the prince—that play is bed-rock, ma'am!" (270–71)

Masculinity and violence are inseparable in this passage. Indeed, per the Virginian's reading, it is an expert use of violence that primarily distinguishes boys from men. Prince Hal literally becomes an adult when he kills Hotspur, quashing his own reservations and, in effect, doing what he has to do. Duty—despite his feeling for his opponent—becomes his paramount concern, expressed in the most basic but momentous of actions: taking another life. The Virginian reads Prince Hal's situation as analogous to his own, though he likely views his circumstances as even graver. Where Hal must face the admirable Hotspur, the Virginian faces cattle rustlers and the despicable villain, Trampas. How much more imperative, then, is the Virginian's own tacit commission to face his enemy in battle? The final showdown is not only what makes him a man but also what saves the surrounding community from crime and violence. Wister simply raises Shakespeare to the level of democracy: the Virginian and Trampas fight less for a crown—the title of fastest gun, as it were—than for the rights of Wyoming residents to dictate their futures free from a savage external threat.

Such readings are in keeping with traditional versions of the frontier narrative, but if Wister is offering a simplistic justification for the Virginian's violence, then it is just as quickly undercut by the events of the narrative. Granted, the hero's speech about Shakespeare does anticipate his confrontation with Trampas, but it more immediately precedes his lynching of the rustlers, including his former friend Steve, an action over which the Virginian expresses continual regret and from which he never fully seems to recover. This relationship has its own Shakespearean echoes, because if *Henry IV* is in part about Prince Hal's assumption of manhood (and regency) through his willingness to enter mortal combat, it is also about his dissociation from those parts of his earlier life that marked him indelibly as a boy. Thus at the end of the play's second part, Hal, now King Henry the Fifth, banishes Falstaff permanently from his vicinity. And as if such banishment does not seem like a serious enough break, given the life-and-death stakes for which the new king plays, Shakespeare reinforces it in *Henry V* when the king must hang Bardolph, his former friend and Falstaffian cohort.

Henry accepts Bardolph's fate with stoicism befitting a king. He simply tells Fluellen, in reference to Bardolph's robbing a French church, that "We would have all such offenders so cut off."[13] As Henry's heir apparent, the Virginian believes that he could execute justice as readily—and he does, despite misgivings, assist in Steve's lynching. But unlike Henry, the Virginian revisits Steve's death again and again. He expresses regret to the narrator over his involvement in the killing and even cries out Steve's name during the delirium when he is tended by Molly. Wister intends such displays partly to humanize the Virginian, to prove that he sympathizes with Steve and is therefore a character with whom readers should sympathize. But in creating his character this way, Wister also manages to revise Shakespeare ever so slightly, calling into question the almost mechanical nature with which Henry accepts Bardolph's fate. "Presume not that I am the thing I was," Henry tells Falstaff, "For God doth know, and the world shall perceive, / That I have turned away from my former self." Henry makes good on this promise with Bardolph, but the Virginian finds it more difficult to dismiss his past. Despite adhering to his sense of duty, he cannot get Steve out of his head. He cannot fully justify the lynching to himself and, by extension, cannot fully justify the simple code to which he has pledged his life. If Henry suggests that changing one's outlook is as simple as changing one's station, then the Virginian undermines that claim. Despite being made foreman and taking on new worldly responsibilities (including his pursuit of a wife), part of the Virginian remains the young man who shared with Steve a kind of affection that he shares with no one else in the novel. The two men had "hunted in couples" since they were "just colts" (322), and Steve is the only person to refer to the Virginian by a name, Jeff. As the Virginian puts it succinctly, "You can't never change your memory!" (312).

Indeed, the Virginian's life often fails to match up to his chosen textual models. He chooses Mercutio over Romeo, for instance, because he believes "there would have been no foolishness and trouble" if Mercutio "had got Juliet," conveniently ignoring his own observation several lines earlier that Mercutio's actions ultimately get him "killed" (217). Such disconnects are not accidental, but seem intentionally employed by Wister to confirm the real danger of the Virginian's chosen lifestyle. And if the central message of the novel seems to be that the Virginian cannot lose— in love, in battle, anywhere—then a subtler narrative strand undoes that certainty. This technique is echoed in Wister's choice of *Kenilworth* as the lone Sir Walter Scott novel that Molly gives to the Virginian. While Scott has been read as a precursor to Cooper—and, therefore, as a precursor to the frontier novel in America—*Kenilworth* lacks the derring-do of *Rob Roy* or *Ivanhoe*. Instead, the novel is a kind of suspense-thriller in which several men compete to see who will control the novel's central female character, Amy Robsart. Amy is the wife of Dudley, earl of Leicester, who for political reasons wants to keep his marriage a secret from Queen Elizabeth. He turns for help to Richard Varney, his servant, who agrees to pretend to be Amy's husband. When Varney begins to fear for his own position, though, he convinces Leicester that Amy has been unfaithful and should be executed. Leicester later reverses this decision, sending several agents to stop Varney and finally telling Queen Elizabeth the truth, but his change of heart comes too late. By the time Varney is captured, Amy is already dead.

On its face, Scott's book seems like a bizarre choice of analogue for *The Virginian*. If its presence in the novel is intended to validate the male-centric and violent action of Wister's narrative, then why did Wister choose a work in which many of the main characters are killed or commit suicide? Why does he choose a work in which the heroine (and chief love-interest) is destroyed through the brutal machinations of the men whom she trusts for her care? Contrary to critical assertions, the Virginian never claims to like Scott's novel; the narrative only confirms that Molly "had provided him with Sir Walter Scott's *Kenilworth*" (109). Even so, *Kenilworth* stands almost as a voice of protest to the action of *The Virginian*, suggesting that the course on which Wister's protagonist has set himself is destined for tragedy. It could be that Molly Wood gives her suitor the book as an objection to violence, the same kind of objection she makes in person throughout the book. It could be that Wister intentionally selected *Kenilworth* because of the way he saw his hero revising the tragic elements of many Victorian novels. But more likely the choice of *Kenilworth* was designed to highlight the potential tragedy of the Virginian's endeavors. It is worth mentioning that, of the many western stories he wrote, only *The Virginian* and *Lin McLean* end "optimistically" with a union. If the Virginian were largely unaware of the jeopardy in which his actions placed himself and others, then Wister clearly was not. The presence of *Kenilworth*, as much as an antecedent to the frontier novel form, serves as a reminder of the danger that plays out differently in other Wister fictions.

Such complexity confirms Wister's place amid the literary western writers of his era. Even though his story may seem simple in comparison to works by Norris or London, his double play on the works of Shakespeare and Scott suggests a writer in command of the literary conventions (frontier and otherwise) that he had inherited, aware of the limitations of the story he was telling. Readers may wonder how seriously to take the undercurrent of doubt in the novel, especially given a main narrative line that successfully fulfills the promise of righteous violence anticipated from the start. But perhaps less important than the degree of doubt in the novel is the fact that it exists at all. Unlike other frontier heroes—both before and after—the Virginian's complacency regarding his own rightness is disturbed several times, by Steve's death especially. He even acknowledges that he might have turned out differently under more "civilized" circumstances. "If I was one of your little scholars hyeh in Bear Creek schoolhouse," he tells Molly, "yu' could learn me to like such frillery. But I'm a mighty ignorant, growed-up man" (250). It is not a big admission, but in a book as apparently single-minded as *The Virginian*, it is more than one might reasonably expect. Despite his hero's self-assuredness, Wister cannot seem to shake his own niggling doubts about the Virginian's (non)responses to Molly's intellectual probing. The presence of this doubt, however subdued, chases the couple throughout the novel and is never wholly resolved. Granted, some scholars would likely ask what greater resolution is necessary; in the final gunfight and marriage, Wister puts aside his own philosophical objections to advance a world-view in which the use of violence always trumps more rational discourse. But on the other hand, Wister needed a place to conclude his story, and faced with tragedy on the one hand (à la Cooper) and apotheosis on the other (à la Miller), he made his choice in favor of a hero who, however flawed, was better than the alternative, Trampas. This choice does not settle debate but merely cuts it short, leaving behind an overt assertion of the Virginian's dominance tinged with unsettling hints that he may not be as perfect as the narrative makes him out to be.

Giving *The Virginian* a new literary lineage, even reading that lineage in a subversive way, does not undo the more explicit racist and sexist transgressions that rest on the surface of the text. But such undoing was not my goal. Rather, I had hoped to unsettle the easy assumptions that invariably pigeonhole the novel as "the first popular western" and, in the process, to call into question whatever else critics might take for granted. One does not have to look far to understand how such assumptions influence readings of the novel; indeed, they are built into the most important themes of the book.

Take, for example, the issue of violence. Critics who assume that violence lies at the heart of *The Virginian* point, in particular, to the final showdown as Wister's sign that public power is negotiated by men through calculated displays of brutality. But if *The Virginian* raises violence to the level of cultural spectacle, it does so in a remarkably subdued way. Atrocities like the lynching and the gunfight, which take place offstage, do not occur quickly and deliberately—as Tompkins suggests—but ponderously. The narrator's anxiety builds to an almost palpable level when he is forced to spend the night with the condemned rustlers before their execution; countless people (all of them men except Molly) spend a period of several hours trying to talk the Virginian out of his final confrontation with Trampas. Violence, when it does occur in front of the audience, is both savage and irrational, as in Balaam's blinding Pedro. And it is never without its consequences, with even "just" violence impacting the main characters in profoundly adverse ways. The Virginian's despair over Steve, for instance, cannot be underestimated; it twice reduces him to tears, making his "the only Western novel . . . in which the hero cries"

(Tompkins 153). Wister seems so concerned about the mixed messages sent by his hero, in fact, that he must enlist the aid of Judge Henry to explain the moral purposes of violence to Molly. The Judge fares no better than his foreman, however; his rambling speech about republicanism spuriously conflates the will of the individual citizen with the will of the government, a claim tantamount to anarchy, which Molly is quick to point out. Moreover, the Judge may unwittingly indict the very process that he seeks to defend. In explaining the difference between hanging Wyoming rustlers and "burning . . . Southern Negroes," he concludes that the latter is "proof that the South is semi-barbarous" (339), conveniently forgetting the Virginian's Southern heritage so often reiterated by the narrator. The Virginian's identity tacitly yokes those two brands of violence, undermining the easy dichotomy articulated by the Judge. Even the tenderfoot narrator recognizes this in his reservations about the Judge's endorsement of lynching: "I cannot say that I believe in doing evil that good may come. I do not. I think that any man who honestly justifies such course deceives himself" (336).

Similarly complex arguments could be made about gender relations. While most critics see the hero's marriage to Molly as a façade—a device used to silence her valid objections to his lifestyle—the novel repeatedly offers up its simple faith that marriage changes a man irrevocably for the better. In particular, marriage sequesters men completely from their former lives of violence; they simply no longer participate in public contests even if, like the Virginian, such contests had practically defined their experience prior to being wed. Readers should note that weddings both begin and end the novel, the humorous opportunism of Uncle Hughey transmuted into the serious determination with which the Virginian wins Molly's affection. Indeed, where even the life and death struggles of the cowboy's work appear to be a version of gaming or play, marriage is a serious business, treated with solemnity and reverence, the one clear demarcation of maturation and progress. This fact is also made clear early in the novel with the episode involving the engineer (whose wife is gravely ill). While all of "the boys" quiet down out of deference to the wife's condition, it is the Virginian especially who collects the flowers and leaves the bouquet anonymously by her door.

None of this is meant to suggest that *The Virginian* should be read, in the first instance, as a protest against violence or, in the second, as a sentimental novel that celebrates the conversionary power of women's lives. It is, however, meant to point out that these tensions exist side by side with their antitheses in the novel and are in a constant state of flux, continually negotiating how characters should view the world and each other. My basic project in this book has been to read fictions about the West against predominant critical trends, but *The Virginian* demands a departure from that system because, finally, the book is not just sexist diatribe or penetrating cultural analysis; it is both. Despite advancing certain opinions deplorable by contemporary standards, the novel never wavers in its commitment to dialogue—both the dialogue between characters where ideas are put forward and refined, and the dialogue between authors where one narrative answers another, sometimes in a variety of ways. Whatever effect Wister's novel may have had on popular literary markets later, it is important to remember the complex cultural interchange in which he engaged with both his contemporaries and even past greats like Scott and Shakespeare. His is a literary endeavor, to be sure, one that places *The Virginian* at the head of the popular western tradition but allows the novel, in its best moments, to transcend that position at the same time.

5

(Re)Writing a
Native American
Western

*John Rollin Ridge
and Zitkala-Sa*

Part of the problem with writing about Native American fiction of
the nineteenth century is that the genre almost does not exist.[1] The reasons for this dearth are complex and somewhat speculative. In part, written stories were not a natural genre for Indian writers, whose storytelling
relied heavily on the spontaneous and performative elements of oral discourse.[2] Moreover, history discouraged fiction: in the face of literal aggression, Natives were forced to operate within those rhetorical forms
that could most readily communicate their situation to an ambivalent,
at best, white reading audience. Accordingly Native writing strategies
mirrored those of other nineteenth-century American minority groups
struggling for recognition, relying heavily on anthropological and autobiographical sketches, moral and political tracts, even economic analyses.[3]
Written fiction was produced by only the tiniest fraction of Native

writers—writers, moreover, who were not considered to be in the van-
guard of the fight for Indian equality and freedom.[4]

In retrospect, these facts only serve to enhance the importance of the
rhetorical and cultural strategies by which early Indian fiction writers, la-
boring in relative obscurity, worked to differentiate themselves from
white counterparts. While certain fictions sought to evoke audience sympathies with a realistic depiction of Native American life—especially its
decline in the face of white aggression—a more common and subversive
narrative strategy was to invert the terms of white western discourse
within Indian novels and stories. Changing the traditionally white hero
into a racial (and sometimes sexual) Other, such narratives used the archetypically heroic movements of frontier texts to valorize their Native
subjective position. Engaging in the same kind of semisavage inter-
changes as their white "cowboy forebears," the protagonists of these stories offered white audiences a window into the Native American text on
the audiences' cultural terms, playing heavily upon the senses of adventure and righteous violence characteristic of white frontier novels. At the
same time, however, these narratives offered a version of reality radically
detached from the one to which most western narratives adhered, for in
valorizing an Indian hero/heroine, they automatically subverted the ethnocentric core implicit in white frontier accounts.[5] Moreover, even as
they depicted protagonists involved in a series of events that closely paralleled white adventure stories, they likewise retained an element of those
mimetic fictions that were designed to accurately represent Native American life. In this sense they doubly undermined the figure of the Indian
common to white western discourse, first by placing minority characters
in roles generally reserved for white male heroes, and second by adding a
sense of depth to such characters (managing to tell a "realistic" Native
story in the midst of white potboiler fiction).

Two accomplished practitioners of this narrative form were John
Rollin Ridge (1827–1871) and Zitkala-Sa (1876–1938) who, though they
lived and wrote almost fifty years apart, can be grouped together as pro-
genitors of an incipient Native American fiction tradition.[6] Neither was
particularly prolific.[7] Ridge's fame rests largely on one novel, *The Life and
Adventures of Joaquin Murieta, the Celebrated California Bandit* (1854, revised 1871), while Zitkala-Sa is best known for *American Indian Stories,* a
collection of short fiction and autobiographical essays written from 1900
to 1902 and first collected in a single volume in 1921. While both authors
wrote intermittent newspaper and magazine articles throughout the rest
of their careers, they never managed to produce works of the same length

or, most likely, importance to literary and cultural scholars as these two volumes. Prolificacy aside, though, the careers of Ridge and Zitkala-Sa follow the same general pattern, with their major works underscoring similar strategies of Native American resistance to and inversion of white cultural and martial oppressions.

A quick overview of these works might suggest their similar designs. In *Joaquin Murieta*, Ridge celebrates the exploits of a Mexican highwayman operating in the Anglo communities of southern California. Repeatedly wronged by whites, Murieta takes to robbery when he can receive justice in no other fashion. His story parallels Ridge's own experiences as a Cherokee Indian, and the author several times draws direct correlations between Murieta's plight and the sufferings of other minorities. The novel, then, subverts white "dime-novel" discourse on two levels. First, it actively attempts to mythologize a nonwhite hero. And second, through the narrative techniques of disguise and transference, it expands the tableau of Murieta's story to incorporate other minorities wronged by whites, thereby suggesting a pan-racial sentiment characteristic of much later minority writing.

An essayist and short-story writer, by contrast, Zitkala-Sa's appropriation of white frontier discourse is more incidental than Ridge's. In fact, the first few essays in *American Indian Stories,* on which critical discussions of the book tend to focus, recount the author's childhood experience moving from a Sioux reservation to a white boarding school in Indiana. Needless to say, the strategies of resistance common to this first section are subtler than the confrontational paradigms of frontier narratives. However, as the book moves from early autobiographical essays to short fiction in its latter half, Zitkala-Sa's narrative technique shifts to emphasize a more active style of resistance than her own experience in boarding school would have allowed. Three stories in particular—"The Soft-Hearted Sioux," "The Trial Path," and "A Warrior's Daughter"— underscore a paradigm of personal struggle and opposition that closely parallels the heroic action of white pulp westerns. Of special note is "A Warrior's Daughter," which focuses on the exploits of an Indian woman compelled to take up arms in defense of her lover. Not only does this plot directly invert both the gender and racial predilections of traditional frontier stories, but it also provides an interesting extension of the subtler discourses of female Native resistance inscribed by the first half of the book.

Obviously, some differences exist between the two authors. Ridge is less concerned with the "gendered" aspect of the Indian question than Zitkala-Sa, who occasionally yokes the concerns of Native women to the concerns of women at large. Moreover, writing in the beginning of the twentieth century, Zitkala-Sa's perspective on the devastation that resulted from imperialism is more complete in many senses than that of Ridge, writing in the 1850s. Nonetheless such differences seem more than outweighed by the similarities between the two writers. Both very specifically invert the strategies of white discourse, expanding the definition of exactly what an Indian story is and might be. Both operate from the same basic discursive impulse, yoking Native concerns to those of larger "marginalized" groups within the country. And finally both represent, in their mixed white and Indian heritage, the first in a long chain of mixed-race writers trying to negotiate a space between cultures.

The point, of course, is not that Ridge and Zitkala-Sa should be read as popular western writers. Rather, this chapter seeks to emphasize the intersections between the literary worlds of the popular western and early Indian fiction. Simultaneously adopting and co-opting the forms and themes of the popular West, these two writers produced fictions that were both familiar and novel to the white audience encountering them. Such strategies are particularly important coming as they do at the beginning of the Native American fiction tradition. Read by critics in isolation, if at all, Ridge and Zitkala-Sa instead form the first link in a chain of narrative resistance leading up to the present day. Their writing is not only important for the way it spoke to white society in the nineteenth century, but also for the way it anticipated the strategies of other Native writers well into the twentieth.

The Life and Adventures of Joaquin Murieta

The publishing history of Ridge's *The Life and Adventures of Joaquin Murieta* is almost as integral to a discussion of the book as the narrative events themselves. First issued in 1854 as a dime novel, the book was quickly appropriated both by other authors and into other forms: subsidiary dime novels (legal and pirated), serialized fiction, stage plays, literary novels, even popular myth. In fact, the enduring popularity of Ridge's story is evidenced not only by *Joaquin Murieta*'s being made into several films at the turn of the twentieth century, but also by the persistence of the Murieta myth up to the present and the willingness of readers (scholarly and nonscholarly alike) to believe in the bandit-hero as an historical figure rather than a fictional protagonist.[8] Understandably, the myriad history of the volume makes it difficult to classify in literary terms. While it demonstrates a number of qualities common to dime novels of the period, it also seeks to promote racial tolerance and, in doing so, undercuts the easy vocabularies of racial dichotomy, righteous violence, and universal morality which most western dime novels took for granted.[9] These subversions likewise beg questions of audience. Given the relatively straightforward and simplistic cultural work that scholars understand most dime novels to do, why were readers so attracted to a work which broke marginally with the anticipated structure and radically with the anticipated themes of a western? Or perhaps more to the point, how did Ridge manage to engage a readership predisposed to racial stereotypes with a narrative largely opposed to those stereotypes? The answer has to do with the complex game of disguise and transference that *The Life and Adventures of Joaquin Murieta* plays, subtly masquerading Murieta as a typical dime-novel hero through the form of the novel in order to implicitly co-opt the racist ideology at the genre's base.

This game of disguise and inversion is itself well disguised throughout the narrative, which presents itself as a straightforward tale about a stereotypical avenging frontier hero. Focusing on a young Mexican seeking his fortune in southern California, Joaquin's story begins as he tries his luck at a series of trades only to be victimized each time by unscrupulous whites. He turns to outlawry only after his mining claim is stolen, his mistress is raped, he is run off several parcels of land, and finally he is whipped (and his half-brother is hung) for a horse theft that neither man committed. Part of this last event is rendered as follows:

> [The crowd] listened to no explanation, but bound him to a tree and publicly disgraced him with the lash. They then proceeded to the house of his half-brother and hung him without judge or jury. It was then that the character of Joaquin changed, suddenly and irrevocably. His soul swelled beyond its former boundaries, and the barriers of honor, rocked into atoms by the strong passions which shook his heart like an earthquake, crumbled around him. Then it was that he declared to a friend that he would live henceforth for revenge and that his path should be marked with blood.[10]

Two aspects of this passage deserve closer consideration. First is Ridge's reference to the "judge or jury" so conveniently overlooked by the white vigilantes. While Joaquin claims to have been victimized by a small class "of lawless and desperate men, who bore the name of Americans but failed to live up to the honor and dignity of that title" (9), the narrative continually stresses an official sanction to the actions of this class. Joaquin fails to get justice not only because of the efforts of a minority of white

thugs, but also because of the complicit courts that offer him no recourse.
Refusing to recognize Joaquin as an American because of his race, official
bodies time and again fail to intercede on his behalf, or on the behalf of
any Mexicans in the book. And it is finally this official inaction—despite
what Joaquin expressly claims about his victimization at the hands of a
few evil whites—which drives him to the life of an outlaw.

The involuntary nature of Joaquin's turn to crime is the second important point emphasized by the passage. Refused any respectable identity by an unjust white society, he becomes a bandit not by choice but by
necessity. Ridge frames this version of Joaquin from the beginning of the
novel when he claims in the opening paragraph that the "character of this
truly wonderful man was nothing more than a natural production of the
social and moral condition of the country in which he lived, acting upon
certain peculiar circumstances favorable to such a result" (7). Again, Ridge
constructs this picture carefully; the circumstances causing Joaquin's devolution into crime are "peculiar" rather than "representative," suggesting
the small minority of whites culpable for Joaquin's situation. But by contrast, the first part of the description seems to indict Euro-American culture as a whole, if not for its active role in Joaquin's persecution, then for
the same kind of apathy as the legal system that breeds the "social and
moral condition" conducive to the rise of racial "mercenaries." Repeatedly Ridge emphasizes the point that Joaquin was made evil by a culture
that, failing to respond to racist attacks, provided no alternative even to
honest and industrious minorities. As the author's first lengthy description of the bandit attests,

> While growing up, he was remarkable for a very mild and peaceable disposi-
> tion, and gave no sign of that indomitable and daring spirit which later char-
> acterized him. Those who knew him in his school-boy days speak
> affectionately of his generous and noble nature at that period of his life and
> can scarcely credit the fact that the renowned and bloody bandit of Califor-
> nia was one and the same being. (8)

Overwhelmed by adverse circumstances, that is, Joaquin is made into
other than what he would naturally be, an assertion that not only points
to the immoral influence of the white community, but also undermines
from the start the conception of minorities as innately less virtuous or
intelligent than their white counterparts.

The effect of this description, rhetorically speaking, is quite compelling. Ridge implicitly condemns white society as a whole while

appearing to condemn only those "bad" whites directly responsible for Joaquin's condition. Moreover, he challenges the central western myth of self-reliance by showing how even those individuals willing to struggle for what they receive are often undone by forces beyond the rather simplistic conception of hard work equaling success. Ridge's apparent purpose is not primarily to debunk the "American Dream"; as a beneficiary of both financial and artistic success in the white world, the author appears to sympathize strongly with Joaquin's desire to enhance his "prospects" by becoming an American businessman. What he truly seeks to debunk are the simplistic categories of race through which the white community assigns human value and decides who will or will not enjoy upward economic and social mobility. Ridge's novel works to depict Joaquin as an exemplary racial type, a man whose energies could have been turned to highly productive social good but, because of white apathy, are mutated into particularly poignant expressions of racial antipathy. In sum, the book delineates the arbitrary and transparent racial categories which allow for Joaquin's exclusion; suggests how much easier life would be for white Americans were a man like Joaquin working with rather than against their interests; and finally enlists the support of that silent white majority which Ridge explicitly distinguishes from outright villains but whose implicit guilt is invoked and played upon at each narrative turn.

Notably Ridge accomplishes these goals almost exclusively through his description of Joaquin as a character. Physically, the bandit's "complexion was neither very dark or [*sic*] very light" (8), and he "spoke very good English" such that people "could scarcely make out whether he was a Mexican or an American" (85). Several times, in fact, Joaquin successfully masquerades as a white American in very public spaces—a home, a courtroom, a saloon. Yet despite his lack of telling characteristics, he is still persecuted for being a Mexican, a label ascribed almost solely out of the greed and envy of the "superior race" (9) that wishes to reserve the protagonist's success for itself. The subsequent violence heaped upon Joaquin lends credence to his decision to become an outlaw, making him a version of the traditional avenging hero of frontier literature who turns to violence when he cannot resolve his problems in any other fashion. In such a narrative, justice is earned at the end of a gun, meted out by that character most qualified to dispense it. And while even the narrator of *Joaquin Murieta* admits that sometimes the hero takes his violent response to the Anglos too far, there is still more than a little truth to the notion that, as a former victim turned avenger, Joaquin is specially qualified to determine who does and does not deserve punishment.[11]

As readers of frontier literature, Ridge's audience would have been predisposed to sympathize with the hero and to accept his moral outlook —even if those readers were somehow implicated in the process. Given its unusual racial dynamic, however, *Joaquin Murieta* must work harder than most frontier novels to inscribe its protagonist as the hero rather than the villain. For this reason, Ridge takes the unusual step of having Joaquin disown his own national and racial "predilections" and accept the value systems of the Anglo community, if only to highlight the intensity of that community's betrayal.[12] As the narrator claims, "Disgusted with the conduct of his degenerate countrymen and fired with enthusiastic admiration of the American character, the youthful Joaquin left his home with a buoyant heart and full of the exhilarating spirit of adventure" (8). This geographical departure suggests a correspondent moral departure from the "degenerate conduct" stereotypically associated with Mexicans, a move signaling Ridge's audience that Joaquin's morals are commensurate with those of more traditional, if avenging, white frontier protagonists.

Joaquin's moral code is highlighted by his assumption of an identity that follows the pattern of not only American frontier heroes but also their Anglo cultural antecedents, Robin Hood especially.[13] Traversing the countryside with his band of hearty male associates, accompanied by his faithful mistress (the Maid Marian–like Rosita), Joaquin echoes a figure straight out of Sherwood. He can be generous to the poor, as when he stops an associate from robbing a ferryman and says to the intended victim, "you are a poor man and you never injured me. Put us over the river and I will pay you for your trouble" (65). And his band lives by the general caveat of robbing only those who deserve to be robbed: "It was a rule with them to injure no man who ever extended them a favor, and, whilst they plundered every one else and spread devastation in every other quarter, they invariably left those ranches and houses unharmed whose owners and inmates had afforded them shelter or assistance" (19). This Robin Hood identity strengthens Joaquin's position within a white moral discourse, working to blur the issue of race and to make the protagonist, at least for the novel's audience, an exact replica of the archetypal Anglo version of the wronged man turned outlaw.[14] In another scene, Joaquin rescues a young woman kidnapped by one of his band and promises to return her to her family. Seeing the woman's surprise at his intention, the bandit claims, "Yes, Señorita, I *am* a man. I was once as noble a man as ever breathed, and if I am not so now, it is because men would not allow me to be as I wished. You shall return to your mother and your lover, if I die bringing it about" (106). Just a man, the quote would suggest, devoid of race and nationality, adhering to a brand of ethics that is largely intuited yet justified, if not always "perfect" in a purely moral sense. This character is the illusion the text works to create for its audience. Having disowned his Mexican heritage and been robbed of his potential place as an American citizen, Joaquin finds himself caught between identities and seeking vengeance for the wrongs committed against him—that is, in one of the classic roles of the frontier hero.

Obviously Ridge must balance a variety of cultural forces in the novel: though a Mexican, Joaquin accepts an Anglo value system and even dissociates himself from his racial heritage, if only to become a "champion" of that heritage when it is reinscribed upon him by the American community of which he seeks to become a part. No doubt such paradoxes did not seem foreign to Ridge, who had ambivalent feelings toward his own Cherokee background as well as toward American Indians in general.[15] A mixed-blood member of a prominent slaveholding Cherokee family, Ridge had his life changed irrevocably when in 1839 tribe members killed his father and grandfather for supporting tribal relocation to Oklahoma. Later, defending himself from the faction that murdered his relatives, Ridge killed a man in a fight, then fled to California for fear that the courts would not believe his claim of self-defense. Feeling betrayed by his own people, yet not completely able to trust the American legal system, Ridge found himself caught between identities—too acculturated to be trusted by Indians yet too Indian-looking to be trusted by whites. In this fashion, Joaquin's story becomes a version of Ridge's own, focusing on a character between cultures with little recourse in either. And like Joaquin, Ridge is forced to balance several seemingly antithetical loyalties. Highly contemptuous of certain Indians and openly embracing acculturation, Ridge nonetheless could not escape his physical Indian identity and often found himself in the position of having to argue for Native rights—not to mention for the simple idea that at least some Indians were capable of becoming civilized intellectuals. Ironically, in his attempt to become "more white," Ridge stood out as a kind of test case for exactly what Indians could be; in trying to distance himself from his heritage, he became at some level its representative. As such, the abuses suffered by Joaquin (which symbolize the abuses suffered by all Mexican Americans) can be translated into the abuses suffered by Ridge that, whether he wanted them to or not, symbolized the abuses suffered by all Indians.[16] Even the smallest details of the novel and of Ridge's biography

are the same; run off his mining claims by fraudulent white legal maneu-
vers, Joaquin's dispossession represents the displacement of the Cherokee,
whose forced migration was the initial cause of Ridge's personal tragedies.

Who was ultimately to blame for Ridge's fate: the whites who took
Cherokee land, or the Cherokee people who retaliated against Ridge's
family? The fact that this question, among others, has no definitive answer suggests why scholars—perplexed by the ambiguities of the author's
life—have failed to agree on the cultural work accomplished by *Joaquin
Murieta*. While the connections between Joaquin and Ridge seem too
blatant to ignore, some scholars still have a hard time resolving Ridge's
lifelong belief in acculturation to his "pure" Indian identity; moreover,
they cannot see how a man who stood against abolition most of his life
could construct a book that seems to speak for a brand of pan-racialism.[17]
The most insightful responses to these issues have called into question the
nature of Native American identity itself. As Maria Mondragon writes,
"In attempting to determine where to place Ridge as holding either 'white
racist ideals' or 'true Indian ideals' we elide questions of our own assumptions about race and authentic history."[18] In reality, there is little question
about the general antiracist sentiment of the novel; it both begins and
ends with a didactic condemnation of the "prejudice of color, the antipathy of races, which are always stronger and bitterer with the ignorant and
unlettered" (9–10). That Ridge cannot see how his description of blacks
as savages inverts the logic he uses to uphold the civility and intelligence
of Indians suggests a largely personal attempt to preserve (or reclaim) his
identity as a part-white Cherokee and former slaveholder. To return to
Mondragon's assessment, however, that paradoxical identity cannot be
overlooked, especially because of the radical revision of our dichotomous
view of race relations that it entails. How does Ridge resolve the racial and
cultural contradictions inherent in his personality? The answer is that,
like Joaquin, he largely refuses to. Joaquin's response to his alienation is to
embark on a career of terror; like other popular western heroes, he navi-
gates the complexities of modern society by falling back on his guns as an
expression of ultimate truth. But unable to react in violent fashion himself, Ridge reserves a few lines in the novel's closing page to plea for
greater *individual* acceptance and tolerance within American society.
Joaquin Murieta, as Ridge writes, "leaves behind him the important lesson that there is nothing so dangerous in its consequences as *injustice to
individuals*—whether it arise from prejudice of color or from any other

source; that a wrong done to one man is a wrong to society and to the world" (158). Finally, Ridge's plea is not for Native Americans, Mexicans, or any other minority group; it is simply, as in Joaquín's original conception of America, a statement that each man should rise and fall by his own merits—dissociated, as Ridge necessarily was, from any particular racial or cultural community.[19]

This idealized individualism sounds ironic at the end of a novel that works largely to highlight its impossibility, and in some senses Ridge's final statement suggests his reluctance to resolve his contradictory stances toward various racial groups. Yet on another level, Ridge's conclusion offers the kind of ambiguous ending common to frontier literature, if slightly transmuted to fit both his and Joaquín's unique situation. A necessarily marginal figure—standing somewhere between civilization and savagery, morality and immorality—the frontier hero is by definition never able to locate a cultural space in which he feels truly comfortable or content. Implicitly valuing individualism in his refusal (inability?) to conform to social norms, he wanders between cultures but rarely exists within them, his oft-expressed desire to be accepted for "who he is" continually thwarted by a civilization which demands a certain conformity and uniformity from its inhabitants. As impossible as his quest may be, the frontier hero is one of American literature's most revered stereotypes both for the unwavering idea of independence and self-reliance that he epitomizes and for his ability, in his best moments, to balance the demands of "civilized" and "savage" worlds. By making Joaquín a version of this hero (which is also a version of himself), Ridge attempts to carve out a cultural identity that does not adhere to any fixed cultural rules but that locates him within both white and Indian discourse. Operating on the fringe of society, the frontier hero is very much a figure of absence and uncertainty, yet it is an absence that many white American readers intuitively take for granted and even respect. Working out of that dynamic, Ridge conflates himself with his protagonist and uses the frontier hero identity to position himself within a multicultural discourse that lacks a vocabulary to define him. Albeit not exactly the same as the frontier hero's navigation of white and Indian worlds, Ridge's parallel situation allows him to use the hero's identity as an approximate gauge of his place within contemporary racial and cultural debates. Hence his heavy emphasis on individuation at the novel's end: not only does he seek to pattern himself after the frontier hero, but he also works to obscure his genetic minority status—asking to be read, like Joaquín, as an individual—in a final attempt to reconfigure white readerly conceptions of who and what a frontier hero might be. Ironically fixed in his liminal space, Ridge asks to be accepted on the same self-defined, if ambiguous, terms through which his audience would have normally accepted the white champion.

Joaquin's death at the novel's end should not signal the futility of these real-world designs. Adhering to the conventions of most nineteenth -century narratives, Ridge no doubt wanted to offer his protagonist's story a definite resolution. Like other frontier writers, though, he had no problem apotheosizing Joaquin after that hero's demise, his admonition about individual acceptance suggesting the central heroic virtue that readers should take away from the text. Many frontier scholars credit Frederic Remington as being the first novelist to extend the frontier tensions of Cooper's novels to their logical end in the hero's death and to use that death as a vehicle to suggest the frontier "virtues" that his readers should perpetuate in their own lives. Writing fifty years before Remington, however, Ridge clearly anticipates such strategies. Where Remington often uses the death of a white hero to lionize the ostensible virtues of the white race, Ridge uses the death of a minority hero to displace the necessary association of specific virtues with particular races. The importance of this dynamic cannot be overstated. Where scholars draw a direct line of descent from ethnocentric, turn-of-the-twentieth-century writers like Remington and Wister to respondent "anti-western" writers in later decades, Ridge represents a frontier novelist who uses the terms of the genre to give voice to his own marginalized position well in advance of the most adamant white attempts to keep minorities marginalized in American frontier discourse. This is not to say that Ridge meant to strike a blow for all minorities or even to offer a narrative strategy by which minority writers might validate their own racial positions; like Joaquin, his efforts seem more than a little motivated by "self-preservation." Nonetheless, *The Life and Adventures of Joaquin Murieta* is a fascinating intersection of early Native American and frontier fictions. Ridge's attempt to conflate these two discourses may have become increasingly difficult for later writers faced with reconfigured racial models and artistic media in the twentieth century. But at the very least, *Joaquin Murieta* belies the popular western claim that Native literature merely reacts to two centuries of white, male-centered frontier narratives. As a dime novelist, writing in one of the most popular venues available to an author of his day, Ridge represents a dissenting voice located firmly in the mainstream of the frontier tradition—a voice to be reacted *against* by later white practitioners of the form, not the other way around.

Writing at the turn of the twentieth century, Zitkala-Sa probably could not bring herself to work within the popular frontier tradition as Ridge did, if for no other reason than that she had seen the literal devastation created by a century of "Manifest Destiny" policy. Her life story remains similar to Ridge's in places, however, and yields much of the same tension in her writing. A mixed-blood Sioux raised on the Yankton reservation, she was sent at age eight to be educated at a Quaker Indian school in Indiana, an experience that marked her indelibly.[20] Educated and acculturated (she became an accomplished musician and educator), Zitkala-Sa still retained both a profound nostalgia for her lost childhood years and severe misgivings about the culturally imperialistic attitudes of white America. Her position between these two personal identities, as with Ridge, left her standing "in exile from both cultures."[21] As Dexter Fisher puts it:

> To her mother and the traditional Sioux on the reservation where she had grown up, she was highly suspect because, in their minds, she had abandoned, even betrayed, the Indian way of life by getting an education in the white man's world. To those at the Carlisle Indian School, where she had taught 1898–99, on the other hand, she was an anathema because she insisted on remaining "Indian," writing embarrassing articles such as "Why I Am a Pagan" that flew in the face of the assimilationist thrust of their education.[22]

Like Ridge, Zitkala-Sa's career thus became a unique venture, an ongoing attempt to find (or create) a cultural identity that could accommodate her status as a mixed-race and mixed-culture Sioux, even as she was determined to preserve traditional Sioux culture in her writing.

Granted, at the turn of the century, American politics of identity had become more complex than in Ridge's era. Confronted with the history of Indian wars in which the Sioux had played a central part, and challenged by the new call for racial solidarity from writers like Remington and Wister, Zitkala-Sa must have seen the schism between white and Indian cultures as even more extreme than did a number of her predecessors. Nonetheless, without a ready-made cultural label by which to identify herself, she was compelled to employ a strategy of self-invention similar to Ridge's. The few scholars who have studied her writing have focused on the way that such self-invention occurs quite regularly in the early autobiographical essays of *American Indian Stories*. Relying on "domestic" conceptions of nineteenth-century women's writing, these scholars argue that Zitkala-Sa uses her relationship with her mother to invite readers into what seems like a traditional tale of redemption through the expression of communal, feminine, and Christian bonds. This tale is subverted, however, not only when Zitkala-Sa overtly rejects Christianity but also when her mother subtly supplants a doctrinaire and static Christian faith with more mutable and elastic Sioux beliefs. The final effect of "Dakota language and custom" in these early sections is "to disrupt the Judeo-Christian discourse, to dispel its repressive power, and to introduce themes that had 'not yet found a [Native] voice' in the English language."[23]

This assessment, however, overlooks two important features of *American Indian Stories*. First, it tends to position Zitkala-Sa in absolute opposition to "white" discourse, neglecting the obvious anxiety of a writer trapped between two worlds. And second, it ignores the latter portion of the book, in which Zitkala-Sa offers strategies of resistance and self-invention in her fiction highly distinct from her nonfiction's "domestic" pattern.[24] In fact, it almost seems that the second half of the book is a direct play on the first. Having used the essays to describe the problems of identity she personally experienced, Zitkala-Sa uses the subsequent stories first to provide a fictional analogue for her own situation (in "The Soft-Hearted Sioux"); then to offer a specifically Indian strategy of resistance (in "The Trial Path"); and finally (in "A Warrior's Daughter") to reconstruct herself—the Indian woman—in an empowered position which relies heavily on both the Native discourse set up in the earlier stories and a white frontier discourse which serves as an implicit subtext to the action of the narrative. Listed in the order they appear in *American Indian Stories*, these three stories not only provide an interesting counterpoint to the trio of autobiographical essays in the book's first half but also act as an extension of that nonfiction, offering an imagined means of identity creation impossible for the author in real life.

The first narrative in this progression, "The Soft-Hearted Sioux," tells the story of a Sioux boy educated in a white Indian school. Returning as a man to his father's home, the protagonist finds himself unequipped to deal with the chores necessary to keep his family alive. Expected to take the place of his dying father as "warrior, huntsman, and husband,"[25] he wrestles with an ancestral identity that flies in the face of his teaching at the hands of the whites:

At the mission school I learned it was wrong to kill. Nine winters I hunted for the soft heart of Christ, and prayed for the huntsmen who chased the buffalo on the plains.

In the autumn of the tenth year I was sent back to my tribe to preach Christianity to them. With the white man's Bible in my hand, and the white man's tender heart in my breast, I returned to my own people.

Wearing a foreigner's dress, I walked, a stranger, into my father's village. (113)

Shortly thereafter, the protagonist argues with the tribal Medicine Man, who denounces him before the people and then disbands the tribe, leaving the soft-hearted Sioux to fend for himself. Unable to either hunt or fight, his family dying from hunger, the protagonist decides to kill one of the cows of a nearby rancher, gets caught, and kills the white man in what he believes to be an act of self-defense. Returning home with the meat, though, he finds his father already dead. The next day, he is imprisoned and sentenced to hang for the rancher's murder; in his jail cell he accepts his death, perhaps acknowledging that his fate is the only one available after being displaced from both white and Native American worlds.

Such displacement is central to the story, and Zitkala-Sa does a good job of balancing the dual cultural pull on the protagonist's sensibilities even at the story's end. Though he has accepted his execution, he asks this final question in his jail cell:

Yet I wonder who shall come to welcome me in the realm of strange sight. Will the loving Jesus grant me pardon and give my soul a soothing sleep? or will my warrior father greet me and receive me as his son? Will my spirit fly upward to a happy heaven? or shall I sink into the bottomless pit, an outcast from a God of infinite love? (125)

Despite his experiences, the narrator is still drawn to certain aspects of his white training, pitting his love of family against his hope for a just and merciful God. This split is the same one chronicled by Zitkala-Sa during her stay at the Indian School, where she was taught that only by abandoning Indian custom could she receive the white God's forgiveness. That the author insists on reiterating this cultural split at the end of "The Soft-Hearted Sioux," despite the obvious malevolence of the white community in the story, suggests how valid both sides of the split may be (not the details of white religion per se but at least the rhetorical notion adopted by the protagonist that violence should be avoided). The story, by extension, seeks not to debunk white beliefs completely but to negotiate the seemingly unnegotiable gap between white and Native American worlds.

The protagonist's impending death signals the failure of both character and story to negotiate that gap successfully. Clearly the story denounces those whites who, having encouraged mercy and taught the soft-hearted Sioux that "it was wrong to kill," nonetheless execute him at the story's end. Perhaps surprisingly, though, the story condemns the Indians as well. After the narrator argues with the Medicine Man, the latter works to turn the tribe against the protagonist, calling him "snake," "fool," and "traitor." His tirade seems motivated not by any legitimate threat to his power or cultural position, but simply by his wounded pride and irrational anger. Allowing his hatred of whites to form his attitude toward the protagonist, the Medicine Man knowingly leaves the entire family to die on the prairie, a lack of compassion that strikingly echoes the similar attitudes of the whites who ultimately hang the protagonist. In fact, the whites' punishment is an ironic "execution" of the sentence first passed on the narrator by the Medicine Man. As such, it becomes difficult to read the story as one that simply valorizes Native American society at the expense of white "civilization." What route of escape is left to the protagonist? The answer, of course, is none.

Finally the story underscores an inexorable sense of powerlessness, where the protagonist is disenfranchised by both "home" and "alien" cultures. And by extension, it decries the presence of those "soft-hearted" qualities that allow for his complete victimization. This latter point is rendered in somewhat gendered terms, echoing the subtler antidomestic discourse of the book's first half. Characteristic of nineteenth-century women's literature, the Christian sensibility espoused by the protagonist makes him into a version of woman—an identity that, the narrative suggests, makes him weak. Indeed his only triumph, albeit temporary, is his successful delivery of the meat after killing the rancher, both stereotypically male actions. There is no denying that *power* in both cultures of the story is defined almost exclusively through physical aggression or martial might—the ability to hunt, fight, or kill. The soft-hearted Sioux's demise occurs because he completely forsakes his warrior identity for a "feminized" Christian version of self, and while the story may not extol that warrior identity absolutely, it emphatically castigates most of the Christian virtues foisted on the protagonist. Suggesting that power is often achieved through acts of physical prowess and even calculated violence, Zitkala-Sa appropriates the themes of many of her white contemporaries, Remington and Wister especially, to articulate Indian cultural ideals and codes of conduct closely resembling those valorized in the heroes of white western texts. Even the rejection of Christian tenets echoes a traditional frontier ideology; as Jane Tompkins has pointed out, the development of the popular western at the beginning of the twentieth century evolved more than slightly out of a masculine reaction to the perceived increase in women's public power.[26] Accordingly, Zitkala-Sa becomes a version of the popular western writer here, rejecting a largely Christian scheme of human intercourse for a system that demands a readiness for physical action and confrontation. Like Remington and Wister, faced with the extinction of a frontier West, her reaction is to elegize the heroic and sometimes violent virtues of Indian culture in an attempt to ensconce and perpetuate those virtues in the subtler, if sublimated, forms of her own historical moment.[27]

This negotiation of frontier themes is equally pronounced in the next story in the series, "The Trial Path." Seemingly a parable on the nature of brotherly love, the story tells of a Sioux warrior who, in a fit of anger, murders his best friend. Rather than execute the murderer outright, the father of the victim arranges the following trial by ordeal:

> A wild pony is now lassoed. The man-killer must mount and ride the ranting beast. Stand you all in two parallel lines from the centre tepee of the bereaved family to the wigwam opposite in the great outer ring. Between you, in the wide space, is the given trialway. From the outer circle the rider must mount and guide his pony toward the centre tepee. If, having gone the entire distance, the man-killer gains the tepee sitting on the pony's back, his life is spared and pardon given. But should he fall, then he himself has chosen death. (131)

As expected, the accused manages to stay mounted and, at the end of his ordeal, is accepted as a son and brother into the victim's family to replace the man he killed.

On one level, this story provides an interesting foil to the swift and unconsidered violence of the hanging in "The Soft-Hearted Sioux"; the sentence in "The Trial Path," after all, seems merciful in its offer of potential life for the accused. But it would be a mistake to view this story as a simple blending of sentimental impulse and Native setting. Notably, the "deliverance" of the murderer is accomplished only through an act of physical prowess that sets him apart from the rest of the tribe, a dynamic suggestive of frontier more than domestic narratives. Moreover, the highly individualistic nature of his ride is made clear by the father before the trial begins; as the old man claims, "But should he fall, then he himself has chosen death." This statement strongly echoes a declaration of western individualism, an echo that is only enhanced by the context of consummately western motifs in which the declaration is made: violent physical confrontation, man against nature, and so forth. Like the showdown in which the western hero engages to determine his fate and the fate of the people around him, the trial brings to bear a variety of cultural and moral forces and distills them into a single man's ability or inability to perform a violently masculine feat (the fact that the trial involves a horse-breaking only adds to the western overtones). Finally, this simple dynamic dictates how power is negotiated in the narrative. The accused, before his ride, is a man outside the tribal culture; he has, after all, committed "the offense of an enemy" (131). It is only through his successful enactment of a valorous conquest that he secures a place within—one might be tempted to say *above*—the rest of the tribe. [28]

Such identity construction suggests the same proactive strategies of self-invention that Ridge uses in *Joaquin Murieta*. In the trial by ordeal, Zitkala-Sa allows her protagonist to wipe clean the slate of history (becoming a version of Adam?) and to redefine himself not through the profound internal conversions common to domestic discourse but through a transient, if highly potent, enactment of physical power. This play on the frontier hero represents a profound attempt to legitimize, if romantically, the Indian figure within a white cultural space. But perhaps more importantly, the trial of "The Trial Path" uses the frontier hero's unflagging individualism as a metaphor for the self-generation of personal identity in general. Isolated from both white and Native American cultures, Zitkala-Sa sought, as did Ridge, an identity which would largely reaffirm her position as Indian but which, at the same time, could inform her ambiguous position between worlds. "The Trial Path" seems to accomplish both these ends. On the one hand, it celebrates the ability of the Indian "transgressor" or "outsider" to reinscribe himself within the confines of the tribe. This is the *product* of the protagonist's ride; he regains his place in society. But on the other hand, he sets himself apart from that society through his heroic action and underscores a *process* of identity construction —personal, individuating, and elemental—which somehow transcends his own cultural moment and speaks to his human essence. As romantic as such a conception may seem, it remains at the heart of any trial by ordeal, where moral and legal relationships are defined by simplistic tests of physicality that are understood by an audience to signify "something greater." This dynamic underwrites every showdown in traditional frontier literature exactly as it does the ride in "The Trial Path." And by extension, it suggests a means through which the author can substantiate her own transcultural position. Having endured the ordeal of living between worlds, Zitkala-Sa uses such endurance to construct an identity which is highly personal and largely intuited (even contradictory) but which is unmistakably her own. As with Ridge, she uses the liminal position and stereotypical actions of the traditional frontier hero not as an analogue to but as a mechanism for defining her own specific identity.

The only problem, if Zitkala-Sa is indeed using the frontier hero/warrior as a paradigm for self-generation, is that such an identity is usually reserved for men in both white and Native cultures. Even Ridge, despite his inversion of stereotypical racial dynamics, does not mention women in his novel except as the respective consorts or victims of male heroes or villains. Accordingly, the third story in Zitkala-Sa's series, "A Warrior's Daughter," works to invert the stereotypical gender paradigms of male-authored frontier fiction by creating a heroic identity which is exclusively female.

"A Warrior's Daughter" begins where "A Trial Path" leaves off, by reifying traditional gender assumptions about the hero's nature. Though the story focuses on Tusee, a young Indian woman, most of the early description is devoted to her father, a man who "had won . . . the privilege of staking his wigwam within the great circle of tepees" and who "never wearied nightly of rehearsing his own great deeds" (137). In the beginning, Tusee seems satisfied with this arrangement; her greatest ambition is to dance for her father, and the narrator is quick to note how the girl has the "finely pencilled eyebrows and slightly extended nostrils" (141) of her mother. Designed to emphasize Tusee's femininity, the physical description is, nevertheless, slightly tempered by the narrator's aside that "in her sturdiness of form she resembles her father" (141).

That small disclaimer shortly leads to a radical revision of traditional gender assumptions and arrangements. Such transposition begins in earnest when Tusee's lover is captured by enemy warriors during a raid and, despite Tusee's pleas, the male members of the lover's raiding party refuse to attempt a rescue. Instead, Tusee straps on a knife and makes her way toward the enemy camp. Unlike previous women in *American Indian Stories,* she is neither gentle nor compassionate. "With desperate hate she bites her teeth," her prayers asking for "swift cunning for a weapon this night" (146). These prayers occasionally suggest that she wishes to be made into a man herself—"All-powerful Spirit, grant me my father's warrior heart, strong to slay a foe and mighty to save a friend!" (146)—a request that on its surface reiterates traditional gender constructions by associating heroic virtues with a masculine nature. Yet importantly, the story never lets its audience forget that Tusee is a woman. She lures the brave who captured her lover away from his camp with her sexual charm and even in her moment of greatest "masculine" triumph, killing her enemy, reaffirms her gendered identity by proclaiming, "I am a Dakota woman!" (150).[29] Moreover, when she unties her lover, he almost faints, so that Tusee is forced to carry him: "The sight of his weakness made her strong. A mighty power thrills her body. Stooping beneath his outstretched arms grasping at the air for support, Tusee lifts him upon her broad shoulders. With half-running, triumphant steps she carries him away into the open night" (153).

Were there any doubt about the gender inversions accomplished by the narrative, this final paragraph makes them clear. Even after his rescue, the man remains weak and the woman strong, suggesting that Tusee's strength is more than transitory or incidental. Moreover, the exhilaration obviously felt by Tusee seems to reflect the author's own excitement at the prospect of liberation and self-generation. The full impact of these qualities is even more striking when one recalls the context surrounding the young lover's raid on the Indian camp. Wanting to marry Tusee, he is told by her father that "Naught but an enemy's scalp-lock, plucked fresh with your own hand, will buy Tusee for your wife" (143). In her victory over the enemy, it is actually Tusee who manages to purchase her lover, and in so doing she changes the entire composition of the male-oriented barter system which fueled the young man's quest to begin with. Where the female body is early seen as a type of currency to be negotiated by men (one enemy scalp equals the price of a daughter/wife), Tusee's victory reverses the terms of that arrangement, making the male body into a commodity purchased by her violent conquest.[30] Not only, then, does the story invert the cultural inscription of the female body in order to demonstrate how women might occupy the position of frontier hero as easily as men; it also reinscribes men as potential subjects to the heroic female in the same way that Tusee is a subject to her father in the early portions of the story. By extension, the story destabilizes traditional gender vocabularies both in the way that it fails to ascribe specific brands of cultural performance to sexed bodies and in the way that it refuses to privilege either "masculinity" or "femininity" as a kind of central cultural model from which the other might be derived.

★

Zitkala-Sa's act of unfixing genders ultimately creates a space where it is impossible to (dis)locate people through simplistic cultural constructions, gendered or otherwise, a development which strongly recalls Ridge's plea at the end of *Joaquin Murieta* for readers to deal with one another as individuals. Zitkala-Sa's strategy, of course, expands frontier discourse one step further than Ridge's, by subverting the gender as well as racial essentialism common to white frontier texts. Accordingly, it seems fair to say that both authors deserve a notable place in the history of popular frontier writing, not only because their work subtly co-opts the ethnocentric and sexist precepts of many white westerns but also because their early historical placement in that frontier tradition makes their anticipation and inversion of white narrative strategies even more impressive.[31] Their place in the canon of Native American writing, however, may be less certain. While Zitkala-Sa has sometimes been viewed as a predecessor of female writers like Louise Erdrich and Leslie Silko, that reputation rests largely on her autobiographical accounts of life between white and Indian worlds. The idea that her fiction offers an interesting counterpoint not only to white frontier discourse but also to that version of a Native American self constructed in her autobiography has, to this point, been largely ignored by critics.

Ridge and Zitkala-Sa may represent something of a literary historical anomaly: two writers who sought to bridge white and Native American frontier discourses in a period when other Native thinkers worked largely to distinguish Indian culture from universalizing white models.[32] However, the fact that contemporary writers like James Welch, Thomas King, and Sherman Alexie have incorporated versions of white frontier discourse into their fiction in an attempt to negotiate this idea of trans- or even extra-cultural identity suggests just how prescient Ridge and Zitkala-Sa may have been. While it is likely presumptuous to call them the "founders" of a Native American literary tradition, it nonetheless seems prudent to emphasize their connections both to each other and to later artists. Two of the first Indian fiction writers, they are concerned with the same problem as many subsequent authors: how to negotiate personal identity between the "pure" constructs of white and Native worlds, indeed how to undermine the legitimacy of such constructions of "purity" in an attempt to bring separate cultural discourses closer to-

gether. Perhaps unavoidably, their strategies for accomplishing these goals
rely heavily on the use of white cultural models, given both the dearth of
Native American fiction in their lifetimes and the intensive immersion
into Euro-American culture which both experienced at an early age.
Nonetheless one cannot overlook the serious challenges they raise to
white cultural ascendancy, challenges implicit in works which trope white
conceptions of race, gender, faith, and culture and even rely on the traditional form of such conceptions to tell a nonwhite story. Though they
may not have acted as a direct influence upon that wave of Indian writers
that followed in the 1930s, their "rediscovery" in the present both offers
historical antecedents for contemporary writers and illustrates one aspect
of Native American identity construction, through a largely white frontier discourse, that scholars had heretofore considered possible only
through a late-twentieth-century sensibility. Finally, *Joaquin Murieta* and
American Indian Stories may not be the most formally accomplished or
structurally unified books available, but their importance as a template of
the minds and mindsets of a particular Indian class in the late nineteenth
century cannot be overstated, a template that for better or worse reflects
similar cultural schisms and methods of identity negotiation even in
works being published today.

Riders of
the Papal Sage

Willa Cather's
"Western"

With recent criticism focusing on feminism and latent lesbianism in Cather novels, it is hard to know exactly where a book like *Death Comes for the Archbishop* fits in. After all, a tale about two priests struggling to restore orthodox Catholicism to the American Southwest does not really suggest the politically liberal themes popular in contemporary academia. Nevertheless, critics across the board still refer to *Archbishop* as one of Cather's greatest novels, if not her masterpiece.[1] The only unanswered question is why.

Reading the novel in "subversive" fashion, gender critics have suggested that the intimacy between Latour and Vaillant represents a deeper, if forbidden, romantic attraction. Modernist critics point to the innovative structure of the novel, which eschews a strong central plotline in favor of loosely collected episodes, vignettes, and fables. Formalists celebrate the book's descriptive passages, the New Mexico landscape offering Cather a model for some of the most sweepingly beautiful passages in her writing. And more conservative religious critics note the sense of purpose that Latour brings to his mission, a moral determination that never wavers in the face of his adversaries.

None of these readings, however, offers a full account of *Death Comes for the Archbishop* because, in reality, the book is all of these things and more. The reason that critics have failed to produce a unified reading of the novel has much to do with academic territorialism, emphasizing one idea over others in an attempt to draw Cather more firmly under a specific critical rubric. In addition, few scholars seem willing to take up the glaring prejudices of the book. While a growing number of multicultural critics have called into question Cather's scathing depiction of Padre Martínez (the most notable of the schismatic New Mexico priests), few readers seem willing to explore the tints of racism, ethnocentrism, and at times misogyny that permeate the novel. Part of this resistance involves respect for Cather's genius. And part involves academic politics, a reluctance to undermine a writer who has become an increasingly important figure in critical writing on gender and sexuality. But for the most part the problem is far simpler: critics are being too literary. Despite the critical tendency to read Cather as "high art," I would argue that the impulses, biases, and events of *Death Comes for the Archbishop* can be understood together if the book is read as a thematically straightforward, if slightly amended, version of the popular frontier novel. [2]

Just consider the critical positions above. If homoerotic tension does exist between Latour and Vaillant, it does so no more than in countless popular frontier texts, where homosocial male bonding and expressions of "manly love" are routinely read with deeper romantic implications. If *Archbishop* is episodic, it is no more so than many popular western narratives, including Owen Wister's *The Virginian,* which uses a series of loosely connected vignettes to follow the heroic exploits of its cowboy protagonist. If Cather's New Mexico landscape is beautiful even as it is dangerous, then that rendition parallels descriptions by writers like Cooper, Wister, and Zane Grey, who often celebrated the splendor of the Western terrain in which their characters fought or died. And if *Archbishop* is finally a book about a man with a moral purpose, willing to sacrifice certain beliefs and even people so that he can meet his sacrosanct final objective, then he is in line with the popular frontier hero who must often choose between two moral imperatives in order to achieve what he sees as a just peace by the story's end.

These observations would no doubt surprise Cather, who expressed disdain for the hastily produced and "lowbrow" fictions that she understood popular westerns to be.[3] And they would certainly raise the eyebrows of more than one scholar who has worked to uncover the strong feminist impulse of Cather's fiction, even if that impulse occurs in coded fashion. But *Death Comes for the Archbishop* is not *The Song of the Lark*, or *My Ántonia*, or even *O, Pioneers!* It lacks the presence of the woman artist finding her place in American society or, for that matter, women finding their place anywhere. The book is first and foremost about men—Latour, Vaillant, Martínez, Lucero, Kit Carson, Eusabio, Jacinto—discovering their purposes, fighting their personal battles, and fulfilling their destinies. Women, when they feature at all, are treated as creatures ruled by vanity (Doña Isabela) or merely as signs of Latour's holy mission (Magdalena Scales, old Sada). Even the Virgin Mary becomes a symbol of Latour's goal, an active agent in the story only insofar as she motivates the priest.

These ideas about gender construction are far from cursory. Along with race relations, they form the main areas in which *Death Comes for the Archbishop* demonstrates striking parallels to the popular frontier narrative. Of course, it is tempting with writers like Cather to excuse more "formula" moments as a necessary coincidence. Certainly literary artists, considering the same landscape, will note some items in common with popular artists. But *Death Comes for the Archbishop* is more than a series of incidental connections. Exploring the novel's attitude toward the two essential features mentioned above should demonstrate that, far from tangential, the connections between Cather's book and popular western writing are both profound and pervasive.

Gender

That all the principal characters in *Death Comes for the Archbishop* are men is a feature that should not be understated. In reality, the impulse to read the novel as one which embraces "women's culture"—as some critics have done—relies on the mistaken notion that Latour's brand of religion parallels the values of women's sentimental narratives, in particular his willingness to sacrifice himself for the larger glory of God. This feature is apparent from Latour's initial experience in New Mexico. Lost in the desert, he comes across the cruciform tree and utters the phrase "I thirst"—an echo of Christ's declaration on the cross that indicates Latour's own missionary self-sacrifice.[4] Having entrusted his venture completely to God, he stumbles upon the hidden spring, *Agua Secreta*,

moments later. Desert gives way to garden in this scene, a literal enactment of Latour's figurative mission—to bring the New Mexico community out of a wilderness of false prophets and back into the grace of the
true church, largely through his own initiative and relinquishment of the
things of this world.

Certainly, Latour leaves behind personal comforts to come to New
Mexico. But to view him as a version of the protagonists who featured in
earlier women's novels is rife with problems.[5] For instance, such protagonists are almost completely self-effacing, doing their Christian work in
private spaces and receiving only that satisfaction which accompanies
doing the Lord's bidding. Latour, by contrast, is an intractably public figure whose Christian work involves multiple confrontations with schismatic priests, political alliances with powerful New Mexico individuals
(including Kit Carson), and a host of other high-profile entanglements.
His mission, despite its advance of Catholicism, increases his personal
fame and stature, to the point that his erection of the cathedral seems as
much a gesture of personal potency as religious zeal.[6] Moreover, women's
novel protagonists are fundamentally concerned with human relationships, often with an eye toward making the right match between individuals, with a wedding signaling one triumph of domestic virtues. Latour,
instead, follows the model of the popular western hero, who enjoys few
close allegiances and is forbidden to take a mate. Whether or not his
friendship with Vaillant suggests a deeper homoerotic desire (as with
other westerns where homoeroticism lurks beneath the surface) is beside
the point. His position as priest forbids him from seeking any match, heterosexual or otherwise, emphasizing the way that his story is about the triumph of the individual despite rhetorical overtures to the religious
community (the proverbial townspeople) whom he has sworn to protect.

More fundamentally, though, I would challenge the notion of Latour
as a man bent on self-sacrifice whose chief concern is following Catholic
doctrine on behalf of his diocese. Time and again, he demonstrates a willingness to sacrifice other people on his behalf. Largely these people are
women, and they pay for Latour's triumphs in literal, often brutal fashion. Ironically these women—Magdalena Scales and old Sada especially
—occupy the roles normally reserved for heroines of women's novels; despite concerns for their own welfare, they act selflessly to assist others and,
in the process, contribute to the higher program of fostering peace and
cultivating faith. Latour's inability to act in the same fashion demonstrates egocentric impulses that suggest his belief in a personal moral purpose more righteous than those of the people around him. Like the classic

western hero, he sees himself advancing a brand of justice and morality that—if not strictly Scriptural—is nonetheless the best navigation of the many moral and practical forces that he must balance.

Latour's first prolonged encounter with a woman occurs when he and Vaillant stop at the house of Buck Scales—unknown to them, a "degenerate murderer" (77)—to rest after a long ride. Shortly after their arrival, Scales's wife, Magdalena, issues an urgent and secretive warning for them to flee.

> Just at the door she turned and caught the eyes of the visitors, who were looking after her in compassion and perplexity. Instantly that stupid face became intense, prophetic, full of awful meaning. With her finger she pointed them away, away!—two quick thrusts into the air. Then, with a look of horror beyond anything language could convey, she threw back her head and drew the edge of her palm across her distended throat. . . . (68)

The priests manage to escape, but only after the "Bishop [draws] his pistol" (69) to threaten Scales. After riding a short distance, they decide that the "warning given them by that poor woman . . . seemed evidence that some protecting power was mindful of them," even though Latour expresses his regret that Scales will probably "suspect . . . and abuse" (70) his wife for giving warning. The dubious nature of the priest's actions is self-evident. While claiming to abhor violence and expressing compassion toward Magdalena, Latour is quite willing to draw a pistol in his own defense yet to leave the woman behind to incur Scales's wrath. Moreover, as if to justify their spurious self-preservation, the priests reconfigure the escape to credit a divine "protecting power" with their deliverance rather than the selfless action of Magdalena, whose courage contrasts favorably to their relative cowardice. Arguably Latour's action is designed to eschew earthly matters for spiritual ones, an idea confirmed when a battered Magdalena appears before him the next day in Mora after escaping her husband.

> She had supposed [her husband] would overtake her and kill her, but he had not. . . . Kneeling before the Bishop she began to relate such horrible things that he stopped her and turned to the native priest.
> "This is a case for the civil authorities. Is there a magistrate here?" (71)

The scene suggests more than a perfunctory distinction between Church and State. Latour divorces himself completely from Magdalena, even refusing to listen as a comforter or spiritual guide to the many evils waged against her. His quick deference to civil authority is another self-serving escape, reminiscent of his failure to use his pistol to rescue the woman earlier. Simply put, although he will deploy violence to save himself and Father Vaillant, he will not use it to save others; although he sets himself up as a model of compassion and salvation, he proves largely averse to or incapable of dispensing either.

This is not to say that Latour's concern for Magdalena is disingenuous or even that his words and actions continually contradict each other. His expressed purpose is to resuscitate the Church in the Southwest, and to do so he must avoid both self-harm and the legal entanglements that would result from his shooting Scales or participating in the criminal's prosecution. Ultimately his mission operates on a grand scale and, despite its de-emphasis of the personal aspects of religion, does seem to be the most efficient way to spread the Church's influence. Latour is concerned with the power of the papacy writ large, not necessarily with his individual parishioners, and he is quite willing to rhetorically sacrifice himself as well as others to bring that dream to fruition. Two points, however, bear reiteration here regarding Latour's so-called sacrifices. First, he gives up the niceties of European culture to be a priest, but this lack of material and intellectual comfort can in no way compare—no matter how much Latour believes it does—to the physical abuse suffered by Magdalena. Second, as the quintessential representative of the papacy in the Southwest, Latour's own fate is inextricably tied to the Church's, and the consolidation of Church power signifies a consolidation of Latour's personal power as well. As such, the personal sacrifices made by Latour are not without their personal rewards; the sacrifice made by Magdalena, however, benefits Latour exclusively. It is true that she is ultimately saved when the local citizens hang Buck Scales. But that salvation is completely self-generated: she escapes with no help from the priests or anyone else, flees to Mora, and offers the confession that will allow for her husband's conviction.[7]

That Latour takes advantage of the misfortunes of women for his own gain—moreover that he falsely views his triumphs as self-generated—is reaffirmed in his encounter with old Sada, the servant/slave who sneaks away from her abusive Protestant masters to the sacristy. Latour knows about Sada in advance, since "more than once Father Vaillant had spoken of this aged captive" (214) who had not been allowed out of the Smith compound for "nineteen years" (214–15). Her situation is so deplorable that Vaillant and others favor rescuing her and giving her asylum, but Latour dismisses this plan because of the inconvenience it might cause the Church: "[F]or the present it was inexpedient to antagonize these people.

The Smiths were the leaders of a small group of low-caste Protestants who took every occasion to make trouble for the Catholics" [216]. Of course, the family does not represent a major threat but, as with Buck Scales, could be a nasty complication to the "expedience" of Latour's goal.

This perspective seems to change, however, when the Bishop worships with the old woman in the sacristy. He is stunned by her devotion, which has been kept secretly alive for nineteen years and even made stronger in the face of the Smiths' tyranny. In Sada, Latour experiences a rejuvenation of his own faith, recalling the exhilaration that he once felt before the altar:

> He was able to feel, kneeling beside her, the preciousness of the things of the altar to her who was without possessions; the tapers, the image of the Virgin, the figures of the saints, the Cross that took away indignity from suffering and made pain and poverty a means of fellowship with Christ. Kneeling beside the much-enduring bond-woman, he experienced those holy mysteries as he had done in his young manhood. He seemed able to feel all it meant to her to know that there was a Kind Woman in Heaven, though there were such cruel ones on earth. . . .
>
> Not often, indeed, had Jean Marie Latour come so near to the Fountain of all Pity as in the Lady Chapel that night; the pity that no man born of woman could ever utterly cut himself off from, that was for the murderer on the scaffold, as it was for the dying soldier or the martyr on the rack. The beautiful concept of Mary pierced the priest's heart like a sword. (218)

Latour's is a pity born of woman yet extended, it seems, to all but women. Sada's devotional allows him insight into the concept of universal pain while, at the same time, keeping the specific pain of the woman beside him at a distance. Again Latour is a man who subordinates the small moments of religious endeavor to the big picture, compassion to concept. Somewhat condescendingly he realizes that "This church was Sada's house, and he was a servant in it" (218), a statement which rings especially strange when his subsequent action is to lead her to the door that will send her back out into the snow and toward the house where she will suffer further abuse. Just before Sada departs, Latour gives her a small silver medallion as an emblem of her faith: "Now she would have a treasure to hide and guard, to adore while her watchers slept. Ah, he thought, for one who cannot read—or think—the Image, the physical form of Love!" (218–19). The irony of this scene cuts many ways. The old faithful woman who has somehow "saved" the Bishop is given a minuscule piece of religion to squirrel away even as Latour himself is reenergized for the magnificent plan of building his cathedral and converting the surrounding populace. His haughty realization that Sada "cannot think" suggests his own feeling that once more a woman was a sign sent expressly to him, important only in that symbolism, incapable of understanding her own significance—which is a job left to Latour, who understands why Sada acted the way she did and can in his larger mission transmute that sensibility into a true homage to the Lord. It is almost as if Latour cannot see the real woman beside him, or any real woman for that matter, but only "the Virgin Mary, woman without the darkness or the odor, woman without desire, need, or stain."[8]

The fact that Latour engages with actual women almost exclusively to his own benefit, moreover that he conceals himself beneath the aegis of spiritual rectitude, brings him dangerously close to being a replica not of the western hero, but of some of its villains. (In particular, I am thinking of the Mormon villains of certain westerns—for example, Zane Grey's *Riders of the Purple Sage*—who use their position in the church to intimidate, extort from, and murder local settlers.) Several factors, however, prevent Latour from being like these characters. First, such villains actively seek to hurt their victims, whereas Latour simply declines to help those in need. Second, *Death Comes for the Archbishop* constructs a religious hierarchy in which a variety of faiths—"true" Catholicism, schismatic Catholicism, Protestantism, and Native belief—compete for primacy. By contrast, more popular westerns feature a power struggle within a single religion, or else they depict an antireligious hero struggling against the dictates of an established faith (and often a particular sect of that faith, like Grey's Mormons, whose leaders abuse their power). Finally, though, Cather's protagonist is not a western villain because he so closely resembles the hero. He operates on the fringe of civilized and uncivilized worlds. He adheres to a sense of purpose that is wholly his own: largely intuited, morally complex, driven by earthly imperatives, and unyielding to any other value system in the novel. He confronts his enemies in public fashion, facilitating their downfalls. And he even has a female love interest, Mary, who in her virginal purity serves as his inspiration and moral touchstone, even if he does not adhere perfectly to her wishes.[9]

This devotion to Mary is important because, in the eyes of some critics, it is Latour's willingness to turn away from earthly matters toward more spiritual ones that makes him greater than the western heroes who understand life largely through its physical details. And in that he rhetorically champions absolute adherence to Christian principle, he is like the protagonists of women's novels, who occasionally suffer adverse consequences due to their passivity. But despite the apparent similarity, Latour cannot be confused with such heroines. To begin with, he carries a gun and is notably prepared to defend himself but not others. He has the powerful backing and official sanction of the Catholic Church; indeed he is the spokesman of his religion where the women around him are subjects, if not victims, of theirs. He allies himself with other powerful male figures, Kit Carson especially. And he is himself a man, not susceptible to the same perils as women—the domestic violence directed toward Magdalena or Sada or, on a lesser scale, the sexual vanity of Dona Isabella. Even the male bias of the Catholic Church, despite its symbolic championship of the feminine Mary, works to protect Latour. Admittedly, certain elements of the New Mexico community threaten the Bishop on a regular basis, but those perils exhibit no striking difference from the forces aligned against any frontier hero—and if anything, the popular frontier hero, operating outside any established rules of law or religion, is far less privileged and far more endangered than Latour. These qualities are not meant to detract completely from Latour's mission but to confirm the advantage from which he operates and to reiterate the real-world costs at which his advances are made. Like his religious forebears, Latour believes in sacrifice, but perhaps like other western heroes he is so caught up in the sacrifices he has made that he fails to see the even greater sacrifices occurring around him—sacrifices with a specific gender tint, often made in his name, on his behalf, or even at his command.

Race

If Latour's dealings with women suggest certain connections to popular western attitudes, then his relationship with Indians in the novel only confirm those echoes. On its surface, *Death Comes for the Archbishop* purports to be a book that dispenses with simplistic depictions of Indians. From the start Cather provides painstaking details about those Native Americans with whom Latour comes into contact; indeed, such heightened realism forms the basis of critical opinions that identify Latour as a friend to nonwhite races. Yet how truly different is Latour's experience from that of other frontier heroes? Despite his literal access to Natives, Latour proves continually unable to confront the possibility that the Indian experience he observes could impact his own theological views.

Instead, reading that experience selectively, he tries his best to conform Native culture to his own culturally biased world-view and ultimately ignores what portions of it he cannot somehow co-opt.[10]

Such a quality is anticipated in the prologue, when the Spanish Cardinal insists that southwestern Natives live in "wigwams" and remarks to Father Ferrand that "I see your redskins through Fenimore Cooper, and I like them so" (13). The Cardinal's beliefs do not represent the entire party, and if in one sense the opening scene prepares an audience for the questionable versions of Native Americans to follow, in another sense it mocks the Cardinal's simplistic world-view and promises better from the missionary Father Ferrand and his appointed delegate, Jean-Marie Latour. And after a fashion, Latour's views on the indigene are more enlightened than the Cardinal's merely because at times he realizes how little he actually understands the Indians around him. As he thinks during one of his meditations, "neither the white men nor the Mexicans in Santa Fe understood anything about Indian beliefs or the working of the Indian mind" (133). Yet despite these brief glimpses of his own limitations, Latour quickly forgets his insights. Directed by God and his own ego to unite the disparate religious factions of New Mexico, he implicitly starts to figure himself as that extraordinary white man who can come to terms with the Natives. Like other frontier protagonists, he takes for granted the absoluteness of his own destiny, such that what began as his dialogic quest to adapt the Church to the needs of the people becomes his monologic attempt to install Catholic hierarchies over the populace. In doing so, he manages to defeat the schismatic priests and their self-serving versions of religion, but at the same time, he closes himself off to the alternative messages about his spiritual purpose that the Indians offer.

Nowhere is this dynamic more evident than in the episode where Jacinto shelters Latour during a blizzard in a cave used by local Indians for religious rites. (This section, commonly known as the "Stone Lips" passage for the way that the cave first appears to the priest, is a central element of practically all critical essays charting Latour's relationship with Indians.) At one point, Jacinto instructs the priest to listen at a fissure in the wall.

> Father Latour lay with his ear to this crack for a long while, despite the cold that arose from it. He told himself he was listening to one of the oldest voices of the earth. What he heard was the sound of a great underground river, flowing through a resounding cavern. The water was far, far below, perhaps as deep as the foot of the mountain, a flood moving in utter black-

ness under ribs of antediluvian rock. It was not a rushing noise, but the sound of a great flood moving with majesty and power.

"It is terrible," he said at last, as he rose. (130)

Later, after Latour has made Jacinto "repeat a Pater Noster" (131), the priest wakes to see his Indian guide "listening with supersensual ear" (132) at the hole in the wall. In one way, Jacinto's "intensity of solicitude" is designed to reinforce the monumental nature of Latour's task in converting the people of New Mexico. But in another way, it is designed to reinforce the highly conditional nature of that task, if not its downright futility. Listening "to one of the oldest voices of the earth," Latour is asked to reckon with the age and depth of a Native religious belief predicated on a union with the physical world, as contrasted against the somewhat cerebral faith and relative youth of the Christianity he seeks to import. Despite the "eternal" nature of his philosophy, he is asked to consider how brief is the glory of man and man's institutions (perhaps even those dictated from above) when contrasted against the absolute durability of the world, a palpable god. The meaning of the "Stone Lips" passage seems even clearer when juxtaposed against the scene in the Pueblo village that immediately precedes Jacinto and Latour's descent into the cave. Seeking a place to sleep, Latour takes refuge in a dilapidated mission whose "great red walls . . . yawned gloomily before him,—part of the roof had fallen in, and the rest would soon go" (120). Confronted by a Christian "ruin," Latour's later experience in the Indian cavern suggests the relative transience of his own (and his people's) accomplishments, no matter how grandiose and enduring they may appear.

Surprisingly, however, Latour fails to read his experience in the way it seemingly demands to be read, instead converting his encounter with the ruined mission and the cave into Christian iconographic terms. Shortly after his return to Santa Fe, he convinces Zeb Orchard—a man who once lived with the Pecos—to explain what he experienced in the cave and even asks "Orchard if he thought it probable that the Indians kept a great serpent in concealment somewhere, as was commonly reported" (134). The serpent, needless to say, is Latour's nemesis, and while it is tempting to read this exchange metaphorically and treat the Pecos religion simply as an extra-Catholic challenge to Latour's papal authority, the tone of his exchange with Orchard suggests that the prospect of an actual snake against which he might wage a religious crusade somehow appeals to the Bishop.[11] His desire is reaffirmed by the final story Orchard tells regarding the Pecos.

Their priests have their own kind of mysteries. I don't know how much of it is real and how much is made up. I remember something that happened when I was a little fellow. One night a Pecos girl, with her baby in her arms, ran into the kitchen here and begged my mother to hide her until the festival, for she'd seen signs between the *caciques,* and was sure they were going to feed her baby to the snake. Whether it was true or not, she sure believed it, poor thing, and Mother let her stay. (135–36)

As a concluding statement on the Pecos religion, this story certainly has its Christian resonance, with the innocent infant and its mother contrasted against the demonic snake and its followers. But also important about this scene is the way Orchard highly conditionalizes his account with phrases like "I don't know how much of it is real" or "Whether it was true or not, she sure believed it." This latter statement, especially, speaks to the way that the entire exchange is written in terms of particular faith, with the facts being less consequential than issues of belief. Latour, in other words, hears what he must. He configures his knowledge of Pecos lore to fit within his own religious system, contriving the serpent out of what he knows to be an underground river in order to create a symbol against which his faith might contend.[12]

When he remarks to Orchard that "veneration for old customs was a quality he liked in the Indians, and that it played a great part in his own religion" (135), Latour applauds that version of the Other in which he sees himself, while conveniently ignoring the more subversive elements of Indian belief. While he does not dismiss all of the aspects of Pecos faith that run counter to his own, he does adapt them to his peculiar theology, recognizing them as a version of evil ("the serpent") to be defeated.[13] Soon after his journey with Jacinto, Latour redoubles his efforts to increase the power of the Church in the Southwest and to showcase that power through the erection of palpable Catholic symbols. His inspiration to build the cathedral testifies to his own fear of failure and misgivings about his purpose as much as to his Christian resolve. Despite the lesson inherent in the ruined Spanish mission, he seeks to make the new building "a continuation of himself and his purpose, a physical body full of his aspirations after he had passed from the scene" (175), over and against both the landscape and the insights of the Native religion which suggest how futile his plan might ultimately be.

Furthermore, Latour's construction of the cathedral in opposition to a more "Indian" vision is ironic given the respect that he continually accords Indian culture. He hypocritically professes to admire not only the

Native "veneration of old customs" but also the Native veneration of the landscape itself. Traveling with Eusabio, he notes how "as it was the white man's way to assert himself in any landscape, to change it, make it over a little (at least to have some mark of memorial of his sojourn), it was the Indian's way to pass through a country without disturbing anything; to pass and leave no trace, like fish through the water, or birds through the air" (233). Elaborating on this point a short time later, Latour thinks:

> They seemed to have none of the European's desire to "master" nature, to arrange and re-create. They spent their ingenuity in the other direction; in accommodating themselves to the scene in which they found themselves. This was not so much from indolence, the Bishop thought, as from an inherited caution and respect. It was as if the great country were asleep, and they wished to carry on their lives without awakening it. . . . They ravaged neither the rivers nor the forest, and if they irrigated, they took as little water as would serve their needs. The land and all it bore they treated with consideration; not attempting to improve it, they never desecrated it. (234)

His perspective only increases the irony that, far from wanting to leave the landscape untainted, Latour is a man fundamentally bent on self-assertion, change, mastery, creation, and even desecration. Latour himself would probably admit as much; he does, after all, refer to the general desire of "the white man" to lay his will over the landscape. But importantly the expression of that will works to unite Latour to those individuals against whom he has been contending, most notably the renegade priests. Rather than a sympathizer with Indian belief and custom, Latour is concerned with founding a theological empire which bears his self-memorializing stamp. Even the line between the Bishop and the God he represents blurs as Latour builds the cathedral, figuring himself as creator while downplaying the primordial benevolence of the surrounding earth.[14]

Toward the end of the novel, Latour expresses pity when his friend, Kit Carson, drives the Navajo from their homes, going so far as to refer to Carson as "misguided" (293). But if Carson ignores his own logical objections about destroying the Navajo in favor of his sense of national duty, then Latour must be seen to repeatedly ignore his logical objections about his methods in New Mexico in favor of his sense of Catholic duty. He does not intercede on the Navajo's behalf, an action which is not entirely unexpected given his tendency to profess his admiration for other cultures but to act in a largely contrary manner. In fact, Carson is one of the few people, besides Vaillant, with whom Latour feels a natural ease and kinship. Take this account of his first meeting with the scout.

> There was something curiously unconscious about his mouth, reflective, a little melancholy,—and something that suggested a capacity for tenderness. The Bishop felt a quick glow of pleasure in looking at the man. As he stood there in his buckskin clothes one felt in him standards, loyalties, a code which is not easily put into words but which is instantly felt when two men who live by it come together by chance. (75)

"Curiously unconscious . . . reflective, a little melancholy"—the description could be of the priest as easily as Carson.[15] The symmetry between the two men extends to an enigmatic intellectual and spiritual level, which Latour intuitively recognizes in "the code" (of gentility? of single-mindedness? of the West?) by which they both live. Carson's position as Latour's mirror image is unexpected. A stereotypical western hero—an explorer, an expert with a gun, "fated" to persecute Native peoples—Carson would seem to stand in stark contrast to the Christian ideals Latour rhetorically champions. The fact that he does not says less about Carson's "code" (which seems to befit a western hero) than about Latour's application of the intrinsic principles he cherishes. It would be a critical commonplace, at this late date, to talk about the central role of Christian doctrine and sanction in the North American imperial process. What is important to this argument, however, is the way that Latour seeks to distance himself from that process and to configure himself as a friend to the indigenous peoples of the Southwest, but then fails to help the Navajo, aligns himself with their chief persecutor, and even engages in his own brand of theological imperialism through the contortion of the landscape. Small wonder that Latour feels comfortable with Carson where with Jacinto he has only "the silence which was their usual form of intercourse" (91–92). In his interactions with the Natives, the Bishop proves himself to be a version of the prejudiced Cardinal from the novel's prologue —at best, a man not opposed to the cultural domination characteristic of more "popular western" counterparts.

This potentially sinister identity is particularly emphasized in the near-final scenes of the narrative, when the Navajo are restored to the Canyon de Chelly after Carson burns the sacred peach orchard. As Latour states to Bernard, his late-life companion, "My son, I have lived to see two great wrongs righted; I have seen the end of black slavery, and I have seen the Navajos restored to their own country" (292–93). That conjunction (the end of slavery and deliverance to a promised land) cannot help but recall the Israelites' deliverance from Egypt—with Latour acting as a symbolic stand-in for Moses. The Natives' original expulsion had seemed to Latour "an injustice that cried out to Heaven. Never could he forget that terrible winter when they were being hunted down and driven by thousands from their own reservation to the Bosque Redondo, three hundred miles away on the Pecos River" (292–93). But if Latour is that figurative Moses who can die only after his children have crossed the river into Canaan, he is conspicuously a Moses who neither suffers his people's fate nor contends for their rescue. In fact, his relief at seeing the Navajo restored rings largely false given his earlier inaction. Latour is again quick to configure the events surrounding the Navajo expulsion in Christian iconographic terms. The image he perceives as most emblematic, when thinking back on the Indians' return to the Canyon de Chelly, is "a young Navajo woman, giving a lamb her breast until a ewe was found for it" (297). This image recalls one of his earliest experiences in the novel, when, at Agua Secreta, he watches a group of playing children and thinks of "the chapter in the Apocalypse, about the whiteness of them that were washed in the blood of the Lamb" (31). With the Navajo woman, however, Latour is so caught up in the imagery of the lamb being suckled by the Virgin that he fails to grasp the depth of the actual disaster that has occurred. Their homes destroyed, their farms burned, their shrines laid waste, the Navajo have absolutely nothing despite being allowed to return. The scene with the woman giving milk to her animal is thus imbued with a greater sense of tragedy than of religious promise; the woman is merely attempting to keep the beast alive rather than seeing in her gesture a signpost of redemption and salvation. As he has all along, Latour reads the Indians through the lens of his own theological mission, and their presence as actual humans is far less important to him than the Christian metaphors they suggest. To be blunt, he dehumanizes them, thereby echoing the imperial logic which held that Indians should be either assimilated (through religious conversion, for instance) or destroyed by men like Carson.[16]

Reclaiming the Garden

Latour's preference for a symbolic reading of the Navajo over a literal one does not come as a surprise given the way that, for him, all experiences constitute part of a metaphorical journey from physical desolation to spiritual salvation. This journey is prefigured in the early moments of his trip to Santa Fe when, after devoting himself to God, he moves immediately from the unforgiving desert into the fertile and verdant *Agua Secreta*. All of *Death Comes for the Archbishop* is about reclaiming "the garden," in fact, imbuing the novel with a hoped-for return to Eden characteristic of many formula westerns. Gardens are important to every priest in the novel, but Latour is especially adept at cultivating his own. He raises fruit trees from "dry switches," and the cuttings from those trees "were already yielding fruit in many Mexican gardens" (201). This physical expansion confirms the success of Latour's other mission, with the Bishop creating "the shapes of redemption out of this vast inimical wilderness: a diocese, a cathedral, a garden."[17] The priests do not simply sustain the garden but also "have their allegorical representatives in [it]: Father Vaillant is connected with the flower of the tamarisk tree . . . and the Bishop is connected with the rare lotus of contemplation, which he nourishes carefully in his garden pond."[18] Thus Latour and Vaillant both populate and perpetuate Eden, becoming versions not only of the prelapsarian couple of the original garden but also of the celestial entity that created it.

The notion of the garden was fundamental to American imperialism, of course. Garden images tinged not only religious but also political, academic, and cultural discourse well into the twentieth century (Turner's Thesis, after all, centers on the redemptive power of the landscape and the values it imparts to settlers who cultivate it). Indeed, Latour is not, as he would believe, a man who passes through the landscape trying not to disturb anything. From his first experience with a tree in the desert (which he turns into a cruciform), he is intent upon finding the symbols of his religion in the landscape, and where those symbols are not readily apparent, he alters that landscape to fit his needs. His figurative garden is no different. Faced time and again with literal inhabitants of New Mexico, he changes their meaning to suit his holy purpose. Old Sada, Jacinto, even the entire Navajo nation become abstractions, conformed by Latour's imagination into beautiful religious icons despite the presence of alternate cultural readings or (as with the Navajo) literal atrocities.

In sum, Latour is a man uncluttered with concern for native species, in both his actual and spiritual cultivations. Even the plants that dominate his imagination are ones originating in more "civilized" places. As J. Gerard Dollar writes,

> But if we look closely at the pervasive garden imagery we find there is a certain mistrust of native species; the French ideal in cultivating—in both a religious and horticultural sense—is to bring in cuttings from elsewhere, to graft the foreign on to the native. Padre Martínez immediately sees this as

wrong when he tells Latour that "our religion grew out of the soil, and has its own roots." But these native roots are distasteful, sometimes even abhorrent, to Latour, whose gardens include cuttings brought in from Saint Louis and exotics such as lotus flowers in his artificial pond. Native rootedness to Latour means a regression to the primal, the pagan, the unchristian. Getting too close to the earth . . . brings . . . a sense of being cut off from divine spirit.[19]

Latour's garden mirrors not so much his literal work in New Mexico as it does the shape of his own soul. His ambition, like religious settlers before him, is to craft a wilderness into a garden not just to claim its inhabitants for Christianity but also to guarantee his own position within the elect garden of God's grace—a grace that is critical given the fact of his death (which, while occurring at the novel's end, is the one event that hangs over the narrative from its beginning in the form of the title). A man highly attuned to religious symbols, he commingles the species of his personal garden in an imaginative attempt to convince himself that conflicting cultural ideals can be merged just as easily. But even this metaphor is undercut by the larger metaphor of the garden and its unwavering Christian implications. Latour cannot help but see those around him eventually joined in a true Catholic faith; the cathedral that he builds to preside over the surrounding landscape suggests as much. The message is clear, then: all species are welcome in the garden so long as they pose no danger to the garden itself. Other cultures are fine so long as they do not contradict God's will, especially as that will is mediated through the consciousness of God's representative: Jean-Marie Latour.

This belief system, yet again, lacks any sense that the garden may be neither permanent nor absolute, as Latour's experiences in the ruined Spanish mission and the Indian cave suggest. In reality, most gardens do not fare well in *Death Comes for the Archbishop*. The Indians at Acoma take great pleasure in watching Friar Baltazar's garden wither away after his death, and Kit Carson completely destroys the orchards of the Navajo. Even Latour's garden after his retirement is ironically erected around an apricot tree that, notably without cultivation, has borne fruit for two hundred years. What Latour takes as a symbol of God's presence in the natural world, much as the cruciform tree is read as an overt sign, can be read more subversively as a negation of that belief: the apricot tree predates Latour and all of his gardening acumen, and it will continue long after his passing. In one sense this fact validates Latour's repudiation of the physical world, but in another sense it more strongly confirms the In-

dians' faith in the land itself over celestial extrapolations. A tree is only a
tree, the Navajo might remind Latour, but that identity is important
enough.

Latour as a Frontier Hero: Implications for a Genre

Like popular frontier heroes, Latour's ethnocentrism, sexism, and cultural biases emanate from his negotiation of a highly conditional moral
universe. While the "good" he seeks is in part the abstracted theological
good of Christian faith, it is also the highly practical good of installing his
specific world-view at the center of public consciousness. Ironically that
installation requires a methodology—of denial, coercion, even force—
contrary to the dictates of the moral code which gave it rise. Latour's
quest bears the stamp of the popular frontier novel in that it compels him
to make hard choices, choices that may ultimately seem paradoxical in
their willingness to sacrifice certain characters so that other characters (or,
in Latour's case, beliefs or religious initiatives) may survive. Nonetheless,
as he keeps his own counsel, Latour's individualism, self-reliance, and unerring singleness of purpose yoke him to the kind of indomitable figure
long a hallmark of the popular frontier. And the sacrifices he makes of
both himself and others, whatever else might be said about them, are necessary to accomplish his task.

There are certainly differences to be drawn between Latour and more
popular heroes. He rides a mule instead of a horse. He never fires a gun.
He eschews displays of personal violence. He is a priest. On the other
side, though, there are similarities. He carries a gun and is willing to use
it, even if he never has cause to do so. He comes to the frontier at a time
when, in his mind, the forces of civilization and savagery are locked in a
precarious battle. He has a sidekick, an intimate confidant, with whom he
interacts so closely that he invites suspicion of homoeroticism. He eschews romantic entanglements—indeed, his position denies him a mate.
He interacts closely with Indians and professes a respect for their values
and skills even if, in the end, his allegiance is wholly to the "civilized"
cause. He demonstrates a concern for the landscape though he ultimately
attempts to domesticate the wilderness into an idyllic garden space. And
despite his repudiation of personal violence, he tacitly accepts certain
large-scale aggressions, especially when those aggressions are directed
against minorities and designed to consolidate the white, male, Eurocen-
tric power structures in the region.

In these ways, Latour is less like the western hero of popular film than like frontier heroes of the nineteenth century, Cooper's Natty Bumppo especially. Caught between two worlds (and two personal identities), Natty is a character who continually presses ahead, refusing to resolve the tensions in his life until he finally dies on the prairie facing west. One never knows how satisfied Natty is upon death, though certainly he does not view his life with the sense of completion that Latour views his own. Unlike Natty, Latour never feels a great pull against his civilized (Catholic) beliefs, and in this regard, he is more like the self-satisfied gunslingers of later fiction—Wister's *The Virginian* in particular—who act upon a world-view that is implicitly right if not purely moral. But the end result of such later westerns is to demonstrate to an audience the absolute certainty of the hero's virtues, the absolute rightness of his actions. Latour may resolve all of the problems of New Mexico in his own mind, but clearly those problems still exist, even at his death. The frontier contest, whatever its exact rules, slogs on, such that Latour can finally do no better than Natty in the end. He dies, having advanced civilization to a degree, but only at the expense of many others whose sacrifices he simply does not acknowledge.

In the end, such observations are not meant to detract from *Death Comes for the Archbishop;* it is a beautifully written book, its setting evocative, the plight of its central character compelling. Rather, I would submit only that the worlds of literary and popular novels are not always as far apart as they seem. The traditional frontier tensions in Cather's novel place it in a direct line of descent from Cooper's Leatherstocking novels, despite subtle amendments made by Cather to the form. That Cooper has been maligned for his many prejudices while Cather's biases are largely overlooked only further suggests a problem with critical methodologies valuing identity politics over textual interpretation. Cather was not, on the whole, a writer of popular frontier fiction, and one would be hard pressed to find in the canon of her work another novel that exploits traditional frontier themes as thoroughly as *Archbishop*. But if nothing else, the fact that a writer of her gifts could not avoid those themes completely—moreover, could not avoid deploying them in somewhat conventional fashion—suggests that there is likely more substance to some traditional frontier novels than recent critics have given them credit for. It is tempting, in the contemporary critical climate, to denigrate or dismiss past works that betray ideologies not commensurate with our own relatively enlightened views on race, class, gender, and sexuality. But *Death Comes for the Archbishop* proves that a book—and an author—can still be considered important, even brilliant, despite holding values that are unarguably prejudiced at some level. Needless to say, celebrating such a novel does not mean that we personally endorse its biases. Rather, it suggests that we should continue to develop complex interpretive strategies that allow us to read books in more than diametric fashion. Accepting Cather, warts and all, may compel us to revisit other texts whose beliefs strike us as outdated. Whatever the product of such investigation, we should value the process itself, which recognizes fine breaks rather than chasms separating the cultural work of most writers and reiterates the continuum of literary influence that, despite differences, flows Cooper into Cather into the most radical Western-region writing being produced today.

The
Many Echoes of
The Man Who Killed
the Deer

Almost sixty years have passed since the initial publication of Frank Waters's *The Man Who Killed the Deer,* but despite many authors and scholars claiming to admire the book, it has yet to inspire a great deal of what might be called traditional literary criticism. There are testimonials and appreciations, to be sure. Much of what serves as Waters scholarship today comes in the form of transcribed interviews, lectures, and panel discussions in which a broad array of readers talk about the importance of the author's best-known novel. Such transcriptions have their place. But too often they succumb to the normal ebb and flow of oral discourse, until what remains is not a unified statement about the novel so much as an echo of the many issues that it seems to raise. Even more formal scholarship tends to be oblique, idiosyncratic, or highly personal. *Frank Waters: Man and Mystic*—arguably the best of recent critical anthologies—begins with eight essays devoted wholly to remembrances of Frank Waters and, even in the ensuing commentaries, relies heavily on personal recollections of readers' first encounters with the author's work.[1]

This is not to say that the present scholarship on Waters lacks merit; indeed, substantial recent works by Alexander Blackburn and Charles L. Adams, among others, continue to offer new windows into the author's artistic and cultural purpose.[2] But Waters's novels, simply put, do not enjoy the same cachet as those of his contemporaries. Despite being nominated several times for the Nobel Prize, and despite Blackburn's claim that he should be read on a par with other literary regionalists (Twain and Faulkner especially), Waters is still regarded by many as a somewhat localized phenomenon.[3] Reflections on his work appear almost exclusively in Western American magazines, with scholarly essays restricted to a handful of journals. Even the myriad of fashionable ideas with which his novels artfully concern themselves—Native American rights, gender equality, environmental policy, and others—have not gained him the fame that he probably deserves within American literary and academic circles.

Part of the problem involves personal identity. Demographically speaking, Waters is a textbook example of the traditional Western writer: white, male, born and raised in Colorado, whose fiction is set almost exclusively in the Southwest. Even though his father was part Cheyenne —and even though Waters lived among various Indian tribes and established a formidable reputation as an ethnographer—his lived experience was not exactly that of his Indian subjects. This identity issue is particularly germane to *The Man Who Killed the Deer*, whose main characters (with the notable exception of Rodolfo Byers) are all Indians, mostly Pueblo. In support of such cross-racial representation, some scholars draw comparisons to Faulkner's depiction of black characters in the South. But Faulkner usually tied his black characters to white ones, with works like *Absalom, Absalom* or *Go Down, Moses* focusing both on interchange between the races and on the brutal and debilitating aspects of racism for all involved. *The Man Who Killed the Deer* is heir to a different tradition. In its singular depiction of Pueblo life, Waters's novel is written in the same vein as other sympathetic (if more patronizing) white-authored novels about Native Americans—Helen Hunt Jackson's *Ramona* or Oliver La Farge's *Laughing Boy*, for example. These connections are important ones because, while Jackson and La Farge are still read today, neither is taken as an authority on Indian experience. Moreover, Jackson arguably enjoys more widespread critical popularity than La Farge or Waters because, as a

156

🐎

The Many

Echoes of

The Man

Who Killed the

Deer

woman writer, her novels also fit within the canon of women's sentimental literature.[4]

My point is not to equate Waters with La Farge or Jackson. *The Man Who Killed the Deer* is a more complex, authentic, and compelling depiction of Indian life than both of its predecessors. Rather, my point is to suggest how contemporary critical categories may have sidelined Waters's novel, relying too heavily on identity politics as a gauge of its aesthetic or cultural value. In a nutshell, the novel is too often dismissed because critical audiences see it as a "western" book and Waters as a "regional" writer, based not on what occurs within the novel but on strong preconceptions regarding both Southwestern fiction and the white guys who write it. Contemporary critical reactions bear this phenomenon out. Though John R. Milton expressly argues that *The Man Who Killed the Deer* should be read over and against the popular frontier tradition, Arnold E. Davidson reverses this logic to claim that, despite its inversion of formula western themes, the novel still exploits the mythic tradition of the American West and is therefore indebted to its more commercial forebears. Davidson's argument, however dismissive, is a vast improvement over the silence of most critics who have simply chosen to ignore the book. Taking a limited view of literary history, self-satisfied with their own sense of cultural correctness, most critics have overlooked *The Man Who Killed the Deer* in favor of more contemporary writers who have latched onto Water's themes, if not exploited them as masterfully.

The real shame in this choice is that *The Man Who Killed the Deer* may be *the* seminal text in America's transition from viewing the West as a mythic space to viewing it as a geographical region full of the same racial, ethnic, economic, and cultural complexities that characterize America as a whole. It does far more than refute the popular western, though part of its genius is the way that it includes elements of that genre as a legitimate expression of Southwestern life. In reading the novel, one has the sense of peeling back the layers of Frank Waters's cultural and philosophical vision to gradually reveal a continuum of human experience. More than a romantic celebration of Indian philosophies or lifestyles, the book takes on the legitimate questions of how people of various racial and cultural backgrounds might fruitfully interact with one another. And while Waters does not supply easy answers to these questions, he shifts the forum in which they are asked to one where a single cultural or racial authority does not predominate over others. Finally the book is remarkable for the deep sense of honesty it brings to matters of human interchange. Like his protagonist Martiniano, Waters is a person straddling several cultural identities, and he uses that liminal position to suggest a way of looking at the world that is strikingly clear even as it is indeterminate and forever evolving.

The Novel as Traditional Frontier Narrative

Remarkably, Waters's vision evolves from a very simple plotline in *The Man Who Killed the Deer*. Martiniano, a mixed-blood Pueblo Indian, kills a deer in violation of tribal ritual and government regulation, a small act that ignites the larger events of the story. Martiniano, who has been educated at the government "away-school," becomes an outcast—navigating the boundary between white and Native worlds, shunned by both sides as he quests for an identity that will express the truth about who he is. In the meantime, the Pueblo people use Martiniano's case as a means to press their demand for the return of the watershed in which Martiniano was arrested; Dawn Lake, a Pueblo holy site and U.S. government reserve, had been promised to the Indians by treaty. Indeed, some critics have read Martiniano's struggle as a replica of the struggle in which all the Pueblo people engage; his ultimate acceptance of Pueblo belief resembles the government's unlikely acceptance of the Pueblo land claims, which cause the return of Dawn Lake.

Such parallel readings seek to reduce the narrative into one that privileges an Indian view of the world over others. But despite the novel's apparent embrace of much Native belief, it does not endorse a Pueblo outlook unequivocally. If nothing else, Martiniano's recurrent complaint that the tribe has mistreated him is not wholly without merit. As he tells Palemon,

> They fined me because I did not cut off the heels of my shoes and cut out the seat of my pants. They whipped me because I did not dance. My use of the thresher they forbade. They ignore me, they shame my wife. We are outcasts. . . . What have we done to deserve all this? What is good about these old ways of yours which you uphold—this cruelty, this injustice to a blood brother?[5]

Part of the problem, Palemon recognizes, is the individual pride that causes Martiniano to elevate his beliefs above those of the tribe. But at the same time, Martiniano's objection is made at the level of Pueblo belief itself. If all life is connected and sacred, then how can the Elders justify their harsh, even life-threatening, treatment of him and Flowers Playing?

158

🐎

The Many

Echoes of

The Man

Who Killed the

Deer

This question becomes even more profound in light of the Pueblo objections to the federal government. The Indians' basic claim is that, despite its superior power, the federal government is unjustified in its persecution of the tribe, namely in its continued control over Dawn Lake. Might does not make right, the Pueblo people insist, but they are all too ready to reverse that equation when they are the ones in charge and it is the individual, Martiniano, who acts contrary to their desires.

Given his intermediate status, Martiniano acts out the drama of the white-educated Indian that often features in Native American literature produced prior to *The Man Who Killed the Deer*.[6] This identity becomes clear in his conversations with Strophy, the Indian agent:

> "I see!" broke out Martiniano hotly. "You grab us boys out of our houses and send us away to school and teach us all this nonsense, all these lies about becoming good citizens, about being like white men. And then you kick us out, and send us back home, and tell us, 'Now be good Indians again! . . . We've had our fun. Now you go back home and pay for it'" (48–49).

But the specific dynamics of Martiniano's dilemma, including his frequent physical resistance to Pueblo demands, make him more than a passive symbol of white/Native relations. Rather, he ironically assumes the position of the traditional frontier hero caught between white and Indian worlds, who must navigate both without ever feeling completely at home in either. Despite his Pueblo-Apache identity, Martiniano becomes the representative of "civilization," a proponent of many of the ideas he has acquired at away-school. As with other frontier heroes, of course, some of these ideas are flawed, and too often Martiniano crosses the line between individualism and stubborn pride. At the same time, though, he serves as a more sympathetic version of "American" philosophy than the distant government in Washington or even the bungling Strophy. Despite his incompetence, Strophy manages to articulate the government line on away-school students returned to the reservation. "There's got to be a bridge," he says. "You young fellows are the ones to make it. Remember it takes time and patience" (49). His mistake—and Martiniano's at first—is to view this process of "bridging" as one of conversion in which the Pueblo are brought around to a white way of life. But Martiniano's experience demonstrates that complete conversion is neither desirable nor possible. Instead, Martiniano serves as an agent of change in the way that he comes to recognize the world's constant state of flux and compromise. Unlike the Pueblo who hold fast to even the most ancient traditions, or the American government that refuses to admit its mistreatment of Indians, Martiniano recognizes the need for constant negotiation between these two worlds. His life—both his removal to the away-school and his return to the Pueblo—teaches him about the necessary give-and-take of existence. Or if not that, he realizes that cross-cultural interchange will occur, whether people want it to or not.

It may be difficult for some to see Martiniano, a figure of negotiation more than conquest, as a version of the traditional frontier hero. But it is worth noting that, by definition, the frontier hero remains isolated in some measure because he chooses to. His preternatural skill with a gun aside, what real cultural power he wields derives from his ability to resist the demands of white and Native worlds at the same time. Martiniano showcases just such an ability when, time after time, he accepts the punishments inflicted by the tribe but refuses to submit to its will. He is not only a sympathetic underdog but also a representative of Euro-American individualism, remaining stalwart in the face of repeated assaults. His anger and his pride, so antithetical to tribal attitudes, become a version of the same righteous and self-assured traits implicit in other western heroes whose actions, while often taking place outside the bounds of conventional justice, confirm the individual as the single most certain arbiter of moral matters. Finally, Martiniano does author his own destiny. While he may gravitate back to the tribe by the novel's end, such movement occurs voluntarily, the product of his epiphany in isolation more than the tribe's autocratic insistence.

Jane Tompkins has written about the importance of the western hero's propensity to engage in physical, often violent confrontation—his ability not only to administer pain but to endure it as well.[7] Here, too, Martiniano fits the bill. His initial act of violence—killing the deer—is only one in a line of infractions for which he is punished, culminating in the scene in which he is lashed by his friend Palemon. That public whipping, above all, highlights the resolute nature of both the Pueblo people as a group and Martiniano as an individual, because Martiniano has basically volunteered for it. He has come to claim his blanket that was confiscated by the tribe during a peyote ceremony from which he was absent, and even though Palemon whips him harder than he has ever been whipped, Martiniano endures the lashing with a strange sense of satisfaction. The importance of Martiniano's decision to receive the lashing cannot be underestimated. While his concession to the punishment suggests his growing willingness to submit to the will of the tribe, the rest of the

160

🐕

The Many

Echoes of

The Man

Who Killed the

Deer

encounter only confirms his strong sense of individuality. In claiming the blanket, he accepts responsibility for his actions, and in enduring the lashes, he offers external evidence of a newfound inner calm and self-reliance. At one point in the process, he looks up to discover Flowers Playing, whose face registers "no anger at Palemon and the old men, no shame for him, neither pity nor sympathy" (161); by the end of the lashing, Martiniano can even describe her look as "triumphant" and "shining" (162). Flowers Playing confirms the individualistic import of Martiniano's action. The lashing finished, he ignores the old men's "conciliatory gestures" and walks "with calm dignity" to his wife. He is a man who has successfully endured pain for what he believes. And as if to confirm his masculine potency, it is at this point that Flowers Playing tells him she is pregnant.

The Novel as an Anti-Frontier Narrative

Nonetheless, violence in *The Man Who Killed the Deer* fails to secure for any of the men who use it the power that they seek. After he poaches the deer, Martiniano loses his fight with Sanchez's agents and must be rescued by Palemon. Palemon's whipping of Martiniano fails to make Martiniano submit. And even the past large-scale violence of the U.S. government against Indians ultimately fails to preserve American land gains, as Dawn Lake is returned to the Pueblo people.

It is not only violence but also more subtle physical displays that do not achieve their desired result. Manuel Rena, in Byers's story, prepares to fight in a battle that is apparently imagined. Napaita's escape from the kiva into the mountains turns into an ordeal from which he must be rescued by Martiniano. And even Martiniano's public attempt to climb the pine pole, which he believes will redeem him in front of the tribe, fails as certainly as the attempts of the six Chiffonetas preceding him. These failures collectively demarcate the boundaries between Waters's novel and more popular westerns, in which the successful completion of physical tasks—winning a gunfight, bringing in a herd of cattle, surviving the harsh terrain—provides the only actual proof of a male character's power. Physical displays in popular westerns are meant to create a social hierarchy, with the highest rungs reserved for those men who can deploy violence in expert fashion. *The Man Who Killed the Deer* reverses this arrangement, however, with acts of violence and physical competition tending to disrupt the Pueblo social order more than maintain it. The only exception to this rule is the race that Martiniano runs at the novel's end, a ceremonial exercise designed not to determine winners or losers but, conversely, to bring the runners together in "the unending race of all humanity with the wonder of creation" (253). Indeed, relative to the formula western, *The Man Who Killed the Deer* inverts not only the nature of male physical performance but also the significance of the landscape in which that performance takes place. In the popular western, the relationship between hero and landscape is mostly inimical, with the majority of action focusing on the hero caught inescapably in the threatening out-of-doors. In *The Man Who Killed the Deer*, the Pueblo people view the landscape as a provider and treat it with reverence, hence their profound desire to recover Dawn Lake.

That reverence does not make the landscape predictable for Waters's characters, though. Where the popular western valorizes the ability of a hero to read and interpret a static terrain—a visual act of appropriation—*The Man Who Killed the Deer* offers a terrain that is frequently incomprehensible to its inhabitants, precisely because it is always changing. Martiniano's experiences out-of-doors, as when he successfully raises crops only to have them trampled by deer, are often ambiguous and frustrating in comparison to the clearer realizations that he achieves through his domestic experiences with Flowers Playing. The novel reinforces the importance of such realizations in subtle yet telling ways. It should not be lost on readers, for example, that Martiniano's story does not begin with Martiniano, the hero, but with his friend, Palemon. It does not begin in the open air, like most westerns, but in a home, with Palemon sleeping beside his wife. Palemon's disturbed sleep is symptomatic of the rest of the novel, in which troubled sleep—Martiniano's, Manuel Rena's—represents deeper spiritual anxieties. And even Palemon's early break with his family (in order to search for Martiniano) suggests things to come; despite the heavy emphasis on tribal duty and public responsibility, it is finally Martiniano's private reconciliation with Flowers Playing and his joy over their new son that compels him to return to the tribal way of life.

There are other things that separate *The Man Who Killed the Deer* from more popular novels, perhaps most obviously the matter of race. To say the least, Martiniano's Indian identity makes him an unusual frontier hero. More traditional frontier novels, even many written in the twentieth century, depended on an audience's predilection to associate civilization with Euro-Americans and savagery with Indians. In this manner, the stereotypical civilization/savagery contest broke down along simple racial lines, with the hero invariably a white man fighting, whatever his misgivings about the values of other whites, to advance Euro-American culture

162

🐎

The Many

Echoes of

The Man

Who Killed the

Deer

using the means of its Indian opponents. Martiniano's position is more ironic. On the one hand, he advocates many of the things that Euro-American culture has to offer, coming into violent conflict with the Pueblo people over these beliefs. On the other hand, his race "always already" inscribes him as a version of those things that Euro-American culture is attempting to eradicate. This paradox is only intensified by his decision to adopt a more conspicuously Pueblo lifestyle at the story's end. While it is tempting to read this change as a brand of racial determinism (despite his white training, Martiniano reverts to the role he was destined to occupy), it is important to recall that Martiniano *chooses* this lifestyle— a choice that comes only after a long period of resisting what he derides as Pueblo foolishness and superstition. In his conversion, Martiniano at a minimum represents a new version of the frontier hero, finally able to express his love for the "savage" culture to which he owes so much of his identity. At a maximum, his choice to "go Indian" calls into question the nature of what is "civilized" or "savage," undermining the cultural vocabulary implicit at the core of so many traditional frontier texts.[8]

Waters does not merely invert the relationship between whites and Indians. The novel offers even-handed portraits of both sides and, perhaps more importantly, expands the racial and ethnic tableau of the story beyond the immediate conflict over Dawn Lake. Mexicans and Mexican Americans figure repeatedly in the narrative, a presence which is crucial to the book's notions of race and ethnicity for two reasons. First, it provides a counterpoint to the central narrative tension between white America and the Pueblo people. Despite giving them only supporting roles, Waters carefully differentiates his Mexican characters from both whites and Indians, thereby breaking down the simple axis of white versus nonwhite. Mexicans are both aggressors (Sanchez) and victims (the sheepherders who lose their land rights), their multiple identities complicating the apparently bipolar tensions of the main narrative line. Second, the Mexican American presence undermines the primacy of racial over cultural or political identity. It emphasizes the issue of borders in the text, not only the perceived boundaries between races but also the political and cultural lines between nations. The fact that the Mexican American characters seem, at some level, more thoroughly integrated into mainstream American culture than the Pueblo characters is likely a statement of both success and failure for Waters. Certainly their better relations with the U.S. government suggest the possibility of productive interchange between people of different racial, cultural, and political backgrounds. But at the same time, their apparent assimilation warns against the kind of cultural domination that the Pueblo most fear. Moreover, such assimilation does not entail complete protection; after all, Martiniano is set adrift from government aid upon his return from away-school, and the Mexican sheepherders are turned off the land around Dawn Lake, despite their ability (at least in some cases) to produce legal documents establishing their right to be there.

Further complicating racial relationships in the novel is the presence of Rodolfo Byers. Like Martiniano, the trader can make a legitimate claim to the title of traditional frontier hero; despite obvious sympathy for the Indians, his race and his position as the novel's most prominent capitalist make him the most obvious symbol of civilization. In some respects, Byers seems like a figure only slightly removed from the nineteenth century, rugged and cantankerous, dressed in buckskins—as if Natty Bumppo had finally given up, settled down, and bought a country store. Contrary to the traditional frontier hero, Byers has taken a mate, but his wife is tellingly "Spanish-American" (36), thereby avoiding Natty's dilemma of being able to marry neither Anglo nor Indian. Beyond superficial links, though, Byers differs from Natty in that he never seeks to be the novel's mediating consciousness. Where Natty often acts as a dual mouthpiece (he's the voice of Indians when talking to whites, and the voice of whites when talking to Indians), Byers self-consciously rejects a role as emissary between white and Indian worlds. While he may describe the Pueblo people, their customs and beliefs, he does not attempt to fit them into a white context or to explain their significance by analogy. He merely claims to find the Indians irresistible and, with this insistence, becomes as inscrutable as any other character in the book.

For Waters, what is important about Byers is not so much his ability to explain one culture to another, but his mere presence (however unqualified) at the nexus of white, Indian, and Mexican worlds. This position is, in fact, the most striking element in the initial description of the trader:

> Few in town liked him; he was a piece of life they did not understand. He had lived so long among Indians that for whites he took on their subtle elusiveness. But knowing them so well, he punctured their own with the analytical mind of the white. Mexicans feared his sharpness in buying, as whites feared his bluntness in selling. Indians cautiously respected both.
>
> Rodolfo Byers was simply a character. Among three races the stories about him kept spreading. (35)

164

🐎

The Many

Echoes of

The Man

Who Killed the

Deer

Again like Martiniano, Byers is a figure of cultural overlap and negotiation, even if he is not wholly conscious of that position and seems unable to articulate why he chooses it. His reasons for staying with the tribe are inexplicable even to him, as the narrator makes clear. "What held him he never knew, but it was always there. In the look of an eye, in a curious phrase, in the beat of a drum—in a thousand irrelevant incidents that slowly built up into a whole he could not see, but which he felt existed" (39). It is precisely because Byers is so comfortable "not knowing," however, that he is such a useful figure to Waters. The trader takes on faith the value of his association with the tribe, not looking for "an imperfect translation of [his own] values" (130) or personal reward in return. This faith lies at the core of Waters's attitude toward cross-cultural contact. Despite his intimate knowledge of the Pueblo people, Byers will never be one of them; rational explanations of their lives ultimately leave off. But Byers recognizes a shared consciousness binding him to the Indians, and it is this sense of a relationship—even if he cannot put its details into words—that keeps him straddling the three worlds of which he is a part.[9]

Unlike Natty, then, whose median cultural status exists almost solely to write Euro-American civilization over Indian culture, Byers's median status serves a less precise purpose. In large measure, the novel needs him simply as a witness to a lifestyle that will inevitably pass, an outlook encoded in the trader's peculiar brand of fatalism. Several times he reminds himself of the inevitability of the evolving world.

> He himself belonged to the vanishing past. But he was no sentimentalist, he reminded himself sternly. No sickly nostalgia! There is no going back. There is no standing still. There is only that everpresent change which keeps life fresh and ever new. (129)

And this observation leads him to larger conclusions about the fate of both Pueblo and white. As he pessimistically observes about the agreement to return Dawn Lake to the Indians,

> Byers saw its falsity. There can be no oases in the desert of ever-shifting time, no idyllic glades of primitive culture in the forests of mankind, no ivory towers of thought. We are all caught in the tide of perpetual change. These pueblos, these reservations must sometime pass away, and the red flow out into the engulfing white. The government had only postponed the inevitable. . . . The victory, even for the Indians, seemed a shabby makeshift.
>
> For it was predicated upon the differences between men, upon the outward form of their lives, their ethnological behavior, and not upon the one

eternally groping spirit of mankind. It was maintained by the white who was content to set the red apart in his tiny zoo, and by the red who, with traditional secrecy and stubborn obduracy to change, himself held aloof. So both must sometime pass: the Indian with his simple fundamental spiritual premise untranslated into modern terms, and finally the white with his monstrous materiality. (261)

Despite these feelings, Byers can do no more to bridge the gap between white and Native in the present than simply to exist, to hold the different qualities of both worlds in complex suspension within himself.[10] If he does serve a larger purpose in the novel, it is to highlight the importance of that "groping spirit of mankind" transcending the racial and cultural boundaries that humans erect. Byers may be a representative of such transcendence, with his obvious allegiance to the Pueblo people and even Mexicans, but he is no advocate. He does not, like Strophy, try to convince the Indians to change. Indeed, he claims to be quite powerless. It is not just that he fails to replicate his median identity; he cannot even begin a meaningful dialogue (witness the perpetual silence between him and Martiniano) with the various sides involved.

The Novel as "Domestic" Fiction

Finally, Byers confirms the productive possibility of cross-cultural contact, but even he realizes that his position is useful only as a kind of real-world compromise. The Pueblo spiritual ideals are beyond his ken, even if he intuitively recognizes their importance.

[P]erhaps there would still be time, thought Byers, to learn from these people before they pass from this earth which was theirs and is now all men's, the one truth that is theirs and shall be all men's—the simple and monstrous truth of mankind's solidarity with all that breathes and does not breathe, all that has lived and shall live again upon the unfathomed breast of the earth we trod so lightly, beneath the stars that glimmer less brightly but more enduringly than our own brief lives. (261)

Byers may not be the only man, though, on whom this sacred connection dawns only marginally. Despite the inordinate public power wielded by men in the novel, women seem more highly attuned to the interconnectedness of human lives, symbolized not only in the idea of childbirth (which dominates a number of passages),[11] but also in a correspondent spiritual connection to the physical world that only women enjoy. By the

166

🐆

The Many

Echoes of

The Man

Who Killed the

Deer

novel's close, Martiniano may have become the redeemed champion of both family and community; his rescue of Napaita—moreover, the way that that rescue reconstitutes both Palemon's family and the kiva—figuratively concludes the rescue mission on which Palemon embarked at the novel's beginning. But Martiniano's progress to this new identity has been made possible by his wife. And finally it is her spiritual acumen, her power to convert her husband where others could not, that makes Flowers Playing one "hero" of the novel and the novel itself a version of earlier sentimental narratives which recognized women's spiritual endeavor at the core of cultural identity.

Women's elevated status—especially in opposition to the limited roles of women in more traditional frontier stories—is evident throughout *The Man Who Killed the Deer*. Even at a conversational level, the Pueblo people guard the sanctity of both genders: they "always referred to a man as 'she' and a woman as 'he' lest direct reference rob the one of his power" (170). But it is in the feminized forms of their religion that the Indians most thoroughly embrace the notion of a female sphere of power. The novel indicates this relationship in its first description of the kiva, set in glaring opposition to the church's "cross, the phallic symbol of the male lustful to conquer" (67).

> On his way through the pueblo to Palemon's house Martiniano had always passed a kiva. The circular, soft adobe walls sinking like a womb into the dark resistless earth, with a ladder sticking out for men to enter by. The female symbol of fertility embedded in Our Mother Earth. The Kiva. This was the Indian church. A form of life whose substance was passivity, not action, and no will to conquer, to even oppose. A creed of supplication and appeasement. And so when water was needed the people merely danced for rain instead of digging more ditches.

The significance of this scene cuts a number of ways. Martiniano, the passage goes on to note, feels "polarized" to neither church nor kiva but "miserable between them." His misery results in part from his away-school training, the rational side of his being that wants to "dig a ditch" when the other Indians merely dance for rain. But Martiniano's outsider status, the book suggests, is more than the simple product of his training; it is written into his genetic makeup as a man. Waters chooses his words carefully when he classifies a lust for power as "male." Despite the close association of Christianity and conquest, the description of the cross as a phallus indicts the male body, Indian as well as white. Male entry into the female sphere, the passage suggests, is always an act of penetration or conquest even in its most righteous incarnations. If the cross serves as a phallus in certain contexts, then it is equally clear that the ladder by which men enter the kiva serves as another. This figurative association of all men is reinforced by the literal violence that the male elders employ in an attempt to change Martiniano's ways. The repeated lashings, always mandated and executed by men, bespeak a doctrine not of "passivity" and "appeasement" but, rather, a doctrine of the same desire for conquest (if on a smaller scale) so contemptible in the church.

At some level, the kiva seems imbued with an ironic hint of sexism; it is, after all, only men who are taken into it for training.[12] But this exclusivity likewise makes a profound statement about gender identity, namely, that where the female connection to the spiritual world is natural and implicit, such links can only be learned by men (and then, it would seem, only imperfectly). The processes of revelation and even maturation require a feminizing influence, the book contends; no man is complete without recognizing the other half of life, the life-giving half, that is woman. It is not surprising, then, that Martiniano, having been kept from kiva training, must undergo a similar process of recognition and acceptance before he can make peace with the tribe. While other methods of spiritual investigation—such as the Peyote Road—move him closer to that goal, they mainly serve to remind him that he has not yet accepted the difficult and humbling aspects of his faith that are required for true conversion. The deer in his peyote vision is not a figure of comfort or reconciliation, but instead, an ominous presence that drives him away with a gesture signifying his continued inadequacy:

> Martiniano was suddenly afraid. He looked around him quickly for a club, and noticed that the tall pines were sadly nodding. But not at him. At the deer. And he knew that he was an intruding stranger who had not stopped to consider what constituted this strange peace, this universal brotherhood between deer and pines and birds. He turned swiftly and fled. (77)

It almost goes without saying that Martiniano fails to recognize precisely what the kiva training is designed to teach—"*the one great truth: the arising of all individual lives into one great life, and the necessary continuance of this one great life by the continual progression of the individual lives which form it*" (100).

Martiniano will not give up his masculine desire for conquest easily; shortly after his peyote experience, he attempts to climb the pine pole but

168

The Many

Echoes of

The Man

Who Killed the

Deer

is again, in his eyes, defeated by the deer at its summit. This string of fail-ures hammers home the futility of masculine anger, frustration, and pride and casts in even finer relief the epiphanic moment when Martiniano, however grudgingly, realizes that he must return to the tribe. That moment—when Flowers Playing invites the three deer into the corral to protect them from hunters—is rendered, like the rest of the novel, in dreamlike language designed to blur the line between physical and spiri-tual worlds. But, importantly, it is the exact kind of experience, a tangible enactment of Pueblo belief, that is needed to bring Martiniano—the doubter, the rational individualist—back to the Pueblo fold. Throughout his entire narrative, Martiniano has sought an irrefutable sign to elevate one side of his identity over the other: "white" or Indian, individual or communal, church or kiva. Flowers Playing offers him such proof not only in her inexplicable connection to the animal world but in the spe-cific form that connection takes: the deer, the animal that Martiniano has been able neither to avoid nor to defeat.

> Flowers Playing was standing quietly in the gathering dusk. Slowly and gently she put out her hand. With a bound the deer cleared the fence and strode across the field.
>
> A snake wriggled up Martiniano's backbone; his knees trembled. A vi-sion clutched him by the throat. He had cut his corn stalks and stacked them in little, upright, conical piles to shed rain. In the dusk they looked like a far, vast village of tepees standing on the plain. Striding between them, distorted and fantastically enlarged by the perspective, came the deer—giant, ghostly figures looming above the highest tips of protruding lodge poles. For an in-stant, as the old myth-wonder and atavistic fear rose up and flooded him, he saw them as his people had long seen them, one of the greatest animalistic symbols of his race: the deer which had populated forest and plain in un-counted myriads on the earth, and gave their name to the Pleiades in the sky; whose hoofs as ceremonial rattles were necessary for every dance; who complimented at once the eagle above and the snake below; gave rise to Deer Clan and Antelope Priests; and lent the mystery of their wildness, swiftness and gentleness to all men. In a flash of intuition it all leapt out be-fore him. And in its brief glimmer stood out a strange woman with the same wildness and gentleness which had first drawn his eyes to her as she danced—a woman no longer his wife, but as a deer clothed in human form and thus possessing the power to draw and control the great shapes that moved toward her.

The next instant it was all gone. There were only two small does standing before him and licking salt from her outstretched hands. (198)

169

Frank Waters

Reverting to the symbolism of earlier passages, this scene again favorably
contrasts the feminized deer to the phallic cornstalks and lodge poles over
which they tower. Flowers Playing's mutation into a deer herself confirms
Martiniano's latent suspicion of the deer's relation to a more feminine
identity and to a clearer awareness of the spiritual plane. Deer and woman
elide in a vision intended to suggest the continuum that flows each life
into all other lives. And in a more practical sense, it suggests the notions of
interdependence and communal will to which Martiniano must inevitably
submit—indeed, to which he has already submitted as a condition of existence, even if he refuses to acknowledge it.

Martiniano does continue to rebel, but after he witnesses Flowers
Playing with the deer, such rebellion is always yoked to the correspondent
knowledge that he must eventually yield. As the narrator confirms shortly
after the deer episode, "The husband in him could not censure the wife.
But the man in him was stirred against the woman. For he felt in her a
strange female power that sought to dwarf his manhood, and against
which he had no means to rebel" (209). These ideas follow the announcement that Flowers Playing will be one of the Deer Mothers in the
annual tribal dance, a figurative reenactment of Martiniano's vision and
further palpable evidence that he must submit to the version of community symbolized in the deer as surely as he submits to the mystery of his
wife's unshakable love for him. It is worth noting that, in some respects,
Martiniano reverses the terms of the Pueblo spiritual order. He values
lived experience over theological precept and submits to a tribal sensibility not as a matter of cultural heredity but through the slow and painstaking recognition of the forms of his religion in his daily life. In this regard,
he differs from Palemon and the elders, who seem to accept tribal custom
on faith and, proceeding from that faith, are able to identify its outward
signifiers in the physical world. The difference is subtle and, in the large
scheme of Pueblo belief, perhaps meaningless. During the Deer Mother
dance, all men (Martiniano included) give way to Flowers Playing "as the
male ever gives way to the female imperative" (213). But in other ways, the
order of Martiniano's conversion is of paramount importance. At its base,
his faith rests not on a grand theological design but on the redeeming
power of one woman, his wife, and her love for him. This relationship exploits the kind of duality common to Waters's fiction, where things of the

170

The Many

Echoes of

The Man

Who Killed the

Deer

physical world are exactly what they seem to be and, in the same breath, representative of far greater things. Inextricably, Flowers Playing is a simple housewife and a celestial Deer Mother at the same time. But just as importantly, Martiniano's emphasis on family reduces the grand rhetoric of the Pueblo (and arguably Waters) back to its human equation. All things in the world are linked, Martiniano would agree, but understanding these links proceeds from smaller moments of insight—from the hard-forged, fought-for relationships between individuals that only in their immediacy can convey the clear simple truths of existence.

It is appropriate, then, that the novel ends with a scene celebrating Martiniano's domestic contentment as much as his newfound place within the tribe. When he leaves Flowers Playing to go watch the people on their pilgrimage to Dawn Lake, it is with the casual remark that he is only "going for a walk" (264). Not a kiva member, he is not allowed to travel with them but only observes from afar, his thoughts tellingly devoted to Juan de Bautista who will one day enter the kiva with Palemon as his preceptor. Even at the end, Martiniano is a man both within and outside the tribal circle, but it is an identity with which he is finally comfortable, owing in large part to the sense of belonging that he feels in his own home. This feeling is implicit in the way that he imagines the night unfolding, after he has returned from watching the pilgrims.

> In a little while Flowers Playing would light a lamp and wash the dishes. The boy would wake up. She would sing to him awhile, a Ute song, an Arapahoe lullaby, the Corn Dance song. Then they would go to bed and he would lie there, his wife warm on one side, and the night breeze cool on the other, wondering how it was that now he had no more worries and if he should fix his fence tomorrow. (263)

The scene is powerful in its simplicity: Martiniano, the fulcrum for various negotiations of public power, rejects the need for a public identity and accedes to the private contentment of home and family. The old divisions are still there, of course. The songs sung by Flowers Playing recall both her and Martiniano's mixed-tribal status, and even Juan de Batista serves as a tacit reminder of Martiniano's isolation, the child's future in the kiva juxtaposed against his father's enduring inability to participate fully in the Pueblo religion. But Martiniano has come to embrace his median position both as an unavoidable truth and, more importantly, as a statement of his connection to the many lives around him. If the end of the novel makes him into the "bridge" that Strophy once predicted, it is certainly not in the manner that the Indian agent wants. Rather than a figure of dichotomy (white/native, modernized/traditional, individual/communal), Martiniano has become a figure of duality and even multiplicity, able to accept the many identities informing his experience, the many other lives that flow into his own. Hence the conjunction of his newfound calmness to his lack of concern about the fence: with nothing more to block out and no reason to hide behind them, fences literal and figurative no longer interest Martiniano. In a telling metaphor for the rest of his life, he keeps Flowers Playing on one side and the breeze on the other (order and chaos, family and individuality), finally balanced not as oppositional forces but as part of the great circle of his identity—the same balance, the book suggests, implicit in all lives.

The emphasis on the home provides the last break between *The Man Who Killed the Deer* and more popular western novels. Certainly Waters's purpose seems self-consciously contrary to the goals of conventional westerns, but it is worth noting how he still employs that formula—the hero caught between worlds, the violent conflict that ensues—if only to invert or undermine it at every turn. *The Man Who Killed the Deer* demonstrates the state of Western writing in the 1940s: not just authors' complete awareness of frontier conventions, but their ability to alter those conventions and even operate beyond them when the situation required it. Despite critics claiming to have discovered the biases of the frontier tradition in the 1970s or 1980s, Waters's generation truly blows the field of Western fiction and literary criticism wide open. Like Martiniano, *The Man Who Killed the Deer* encompasses multiple identities, and its particular genius involves the way that it manages to collapse traditionally disparate forms (western, anti-western, sentimental novel, philosophical tract) into one another, subtly intertwining them until their natural oppositions rise up in the voices of characters: declaring, challenging, doubting, revising. To read *The Man Who Killed the Deer* is to watch the Western novel evolve before your eyes into a complex site where numerous belief systems vie for supremacy but never really attain it. For if one result of the novel is Martiniano's assumption of the identity he has always desired, then another result is his continued inability to demarcate that identity in language. As at his story's beginning, he remains an agent of multiplicity, flux, and change—as does the novel, which inquires repeatedly about the nature of personal, group, and human identity but never fully answers itself. *The Man Who Killed the Deer* is one of the first

172

🐎

The Many

Echoes of

The Man

Who Killed the

Deer

Western fictions to ask more questions than it answers, to celebrate inde-terminacy, and to forego an easy blueprint for how characters—and, by implication, readers—should live their lives. It is a landmark moment in writing about the West, a celebration not of what is known but of what might be known, of an expansive and inclusive vision of the world whose simultaneous difficulties and promises (even today) signify well beyond the pages of the book.

Epilogue

*Reading the Western
and the Importance
of History*

The 1930s and '40s were watershed decades for both "actual" and "mythic" Wests. On the more serious side, literary writers continued to expand the boundaries of characters and themes suitable for Western fiction, while a new breed of critics started to eschew grand studies of the frontier for more localized treatments of specific Western authors and regional literatures.[1] On the popular side, directors like John Ford and Howard Hawkes continued to make monolithic films about the West, and the genre western expanded directly into American homes through the popular media of radio and television. Americans' attraction to the form was even intensified, arguably, by the nation's central involvement in World War II. As a people, we reveled in a "superpowerful" self-image that made us the frontier heroes of the globe, an image that would not be substantially shaken until the military escalations in Vietnam in the late sixties.

For this reason, though, *The Word Rides Again* should end in the 1940s, at a time when the compartmentalization of Western Studies had not taken complete effect. It probably goes without saying that the popularity of the mythic West began to decline as counterculture movements gained power in the 1950s and '60s. Closely associated with conservative values—including the hawkish impulses at the root of the Cold War—the popular West seemed like an anachronism when set against American disillusionment over the arms buildup and Vietnam. With the prospect of complete annihilation on the one hand, and the reality of a war whose rules differed from previous conflicts on the other, the lone gunfighter—the man who made absolute sense of the world simply by drawing his gun from its holster—no longer seemed relevant or potent. Not that he would ever die completely, of course. Hollywood has continued to produce a handful of westerns into the new millennium and, perhaps more importantly, transplanted the frontier hero's ethos into the words and actions of science-fiction characters, the heroes of the final frontier. But beginning in the 1930s, the frontier hero began to lose the absolute cultural authority that he once enjoyed in many circles. By the 1970s, it was impossible to talk about him without a great deal of skepticism. And by the 1990s, he had become intellectual anathema, a symbol for many academics of the racism, sexism, and imperialism encoded more subtly in a host of other Euro-American texts.

The conscious design of the *The Word Rides Again,* therefore, was to return to its own brand of yesteryear in which discussions of frontier literature were not automatically polarized and charged with the political voltage that they are today. I began with the simple premise that, historically speaking, works of Western fiction did not always fall into the ready-made contemporary categories of "popular" or "literary"—that there was often a gray interpretive area where even novels that seemed single-minded could engage in subtle, if not subversive, inner dialogues. I hope that the foregoing textual studies have helped to highlight that gray area. Reading authors like Harte and Wister against their traditional formula status, or writers like Child and Cather against their supposed revisionist status, may not change the critical categories that we employ in discussions of the literary West. But it should change the easy, preset method by which we too often assign novels to those categories.

Bakhtin reminds us that most novels are, by their nature, polyphonic. The novel's characters compete for narrative primacy, each bringing to the text his or her own unique way of looking at the world and revising

175

Reading

the Western

and the

Importance

of History

that vision as it interacts with others. While some fictions manage to be monologic—that is, advancing a single message or idea—they are few and far between. Thematic tension relies on the interplay of opposing cultural voices, and this larger sort of dialogue is not something that an author creates consciously. Instead, it is embedded in the novel as a form. However definitively a novel may be read in a particular time or place, however an author may insist on one reading over another, the novel's multivoiced quality creates slippage, and it is out of such indeterminacy that critical opinion evolves over time. Even with the frontier novel, to defend absolute and diametric readings is a mistake as a matter of intellectual policy.[2] Critics are certainly entitled to strong opinions, but at the same time they should recognize themselves as part of a larger dialogue in much the way that characters in a novel negotiate ideas competing for cultural primacy. Critical vocabularies, perhaps especially in a field as contentious as Western Studies, should not be constructed with the sole aim of separating wheat from chaff, the elect from the damned. Such practices, while expedient in a given cultural moment, quickly become obsolete and, all too often, as oppressive as the methodologies they seek to displace.

In earlier writing on this subject, I have tried to conclude with some idea of how Western Studies might fruitfully proceed. My answers, though, are pretty much what one might expect. Even as we continue to explore cutting-edge aspects of the field—Native American literature (including oral traditions), women's pioneer writing, ecocriticism, and the like—we should continue to revisit more traditional "frontier" narratives, reading them in isolation and against one another in an ongoing effort to account for their full complexity. As I write this, it even occurs to me that these two efforts—discovering "new" texts that challenge conventional notions about the West and rereading conventional texts in new and subversive ways—are of an epistemological piece. They both delve into the past through an interpretive process intent on understanding the interplay of real-world cultural forces, whether such forces manifest themselves in the space between separate narratives or within individual ones.

★

Rather than reiterate these ideas ad nauseam, though, I would like to end with a personal anecdote that I hope will contextualize my more complex view of Western Studies and the relation of this book to the world at large. Like other teachers, I have watched with dismay over the last decade as my students grow less and less interested in history. Each semester, in my American literature courses, I quiz class members on the relevant dates of not only literary history but also American history proper. The quizzes have grown increasingly simple over time. What were the years of the Revolutionary War? What did the Emancipation Proclamation do? When did women get the right to vote? Recently I asked three upper-level classes to tell me the years of the Civil War, and out of almost one hundred students, not one gave the right answer. It was, however, what followed that really scared me. In explaining her incorrect response, one student remarked, "I'm not worried about the facts of history, just the truth." I expected her remark to foment controversy or, at least, raise a few eyebrows. But in the next few minutes of what passed for discussion, it became clear that several students actually agreed with her, while most others regarded the whole proceeding with various degrees of detached bemusement.

Thinking about the comment later, I could not say that I blamed the student very much. In an age of cultural and intellectual relativism (not a bad thing in itself), she was merely responding as she had been taught. History for her, it seemed, was no longer a playground of events and the ideas that gave them rise but, rather, an ideological war zone. Beyond sheer laziness, it made perfect sense to her that the best response to such competing ideas was simply to pick the version of the past that she liked best, the one that made most sense in the context of her limited personal experience, and call it the truth.

Again, I am not stumping for some monolithic version of history—some brand of the "truth" on which we all (are compelled to) agree. But at the same time, I could not help noting the symmetry between this student's idiosyncratic and highly politicized response to historical study and the attitudes of some professional academics who—albeit with fuller vocabularies—arrive in the same place. This symmetry is clearest in Western literary circles, I think, where (as the quotes from the preface suggest) certain scholars view literary study as a means to a political end. Analysis, in this instance, becomes secondary. Interpretation is an act not so much of exploration as of building a superhighway toward the desired ideological goal. The former technique celebrates the intellectual journey; the latter focuses inexorably on the personal or political destination.

The impulse is understandable, of course. Contemporary Western scholars would likely argue that Turnerian theories of the frontier were political at their base, designed to advance a white male vision of the

world, and they would be largely correct. Beyond this cultural quid pro
quo, though, the problem might be inherent in an ages-old methodology.
If the study of history, literary or otherwise, is to have any real meaning,
then it must offer some guidance for how we can live our lives in the present while avoiding the mistakes of the past. In this scheme, if all history
is relative, if all narratives enjoy the same cultural cachet, then one logical
approach is simply to select whose version of history one likes best and
build one's philosophy around it.

The only problem with this approach, however, is that it values the
conclusions of historical study more than the process by which such conclusions are formed. Even if intellectuals faithfully engage in a fact-finding
mission before forming their opinions, it is less likely, as my student's response suggests, that other people do the same. For more and more
students, studying history is less about investigation than about locating
the facts and analyses that meet a specific ideological standard. In its best
(and often liberal) incarnation, this approach compels students to
consider perspectives that they have not encountered in more traditional
programs of historical study. But in its worst incarnation, this approach
breeds a pedagogical tyranny where only right-thinking students are ad-
judged worthy. And we should make no mistake: this tendency becomes
all too easily encompassing, conflating our research, teaching, and other
public interests. Too often—especially when confronted by an American
culture that seems ambivalent or even narrow-minded—it is tempting to
take a stand for or against this or that literary work as a matter of political principle. The dilemma is that, however slowly or dully, much of the
public takes its cue from its intellectuals; scholarly endorsement of an
"ends-justifies-the-means" methodology only encourages others to adopt
the same.

And lest this debate seem far-flung from the field of Western Studies,
or lest it seem that I am pushing a "too" traditional brand of academic in-
quiry, let me add that one reason I disrelish bipolar readings of frontier
literature is because of the inordinate power that such readings give to the
mythic West. By making the canon of "Western writing" an automatic
alternative to the formula western, scholars tacitly reaffirm the cultural
centrality of those popular stories, both today and historically. The validity of such a claim is questionable, of course, in both literary and larger
cultural senses. Per my readings of nineteenth-century Western narratives
especially, it is clear that there was a great deal of interchange between
popular and nonpopular ideas about the frontier *within* the very novels

that were purported to support one side or the other. Writing about the popular side of this equation—on subjects like *The Last of the Mohicans, The Sea-Wolf, The Virginian,* and *Shane*—Forrest G. Robinson has made a similar point:

> If these books reinforce our sense of the heroic, they also challenge it. If they dramatize the triumph of traditional American values, they also explore the dark side of a dominant self-image. If they dwell on the exploits of white men, they are also attentive to the grave injustices of the social order they portray, especially as those injustices bear on people of color, and on women. But while these texts feature sharp contrasts in shading and emphasis, none appears to do so in a fully controlled or premeditated way. Rather, each of the novels seems on its face to celebrate leading articles of the popular faith, yet each betrays an impulse, a self-subversive reflex, to undermine what it appears so clearly to approve.[3]

Robinson's observation can be extended to American culture at large, where a self-image fashioned out of the frontier experience has regularly competed with and given way to other self-images. Even Jane Tompkins, whose *West of Everything* so firmly ensconces the popular West in opposition to more literary treatments, reminds us that the dominant culture of the nineteenth century was sentimental culture, which focused not on the out-of-doors and territorial expansion but on private domestic affairs and the particularly female work of "saving souls."

We read history through a contemporary lens and take from it selectively those items that bear most centrally on our lives. It is inevitable, and not always unfortunate, that some readers will use tidbits of the past to create or justify a privileged position for themselves in the present. Finally, though, we need to view history through a shifting crucible that constantly challenges earlier conclusions (however subtly), that continually seeks out different vantages from which to analyze old and new data. There is a glib axiom, variously restated, that to invent our future we must first discover our past. It only stands to reason that if we want our future to be a complex one—multicultural, multiracial, as much as possible without division—then we must entertain a view of the past that is equally complex and not merely the product of a binary system predicated on race, gender, or both. Western American literature has thrived for four centuries precisely because of its ability to accommodate extreme and often contradictory positions.[4] But in that regard it also offers one of the most fruitful sites for scholars interested in exploring the complexities of American culture. Breaking down the pendulum of race, class, and gender—searching out moments of overlap, symmetry, and interchange between Western authors of different backgrounds, recognizing the internal dialogues implicit in most narratives—will assist in this process. Without dismissing or downplaying the overt prejudices of certain texts, this approach will create a better sense of balance in Western Studies, accentuating the broad discursive continuum on which critics mutually operate while reducing the sense of competition created by bipolar views of the field.

179

Reading
the Western
and the
Importance
of History

NOTES

Preface

For the purposes of this book, the various meanings of the word "western" will be differentiated by uppercase and lowercase notation, where "Western" refers to the geographical region (the American West) and "western" denotes artistic, popular, or mythic applications of the term, in particular the literary genre. Proper phrases (e.g. "Western Studies") and quoted material remain unchanged.

1. For a good introduction to Canadian Western literature, see Arnold E. Davidson's *Coyote Country* (Durham, N.C.: Duke University Press, 1994); Dick Harrison's *Unnamed Country: The Struggle for a Canadian Prairie Fiction* (Edmonton: University of Alberta Press, 1977); and Laurence Ricou's *Vertical Man, Horizontal World: Man and Landscape in Canadian Prairie Fiction* (Vancouver: University of British Columbia Press, 1973).

2. These two terms can be used almost interchangeably. The phrase "anti-western" was originally coined by Leslie Fiedler to indicate any fiction that self-consciously uses the conventions of the popular western to challenge the point of those conventions (*The Return of the Vanishing American* [New York: Stein & Day, 1969]). More recently, Christine Bold has used the term to delimit a group of novels within the canon of Western writing that both employ and react to popular western conventions—see chapter 5 of *Selling the Wild West: Popular Western Fiction, 1860 to 1960* (Bloomington: Indiana University Press, 1987).

3. Richard W. Etulain, "The Historical Development of the Western," in *The Popular Western: Essays toward a Definition*, ed. Richard W. Etulain and Michael T. Marsden (Bowling Green, Ohio: Bowling Green State University Popular Press, 1974), 75.

4. John G. Cawelti, *The Six-Gun Mystique* (Bowling Green, Ohio: Bowling Green State University Popular Press, 1977), 62.

5. Will Wright, *Sixguns and Society: A Structural Study of the Western* (Berkeley: University of California Press, 1975), 164.

6. James H. Maguire, "Fictions of the West," in *The Columbia History of the American Novel,* ed. Emory Elliot (New York: Columbia University Press, 1991), 439–40.

7. Etulain, "Historical Development," 75.

8. The first argument loosely parallels a portion of W. K. Wimsatt and M. C. Beardsley's essay, "The Intentional Fallacy" (see Marlies K. Danziger, ed., *An Introduction to Literary Criticism* [Boston: D. C. Heath, 1961], 247–61). The second argument loosely parallels the ideas of dialogism and polyphony found in the work of Mikhail Bakhtin, about which I will write more in the closing chapter. For a good introduction to Bakhtin, especially the way that his work can be applied to the West, see Reuben Ellis's "A Thousand Frontiers: An Introduction to Dialogue and the American West," *Western American Literature* 33, no. 2 (1998): 117–24.

9. Don D. Walker, "Notes toward a Literary Criticism of the Western," in Etulain and Marsden, *Popular Western,* 89.

10. Michael Kowalewski, ed., *Reading the West: New Essays on the Literature of the American West* (New York: Cambridge University Press, 1996), 6, 11. Kowalewski is not alone in such assessments. More generally, Timothy B. Powell has made this argument regarding the entire field of Cultural Studies (*Beyond the Binary: Reconstructing Cultural Identity in a Multicultural Context* [New Brunswick, N.J.: Rutgers University Press, 1999]), to wit:

> Cultural studies has reached a theoretical impasse. For the past twenty years, the central project of Cultural Studies has been to deconstruct the epistemological structures of Eurocentrism and to recover historical voices that were overlooked because of an entrenched ethnocentrism that privileged the elite, white, heterosexual, abled, male, European perspective. One of the most effective strategies in this initial phase of cultural *deconstruction* of Eurocentrism was the identification of theoretical binaries such as Self/Other, Center/Margin, Colonizer/Colonized that helped scholars to delineate the inner workings of oppression and to establish a critical paradigm that would allow minority voices not only to be heard but to be esteemed as a critically important point of view. It has become clear in recent years, however, that a binary form of analysis that collapses a myriad of distinct culture voices into the overly simplistic category of "Other" defined in relationship to a European "Self" is theoretically problematic. The time has come, therefore, to initiate a new critical epoch, a period of cultural *reconstruction* in which "identity" is reconfigured in the midst of a multiplicity of cultural influences that more closely resembles what Homi Bhabha has called the "lived perplexity" of people's lives and that more accurately reflects the multicultural complexities that have historically characterized "American" identity. (1)

11. A complete definition of the New Western History (NWH) would be impossible here. It is important to note, however, that the NWH—like other branches of Cultural Studies—involved a multidisciplinary revisiting of the frontier, through history and literature especially. For the most part, the goal of the NWH has been to investigate the largely hegemonic, white, mythic claims about how the West was settled,

by whom, and in what ethical fashion. As Phyllis Fruss and Stanley Corkin write ("Willa Cather's 'Pioneer' Novels and [Not New, Not Old] Historical Reading," *College Literature* 26, no. 2 [1999]: 36–58):

> The key to New Western History's methodology may lie in its overturning of Frederick Jackson Turner's frontier paradigm, under which the frontier is deemed formative of American character, for that led to the West of heroic myth. In this formulation, the frontier becomes the crucible of individualism, self-reliance, democracy, and the cause of national decline because it closed by the end of the nineteenth century. When the continuous process of empire building and colonial treatment is substituted for the finite process of an advancing frontier as the means of determining how the West would be explored, settled, and developed, we get Elliot West's list: "cultural dislocation, environmental calamity, economic exploitation, and individuals who either fail outright or run themselves crazy chasing unattainable goals." (42)

I will address Turner's Thesis, and its shortcomings, at greater length in the next chapter. But the idea that the NWH seeks primarily to overturn the cultural imperatives of Turner—especially as they have endured in film, literature, and myth through the twentieth century—is accurate. For a more extensive discussion of the goals and achievements of the NWH, the following two articles are most helpful: Patricia Nelson Limerick's "Layer upon Layer of Memory in the American West," *The Chronicle of Higher Education* 3 (March 2000): B4–B7; and Carl Gutierrez-Jones's "Haunting Presences and the New Western History: Reading Repetition, Negotiating Trauma," *Arizona Quarterly* 53, no. 2 (1997): 134–51.

12. In 1996, John Cawelti wrote: "It's striking, though perhaps not surprising, that these deeply critical [of the popular western] literary movements have emerged almost simultaneously with a new surge of political conservatism and fundamentalism in America, also centered in the South and the West and seeking to manipulate the same symbolic and ideological traditions for their own very different purpose." ("What Rough Beast—New Westerns?" *ANQ: A Quarterly Journal of Short Articles, Notes, and Reviews* 9, no. 3 [1996]: 13–14.) For further discussion, see Cavelti's *The Six-Gun Mystique Sequel* (Bowling Green, Ohio: Bowling Green University Popular Press, 1999).

13. Barbara Howard Meldrum, ed., *Old West—New West: Centennial Essays* (Moscow: University of Idaho Press, 1993), 4.

14. Susan J. Rosowski, "The Western Hero as Logos, or, Unmaking Meaning," *Western American Literature* 32, no. 3 (1997): 269–92.

15. Ann-Janine Morley-Gaines, "Of Menace and Men: The Sexual Tensions of the American Frontier Metaphor," *Soundings: An Interdisciplinary Journal* 64, no. 2 (1981): 148.

16. Susan Lee Johnson, "Gift Horses: Influence, Insurgence, Interdisciplinarity in Western Studies," *Western American Literature* 34, no. 1 (1999): 78–79.

17. Jan Rousch, "Research in Western American Literature, 1997–1998," *Western American Literature* 34, no. 1 (1999): 5.

18. In many respects, these books build on the fine scholarship regarding gender and the frontier that appeared a decade earlier, the best examples of which include L. L. Lee and Merrill Lewis's edited collection *Women, Women Writers, and the West* (Troy, N.Y.: The Whitson Publishing Company, 1979); Helen Winter Stauffer and Susan Rosowski's edited collection *Women and Western American Literature* (Troy, N.Y.: The Whitson Publishing Company, 1982); and Annette Kolodny's groundbreaking *The Land Before Her: Fantasy and Experience of the American Frontiers, 1630–1860* (Chapel Hill: University of North Carolina Press, 1984). Both Tompkins's and Mitchell's books have been criticized for being politically biased as well as for the way, perhaps more important, that they distinguish very little between western novels and western films. This problem of categorization notwithstanding, both books deftly explore the methods used by many westerns to construct notions of masculinity over and against cultural notions of femininity. (Jane Tompkins, *West of Everything: The Inner Life of Westerns* [New York: Oxford University Press, 1992]); Lee Clark Mitchell, *Westerns: Making the Man in Fiction and Film* [Chicago: University of Chicago Press, 1996].)

19. While a complete list is impossible, a quick glance at the entries in the definitive reference volume edited by Max Westbrook et al., *A Literary History of the American West* (Fort Worth: Texas Christian University Press, 1987), as well as its sequel *Updating the Literary West* (Fort Worth: Texas Christian University Press, 1997), should be enough to confirm the broad and inclusive range of topics being addressed by contemporary Western scholars.

20. See note 8.

21. Just how simplistic the cultural work of western film is relative to western fiction is up for debate. Recent western films, especially, have claimed to regard their subject matter with a bit more care and suspicion than earlier incarnations. However, in his article "Shootout at the Genre Corral: Problems in the 'Evolution' of the Western," Tag Gallagher is quick to point out two things: first, that almost all self-proclaimed "revisionist" western films change the standard plots of the genre only slightly, often producing the same outcome as more traditional western films; and, second, that there are a miniscule number of western films, even today, that strive to be revisionist (despite the unfounded insistence of film critics that a significant change has taken place within the genre). For the full article, see Barry Keith Grant, ed., *Film Genre Reader II* (Austin: University of Texas Press, 1995), 246–60.

Introduction

1. Numerous critics agree on the pivotal importance of this period, including among others Henry Nash Smith (*Virgin Land: The American West as Symbol and Myth* [Cambridge: Harvard University Press, 1950]); Richard Slotkin (*Gunfighter Nation: The Myth of the Frontier in Twentieth-Century America* [New York: Harper Perennial, 1993]); Max Westbrook et al. (*A Literary History of the American West* [Fort Worth: Texas Christian University Press, 1987]); and Richard W. Etulain and Michael T. Marsden, eds.

(*The Popular Western: Essays toward a Definition* [Bowling Green, Ohio: Bowling Green State University Popular Press, 1974]). As the opening paragraph of this chapter suggests, I am not arguing that the cultural icons and values long associated with the frontier were *created* in this period, but that they came to enjoy a widespread and uniform acceptance at this time that they had not enjoyed previously.

2. "Up to our own day American history has been in a large degree the history of the colonization of the Great West. The existence of an area of free land, its continuous recession, and the advance of American settlement westward, explain American development" (Frederick Jackson Turner, *The Significance of the Frontier in American History* [New York: Holt, Rinehart, and Winston, 1920], 1). Subsequent references to this volume will be made parenthetically in text.

3. Fundamental to Turner's Thesis was the idea that the frontier advanced westward in stages (from the Ohio Valley to the Great Plains to the Western Interior, and so forth), and that each stage represented a further move from European attitudes toward a purer expression of American democracy, to wit: "As successive terminal moraines result from successive glaciation, so each frontier leaves its traces behind it, and when it becomes a settled area the region still partakes of the frontier characteristics. Thus the advance of the frontier has meant a steady movement away from the influence of Europe, a steady growth of independence on American lines" (4).

4. Turner's descriptions were not completely sanitized. In describing the ideal frontier settler, for instance, he writes: "The wilderness masters the colonist. . . . It strips off the garments of civilization and arrays him in the hunting short and the moccasin. It puts him in the log cabin of the Cherokee and the Iroquois and runs an Indian palisade around him. Before long he has gone to planting Indian corn and plowing with a sharp stick; he shouts the war cry and takes the scalp in orthodox Indian fashion" (4). For Turner, like James Fenimore Cooper before him and Frederic Remington after, the relationship between colonist and Indian is bipolar. On the one hand, the colonist accepts the manner of the Indian in dress, agriculture, and hunting in order to survive, but on the other hand, he learns to "war" against and "scalp" the Indian, his sworn cultural enemy. Granted, Turner's work is a history; the events he describes had already happened. But at the same time, there is a rhetorical schism between his glorification of the frontier's democratic ideal and his complete disregard for "the Indian problem." Worse still, unlike the apologetic racial determinism in Cooper or the enthusiastic race hatred in Remington—both novelists—Turner's clinical "history" gives white racism a validation in fact. The ends justify the means, as Turner sees it, using America's republican glory to excuse the violence against Indians that it entailed.

5. Turner argued that settlers' desire for free land in the West had more radically influenced their position on slavery and its territorial expansion than moral precept. Had slavery been allowed to move westward, he argues, half of the land that eventually fell to individual white settlers would have been largely claimed by plantation-style farms instead. The economic thrust of this argument is intriguing and helps to explain why, after slavery's abolition, institutionalized racism remained such a large problem

throughout the nation. Turner still fails to note, though, the rupture between his assumption of universal human equality (if only at the frontier) and this ongoing systematic discrimination.

6. Quoted in Turner, *Significance*, 1.

7. As Henry Nash Smith confirms, Turner "turned to the rather unconvincing idea that the Midwestern state universities might be able to save democracy by producing trained leaders, and later he placed science beside education as another force to which men might turn for aid in their modern perplexity" (*Virgin Land*, 258).

8. Bernard DeVoto notes that "[d]own to about 1880 the West in general and the cattle business in particular were realistically reported by the press. Fashions in journalism changed, however, and the roving correspondent began to find in cows and cowpokes a glamor which up to then had escaped his attention" ("Birth of an Art," in *Western Writing*, ed. Gerald W. Haslam [Albuquerque: University of New Mexico Press, 1974], 9).

9. Smith, for example, records the way that American leaders had always linked the frontier to specific myths of national evolution, including the "garden" myth so lauded by Turner. And Eric Heyne's *Desert, Garden, Margin, Range* points out the paradoxes inherent in American vocabularies used to define the frontier from its earliest explorations, where the "four terms represent the four poles of two figurative axes: *desert* and *garden* on the axis of utility, and *margin* and *range* on the axis of spatial representation" (*Desert, Garden, Margin, Range: Literature of the American Frontier* [New York: Twayne, 1992], 1).

10. Remington had taken brief and isolated trips through the West before 1885, but this period marked his first extended stay there.

11. Sherman's full statement follows:

I now regard the Indians as substantially eliminated from the problem of the Army. There may be spasmodic and temporary alarms, but such Indian wars as have hitherto disturbed the public peace and tranquillity are not probable. The Army has been a large factor in producing this result, but it is not the only one. Immigration and the occupation by industrious farmers and miners of land vacated by the aborigines have been largely instrumental to that end, but the *railroad* which used to follow in the rear now goes forward with the picket-line in the great battle of civilization with barbarism, and has become the *greater* cause. I have in former reports, for the past fifteen years, treated of this matter, and now, on the eve of withdrawing from active participation in public affairs, I beg to emphasize much which I have spoken and written heretofore. The recent completion of the last of the four great transcontinental lines of railway has settled forever the Indian question, the Army question, and many others which have hitherto troubled the country. (Francis Paul Prucha, ed., *Documents of United States Indian Policy* [Lincoln: University of Nebraska Press, 1990], 159)

Sherman's sentiments are confirmed by historian Robert M. Utley, who writes:

Every important Indian war since 1870 had been essentially a war not of concentration but of rebellion—of Indians rebelling against reservations they had already accepted in theory if not in fact. Geronimo and his tiny band of followers were the last holdouts. . . . Thus the wars of the Peace Policy, and indeed the Indian Wars of the United States, came to a close in Skeleton Canyon, Arizona, on September 4, 1886 [the day Geronimo surrendered to General Nelson Miles]. (*The Indian Frontier of the American West, 1846–1890* [Albuquerque: University of New Mexico Press, 1983], 201)

12. It should come as no surprise, however, that Remington did his best to immortalize Wounded Knee as part of American military history. In "The Sioux Outbreak in South Dakota" (*Harper's Weekly*, January 24, 1891), he describes how the Natives worked themselves into a "devotional" religious frenzy before opening fire, then records personal testimony from a number of cavalry soldiers who "got square with [the] Injuns" (Peggy and Harold Samuels, eds., *The Collected Writings of Frederic Remington* [Garden City, N.Y.: Doubleday & Company, 1979], 69). Of course, as was often the case with his writing, Remington received these reports secondhand. He was often disturbed by actual fighting, and his art seemed to depend ironically upon a certain mythologizing of events before he could begin to represent them.

13. David McCullough, *Brave Companions: Portraits in History* (New York: Prentice Hall, 1992), 75.

14. Frederic Remington, *Frederic Remington: Paintings and Sculpture* (New York: Wings Books, 1993), 6.

15. G. Edward White deals with this sociocultural context at length in *The Eastern Establishment and the Western Experience: The West of Frederic Remington, Theodore Roosevelt, and Owen Wister* (New Haven: Yale University Press, 1968):

> The Roosevelt generation's sense of instability led to a general search for stabilizing forces in a fluctuating age. Businessmen sought to explain the presence of panics and depressions by a pendulum theory of economics. . . . Sociologists such as William Graham Sumner discussed the ever-varying American social scene in terms of rigid patterns of behavior which emphasized the interrelation of classes and the balance of nature. Members of the eastern upper class attempted to preserve their status and prestige by forming self-perpetuating, stabilizing, elitist institutions. But economic depression (the panic of 1893), violence (the Pullman strike), 'mongrelization' (the heavy influx of immigration in the late eighties and nineties), and a whole host of other problems associated with an urban and industrial civilization constantly threatened stability. (185)

16. Richard Slotkin, *Gunfighter Nation*, 163. Slotkin's assertion is substantiated by Remington's own writing on the subject. In "Indians as Irregular Cavalry" (*Harper's Weekly*, December 27, 1890), he writes, "After we regard Indians as children in their relation to us, we must understand another thing, and that is that they are only second to the Norsemen of old as savage warriors. They possess all the virtues and some of the weaknesses of that condition" (Samuels and Samuels, *Collected Writings*, 59). Claiming that Indians will never be more than "warriors," Remington goes on to argue that if they are ever to serve a useful function in American society, it will be only as part of the military, specifically as cavalry scouts.

17. Samuels and Samuels, *Collected Writings*, 154.

18. Ben Merchant Vorpahl, ed., *My Dear Wister: The Frederic Remington–Owen Wister Letters* (Palo Alto, Calif.: The American West Publishing Company, 1972), 30.

19. Alexander Nemerov, *Frederic Remington and Turn-of-the-Century America* (New Haven: Yale University Press, 1995), 121. Subsequent references to this volume will be made parenthetically in text.

20. It should be noted that, like Turner, Remington associated frontier physicality with an automatic set of virtues; violent Westerners were also, paradoxically, more moral. Consider this description of the cow-puncher, which concludes his article "Life in the Cattle Country" (*Collier's,* August 26, 1899):

> And indeed I must say at the last that the 'cow-punchers' as a class . . . possess a quality of sturdy, sterling manhood which would be to the credit of men in any walk of life. The honor of the average 'puncher' abides with him continually. He will not lie; he will not steal. He keeps faith with his friends; toward his enemies he bears himself like a man. He has his vices—as who has not?—but I like to speak softly of them when set against his unassailable virtues. I wish that the manhood of the cow-boy might come more into fashion further East. (Samuels and Samuels, *Collected Writings,* 388)

21. Christine Bold, *Selling The Wild West: Popular Western Fiction, 1860 to 1960* (Bloomington: Indiana University Press, 1987), 57.

22. Two good examples are Thomas Moran and Charles Russell. Moran, like his Romantic predecessor Albert Bierstadt, created landscapes reminiscent of the Hudson River School, where humans occupy only a minor part of the canvas (if at all) in relation to the majestic and often luxurious spread of nature around them. Russell, somewhat ironically, was a popularizer of the West like Remington. His paintings, however, evidence a greater compassion for other ethnic groups in America, especially the Natives with whom he sporadically lived and who are depicted in his works in all aspects of life, not just combat.

23. Jane Tompkins, *West of Everything* (New York: Oxford University Press, 1992), 145.

24. Richard W. Etulain, "Riding Point: The Western and Its Interpreters," in Etulain and Marsden, *Popular Western,* 5.

25. John Seelye, introduction to *The Virginian,* by Owen Wister (New York: Penguin, 1988), x.

26. Owen Wister, *Roosevelt* (New York: Macmillan, 1930), 29.

27. Owen Wister, "The Evolution of the Cow-Puncher," in *Owen Wister's West, Selected Articles,* ed. Robert Murray Davis (Albuquerque: University of New Mexico Press, 1987), 37.

28. Despite my argument here—which is a reiteration of popular views of Wister —I will argue in chapter 4 that Wister's novel was more complex than this reading gives it credit for, whether Wister intended that complexity or not.

29. Slotkin, *Gunfighter Nation,* 175.

30. And in this regard, Wister may have more carefully followed the full ideal of

Turner's Thesis. Even Turner, one should remember, expressed concern about how Western individualism—if unchecked—breeds greed, dispassion, and savagery.

31. Seelye notes in some detail the way that "Wister's western experience was filtered through the biases of the eastern establishment" and how "he was relieved to discover that the new Promised Land was inhabited by a Chosen People of proper origins [i.e. New Englanders]" (introduction, xv).

32. See note 25.

33. Actually, Roosevelt had visited the West briefly once before, for a buffalo hunt the previous year (McCullough, *Brave Companions,* 60).

34. Ben Merchant Vorpahl, "Roosevelt, Turner, Wister, and Remington," in Westbrook, *Literary History,* 279.

35. Take, for example, this excerpt from his *Autobiography* (New York: Charles Scribner's Sons, 1929), in which he describes the importance of his Western experience:

> In that land we led a free and hardy life, with horse and with rifle. We worked under the scorching midsummer sun, when the wide plains shimmered and wavered in the heat; and we knew the freezing misery of riding night guard round the cattle in the late fall roundup. . . . There were monotonous days, as we guided the trail cattle or the beef herds, hour after hour, at the slowest of walks; and minutes or hours teeming with excitement as we stopped stampedes or swam the herds across rivers treacherous with quicksands or brimmed with running ice. We knew toil and hardship and hunger and thirst; and we saw men die violent deaths as they worked among the horse and cattle, or fought in evil feuds with one another; but we felt the beat of hardy life in our veins, and ours was the glory of work and the joy of living.
>
> It was right and necessary that this life should pass, for the safety of our country lies in its being made the country of the small home-maker. . . . [T]he homesteaders, the permanent settlers, the men who took up each his own farm on which he lived and wrought up his family, these represented from the National standpoint the most desirable of all possible users of, and dwellers on, the soil. Their advent meant the breaking up of the big ranches; and the change was a National gain, although to some of us an individual loss. (94)

All of the elements of his Western doctrine are present: an elegy for the passing of the "strenuous" cattleman's life, a celebration of the glory of hard and often violent physical work, and a final paean to individualism and self-reliance in the person of the virtuous homesteaders who, though displacing the big cattlemen, represented the assumption of a strenuous lifestyle by the general public. One cannot help but feel how uncluttered life is in this excerpt—men, cows, work, hunger, thirst, life, death—an elemental existence. As in Remington, the landscape does not confuse the viewer with contrasting images. It is simple, straightforward, and rugged, qualities that Roosevelt came to expect of all good Americans.

36. Theodore Roosevelt, *The Roosevelt Book: Selections from the Writings of Theodore Roosevelt* (New York: Charles Scribner's Sons, 1909), 21–23.

37. This idea is made explicit in other writings, such as "Women and the Home," where Roosevelt claims that "the most honorable and desirable task which can beset any woman is to be a good and wise mother in a home marked by self-respect and mutual forbearance, by willingness to perform duty, and by refusal to sink into self-indulgence or avoid that which entails effort and self-sacrifice" (Mario R. DiNunzio, ed., *Theodore Roosevelt: An American Mind: A Selection from His Writings* [New York: St. Martin's Press, 1994], 315). Among other pronouncements later in the essay, Roosevelt says of women who refuse to bear children that the "existence of women of this type forms one of the most unpleasant and unwholesome features of modern life" (317).

38. By contrast, however, many of Roosevelt's later writings betray his concern regarding what he considered to be the imminent militaristic dangers facing America on various fronts. In "The War of America the Unready" he writes, "I suppose the United States will always be unready for war, and in consequence will always be exposed to great expense, and to the possibility of the greatest calamity, when the Nation goes to war. This is no new thing. Americans learn only from catastrophes and not from experience" (*Autobiography*, 204). While not necessarily contradicting his doctrine of "the strenuous life," this quote does suggest how that doctrine was born out of Roosevelt's reaction to a perceived external threat as much as unilateral conviction.

39. As a general overview of how Roosevelt's "straight-shooting" Western ideals influenced his later policies, consider this brief statement by William B. Gatewood Jr.:

> Whatever the differences regarding Roosevelt's impulsiveness, both friend and foe agreed on another facet of his personality—his affinity for controversy. Combative by instinct and early training, Roosevelt throughout his career was a storm center of controversy. His term as President opened with a disturbance caused by his dinner with Booker T. Washington and ended amid a bitter quarrel with Congress over the Secret Service. Jules Jusserand, the French ambassador, declared, "Until the end of his presidency Mr. Roosevelt remained *qualis ab incepte:* same ideal, same means, for better for worse, for reaching such an ideal. That means was to give battle." Commenting on his penchant for controversy, one Roosevelt scholar has written, "He created it, he fell into it, and he searched it out. When he was not rebuking his once trusted friends, he was taunting his long-sworn enemies, and if he was fleetingly at peace with both, as occasionally he was, it was rarely the peace that passeth understanding." (*Theodore Roosevelt and the Art of Controversy: Episodes of the White House Years* [Baton Rouge: Louisiana State University Press, 1970], 26–27)

40. In sum, Etulain writes that Roosevelt "vociferously advocated a federal government strong enough to deal with the powerful forces that the cities and industrial capitalists had unleashed" ("Origins of the Western," in *Critical Essays on the Western American Novel*, ed. William T. Pilkington [Boston: G. K. Hall & Co., 1980], 58).

41. From "A Note on Helen Hunt Jackson and Other Writers on Relations with the Indians" (DiNunzio, *Theodore Roosevelt*, 52).

42. DiNunzio, *Theodore Roosevelt*, 329.

43. Thomas G. Dyer sees Roosevelt as a man who, unable to negotiate such complex issues, ultimately fell back on a naïve faith in the indomitable, and Anglo, "American race" (*Theodore Roosevelt and the Idea of Race* [Baton Rouge: Louisiana State University Press, 1980], 168). According to Dyer, though his democratic rhetoric sometimes suggested a platform of racial equality, Roosevelt never acted out this philosophy in practical terms and, by the end of his life, had mostly lost faith in the ability of the races to coexist harmoniously.

44. DiNunzio, *Theodore Roosevelt*, 340.

45. For more on Roosevelt's handling of foreign policy matters, see Howard K. Beale's *Theodore Roosevelt and the Rise of America to World Power* (Baltimore: The Johns Hopkins Press, 1956); C. Wallace Chessman's *Theodore Roosevelt and the Politics of Power* (Boston: Little, Brown & Company, 1969); Lewis L. Gould's *The Presidency of Theodore Roosevelt* (Lawrence: University Press of Kansas, 1941); and Frederick W. Marks III's *Velvet on Iron: The Diplomacy of Theodore Roosevelt* (Lincoln: University of Nebraska Press, 1979). While there is some disagreement among these scholars over the effects of Roosevelt's diplomatic style, there is no disagreement as to what shape that style took. Roosevelt favored an invasive brand of foreign policy that, as he put it, maintained the "balance of power" in various spheres of the globe. Despite his respect for the Japanese, he feared Japanese aggressions against China and Hawaii—and likewise German aggressions against neighboring European states. His policy thus became one of containment, balancing regional rivals against one another and suggesting the American martial response that would result should any nation break the peace. Not without its diplomatic nuance, Roosevelt's policy nonetheless failed because of America's inability to maintain such fragile relationships through rhetoric alone. His oxymoronic policy toward the Japanese—his fear of both Japanese expansion in the Pacific and Japanese immigration to the United States combated against his distaste for the Russians and deployment of American forces so as to give the Japanese a clear tactical advantage in the Pacific—caused an underlying tension between the two nations even as it created a surface sense of amicability and allowed for a Japanese military buildup. Contrary to portraits that paint him as an invariable hawk, Roosevelt's foreign policy attempted to avoid conflict where possible, but the saber-rattling aspect of his rhetoric poised America on the brink of combat with little room for escape. His belief that world affairs could be conducted by nations negotiating from positions of strength all too often created a kind of tension that, whatever its benefits in the short term, perpetuated an international climate where distrust and thinly veiled aggressions threatened incessantly to break out into full-blown war.

46. Critics have pointed to many reasons why the American populace was so enamored with the western. Richard Etulain, for instance, argues that the Old West offered a palatable set of political icons to early-century Progressives, who longed for a simple, almost primitive society to counteract the complexities of urban industrialism. Similarly, John Cawelti claims that the western appealed to the lower classes by providing them with a fantasy world in which they had more freedom and economic opportunity than industrial capitalism allowed. (Interestingly, Cawelti goes on to argue that

the violence of westerns allowed the lower classes to sublimate their anger at their situation, imagining themselves in the role of the righteous avenger for a change.) Jane Tompkins points to how the western's emphasis on masculinity acted as a counterpoint to the cult of domesticity and its feminine ideals popular through the nineteenth century. And W. H. Hutchinson has suggested that the cowboy was a useful symbol for an American military that had significant imperial designs—a warrior hero whose triumphs encouraged martial efforts among real men. Added to these factors was fortuitous timing: the frontier came to its literal close just as the telephone and, slightly later, film were gaining widespread use. These new methods of information exchange and dissemination made it that much easier to spread the word about the West to a public starved for simple explanations of their place in the nation and that nation's place in the world.

47. John G. Cawelti, *The Six-Gun Mystique* (Bowling Green, Ohio: Bowling Green State University Popular Press, 1977), 58. Subsequent references to this volume will be made parenthetically in the text.

48. In her essay "How the Western Ends: Fenimore Cooper to Frederic Remington" (*Western American Literature* 17, no. 2 [1982]: 117–35), Christine Bold writes:

> While Cooper established the dualistic pattern at every level of his text, he never explored either of the consequences suggested by the condition he constructed: that is, he neither involved his wilderness hero in a sentimental reconciliation with either of the two environments, nor did he develop the potential for tragedy or self-destruction. He froze one hero into unresolvable stasis in plot, theme, imagery, and structure; he also ended each novel with the conventional wedding of the romantic hero and heroine. Thus his conclusion embraced both the irreconcilable polarities which trap the frontiersman and the harmonious resolution of the romantic couple. All subsequent writers inherited the predicament of problematic duality, but none, until Remington, took further the implications of polarization. (122–23)

49. The idea, of course, was to domesticate the wilderness. While the "pastoral idea has not yet lost its hold on the native imagination," as Leo Marx puts it, one must recall that the pastoral idea requires a tame natural space, closely united with hearth and home, where people can escape an urban industrial world and have recourse to their own uninterrupted thoughts (*The Machine in the Garden: Technology and the Pastoral Idea in America* [New York: Oxford, 1964], 3). The wilderness, by contrast, is untamed nature that must be conquered before it can become a garden—if not, in the Puritan view, *the* Garden, a new Eden.

The phrase "regeneration through violence" first appears in William Carlos Williams's description of Daniel Boone (*In The American Grain* [New York: New Directions, 1956], 130) and is taken up by Richard Slotkin in his book of the same title to indicate the conscious acts of violence which have long been synonymous with the concept of the New World as a potential "garden" in American culture.

50. For more on the idea of the garden/wilderness in early American life, the following books are most useful: Perry Miller's *Errand into the Wilderness* (Cambridge: The Belknap Press of Harvard University Press, 1956) details several ways in which the Puritans saw themselves as a chosen people destined to create a garden from the surrounding Indian wilderness; Richard Slotkin's *Regeneration Through Violence: The Mythology of the American Frontier, 1600–1860* (Middletown, Conn.: Wesleyan University Press, 1973) traces the development of these nature/frontier themes from the Puritan era through the American Civil War; and Smith's *Virgin Land* demonstrates how such themes were deployed in literature and the culture overall through Turner's announcement of his frontier thesis. In addition, R. W. B. Lewis's *The American Adam: Innocence, Tragedy, and Tradition in the Nineteenth Century* (Chicago: University of Chicago Press, 1955), while not directly addressing the garden myth as figured in Puritanical doctrine, discusses some ways that the myth played out in early nineteenth-century American literature, especially when read through the lens of an American victory in the Revolutionary War, which signaled the new nation's "break" from European history and its assumption of an "Adamic" identity.

51. Jefferson, for example, wrote to John Jay in 1785 that "Cultivators of the Earth . . . are the most valuable citizens. They are the most vigorous, the most independent, the most virtuous, & they are tied to their country & wedded to it's [*sic*] liberties & interests by the most lasting bonds" (Thomas Jefferson, *Writings* [New York: The Library of America, 1984], 818). Later Jefferson would go on to state that "I think our governments will remain virtuous for many centuries; as long as they are chiefly agricultural; and this will be as long as there shall be vacant lands in any part of America. When they get piled upon one another in large cities, as in Europe, they will become corrupt as in Europe" (*Writings,* 918).

52. Justice in the popular western is, after all, more than mere justice. Were the hero to apprehend the villain, bring him in for a lengthy and costly trial, endure an interminable appeal process, then watch him hang, the effect on the western audience would probably not be as invigorating or galvanizing as the kind occasioned by the inexorable "final gunfight." Form more than content is essential to the western's power. It is not so much the hero's moral code as the violent ritual in which he assumes the lead that gives his narrative and its resolution their ultimate meaning.

53. Tompkins, *West of Everything,* 47–67.

54. This particular reading is heavily influenced by Roland Barthes's linguistic construction of myth. According to Barthes, myth evolves when the "sign" in any given signifying chain is emptied of its literal meaning and replaced with one or more figurative meanings, thus becoming a myth-sign. As a myth-sign, the cowboy hero is able to communicate a variety of meanings—some of them contradictory—to a variety of readers. Language, however, complicates this system by reimposing a very literal linguistic sign system over the mythic one. In short, the influx of words prevents the myth-sign from being able to speak for itself. For more on this subject, see "Myth Today" in *A Barthes Reader* (New York: Hill and Wang, 1987), 93–149.

55. Owen Wister, *The Virginian* (New York: Viking Penguin, 1988), 287.

56. David B. Davis, "Ten-Gallon Hero," in *The Western,* ed. James K. Folsom (Englewood Cliffs, N.J.: Prentice Hall, 1979), 29.

Chapter 1

1. Judith Fetterly, "'My Sister! My Sister!': The Rhetoric of Catharine Sedgwick's *Hope Leslie*," *American Literature* 70, no. 3 (1998): 492. Subsequent references to this article will be made parenthetically in the text.

2. Lydia Maria Child, *Hobomok and Other Writings on Indians by Lydia Maria Child,* ed. Carolyn Karcher (New Brunswick, N.J.: Rutgers University Press, 1986), xx and xxiii. Subsequent references to this volume will be made parenthetically in the text.

3. Carolyn Karcher, *The First Woman in the Republic: A Cultural Biography of Lydia Maria Child* (Durham, N.C.: Duke University Press, 1994), 32.

4. It bears noting that the novel also works early on to undercut the potential image of the Englishmen as hearty frontier heroes. Upon first sight of Naumkeak (later Salem), the narrator registers his horror with the settlers he encounters: "The scene altogether was far worse than my imagination had ever conceived. Among those who came down to the shore to meet us, there were but one or two who seemed like Englishmen. The remainder, sickly and half starved, presented a pitiful contrast to the vigorous and wondering savages who stood among them" (8).

5. This dynamic is confirmed when little Hobomok, having graduated from Harvard, ceases speaking of his father and drops all hint of an "Indian appellation" (150).

6. This quality also brings Child's novel more in line with Cooper's works, where Indians are often divided into the "good" and the "bad"—a paradigm where good Indians adhere to Judeo-Christian moral structures, helping to advance Euro-American civilization, while bad Indians (drawn as violent, temperamental, and self-serving) oppose that advance.

7. Lora Romero, "Vanishing Americans: Gender, Empire, and New Historicism," *American Literature* 63, no. 3 (1991): 385.

8. Deborah Gussman, "Inalienable Rights: Fictions of Political Identity in *Hobomok* and *The Scarlet Letter*," *College Literature* 22, no. 2 (1995): 68.

9. Milton Meltzer and Patricia G. Holland, eds., *Lydia Maria Child: Selected Letters, 1817–1880* (Amherst: University of Massachusetts Press, 1982), 496. Further references will be made parenthetically in the text.

10. Domhnall Mitchell, "Acts of Intercourse: 'Miscegenation' in Three 19th Century American Novels," *American Studies in Scandinavia* 27 (1995): 136. Further references will be made parenthetically in the text.

11. A review of the Modern Language Association Bibliography for the last thirty-eight years lists sixty-six articles published on *The Last of the Mohicans* compared to forty-two articles on *The Pioneers.* Each of the other Leatherstocking novels has inspired fewer than ten articles; *The Spy* earns sixteen entries, and *The Pilot* and *Wyandotte*

garner two apiece. Criticism on Cooper's social novels, histories, and travel narratives is practically nonexistent.

Chapter 2

This chapter first appeared in slightly different form as J. David Stevens, "'She war a woman': Family Roles, Gender, and Sexuality in Bret Harte's Western Fiction," *American Literature* 69, no. 3 (1997): 571–93. Copyright 1997, Duke University Press. All Rights Reserved.

1. The simple and readily apparent dichotomy that the western constructs between good and evil has become something of a critical commonplace. As Richard Etulain, echoing John Cawelti, writes, "the narrative structure of most westerns is like a game: the good man pitted against the bad man on a field of competition that is definable and predictable. The game operates under a set of rules that are [*sic*] clear to all those involved in the game—and to the reader" ("The Historical Development of the Western," in *The Popular Western: Essays toward a Definition*, ed. Richard W. Etulain and Michael T. Marsden [Bowling Green, Ohio: Bowling Green State University Popular Press, 1974], 76).

2. Wallace Stegner, introduction to *The Outcasts of Poker Flat and Other Tales*, by Bret Harte (New York: New American Library, 1961), ix. Stegner's assessment is echoed by a number of critics, most notably John Seelye, who writes that Harte's stories "are justly famous, and they established the formulas and conventions for much Western fiction written thereafter—including Harte's own" (*Stories of the Old West: Tales of the Mining Camp, Cavalry Troop, & Cattle Ranch* [New York: Penguin, 1994], 3).

3. Geoffrey Bret Harte, ed., *The Letters of Bret Harte* (Boston: Houghton Mifflin, 1926), xiv. Family ties no doubt have something to do with this perhaps inflated view of Harte's importance, but Geoffrey Harte's position is substantiated by other critics who see Bret Harte as playing a major role in founding the popular western tradition. For further discussion, see John R. Milton's *The Novel of the American West* (Lincoln: University of Nebraska Press, 1980); James C. Work's *Prose and Poetry of the American West* (Lincoln: University of Nebraska Press, 1990); and W. H. Hutchinson's "Virgins, Villains, and Varmints," in *The Western: A Collection of Critical Essays*, ed. James K. Folsom (Englewood Cliffs, N.J.: Prentice Hall, 1979).

4. George R. Stewart Jr., *Bret Harte: Argonaut and Exile* (Boston: Houghton Mifflin, 1931), 85–89. For further discussion of Harte's liberal stances on race, see Margaret Duckett's "Bret Harte and the Indians of Northern California" (*Huntington Library Quarterly* 18 [November 1954]: 59–83); "Bret Harte's Portrayal of Half-Breeds" (*American Literature* 25 [May 1953]: 193–212); and "Plain Language from Bret Harte" (*Nineteenth Century Fiction* 11 [March 1957]: 241–60); as well as Oliver S. Egbert's "The Pig-Tailed China Boys Out West" (*Western Humanities Review* 12 [spring 1958]: 175–77) and Richard O'Connor's *Bret Harte: A Biography* (Boston: Little, Brown, 1966).

5. "Muck-a-Muck" can be found in Harte's *Condensed Novels. New Burlesques* (New

York: Collier, 1902) or reprinted in John Seelye, ed., *Stories of the Old West: Tales of the Mining Camps, Cavalry Troop, & Cattle Ranch* (New York: Penguin, 1994), 4–9.

6. Even Harte admirers agree on this point. Gary Scharnhorst writes that "Harte depicted the West through a filtered lens and in soft light and his characters—whether dandy gamblers, rough miners, genteel schoolmarms, inscrutable Orientals, or gruff stagedrivers—rarely transcend the stereotypical" (*Bret Harte* [New York: Twayne, 1992], 25). Likewise, Patrick D. Morrow says that Harte's stories "can probably be read most accurately as topical parables that reinforced the value of the *Overland's* [Harte's newspaper's] market, the idealistic eastern audience. . . . Parables are designed to illustrate truths, i.e., support an audience's values and expectations; they are typically not well-wrought individualistic statements from a gifted, articulate consciousness" ("Bret Harte, Mark Twain, and the San Francisco Circle," in *A Literary History of the American West*, ed. Max Westbrook et al. [Fort Worth: Texas Christian University Press, 1987], 348).

7. Here I should clarify my terminology somewhat. For the purposes of this chapter, the terms "sexed inscription" and "biological inscription" are taken to be absolutes, indicative of one of two kinds of genitalia available to a person: penis to a man, vagina to a woman. Terms like gender or cultural inscription, on the other hand, incorporate those ideas of sex but also link them to specific kinds of cultural performance. Thus the words "male" and "female" refer to anatomical difference (sex) only, while the words "masculine" and "feminine" refer to cultural categories of difference (gender) *ascribed* on the basis of sex.

8. In *West of Everything* (New York: Oxford University Press, 1992), Jane Tompkins argues that the western evolved out of a masculine reaction to women's culture of the nineteenth century. Whether or not the western is as expressly reactionary as Tompkins claims, the salient point for this chapter is the way in which she sees the "elements of the typical Western plot [arranging] themselves in stark opposition to this pattern [of sentimental novels and women's culture overall], not just vaguely and generally but point for point" (38). Where the action of sentimental novels "takes place in private spaces, at home, indoors, in kitchens, parlors, and upstairs chambers" and largely "concerns the interior struggles of the heroine to live up to an ideal of Christian virtue," the western takes place in almost exclusively public arenas, focuses on a male hero, valorizes interpersonal confrontation and conquest, and derides many Christian ideals, chief among them the advocacy of peace and the preservation of chastity. In fact, as Tompkins notes, women appear relatively infrequently in the western, and then almost always as a fixture in the home, removed from the public sphere of male power (though not the private sphere of male desire).

9. By contrast, Leslie Fiedler's *Love and Death in the American Novel* (New York: Criterion, 1960) and D. H. Lawrence's *Studies in Classic American Literature* (New York: Penguin, 1961) both point to the kinds of homoerotic desire which white protagonists, especially in frontier fiction, seem to feel for a racial or cultural Other. Two points, however, must be made about such arguments, especially as they relate to larger assumptions about the popular western. First, as John Cawelti claims in *The Six-Gun Mystique*

(Bowling Green, Ohio: Bowling Green State University Popular Press, 1977), the western guards very carefully against the enactment of homosexual desire. While homosociality may pervade western texts, a very definite line, at least in the minds of most critics, must be drawn between this impulse and implications of homosexuality. The hero never capitulates to nonheterosexual desire, but always accepts "the monogamous sexual pattern of modern middle-class life" (75).

Second, Fiedler's and Lawrence's analyses are both based largely on readings of Cooper, where there is a very clear racial Other for the hero to befriend and even "eroticize." Many later westerns, however, dispense with this character. Take, for example, Owen Wister's *The Virginian,* another classic western published at the turn of this century. The sexual tension is always between Molly Wood and the Virginian, as inevitable as it is heterosexual. While the hero's novel-long struggle with the villain, Trampas, might be read as a kind of homosocial engagement, the Virginian's desire is always unequivocally to kill Trampas and to love Molly. The two impulses are separate and ultimately distinct.

10. Bret Harte, *The Luck of Roaring Camp and Other Stories* (New York: Lancer Books, Inc., 1968), 22. Subsequent citations will be made parenthetically in the text.

11. Allen S. Brown, "The Christ Motif in 'The Luck of Roaring Camp,'" *Papers of the Michigan Academy of Science, Arts, and Letters* 46 (1961): 629.

12. J. R. Boggan, "The Regeneration of 'Roaring Camp,'" *Nineteenth-Century Fiction* 22, no. 3 (1967): 271.

13. Fred E. H. Schroeder, "The Development of the Super-ego on the American Frontier," *Soundings* 57 (Summer 1974): 198.

14. Cawelti, *Six-Gun,* 85.

15. I am not making Harte out to be a "sentimental" writer in the mold of, say, Catharine Sedgwick or Louisa May Alcott; these latter writers as a rule were consciously concerned with women and women's issues, while there is no substantial evidence to suggest that Harte saw himself reshaping conventional notions of domesticity or femininity, even if some of his stories manage to accomplish just that. Such comparisons, however, are not completely fruitless. After all, Tompkins contends that one of the great differences between Western and Domestic fictions is setting: Westerns take place out-of-doors and beyond the constraints of "feminine virtue," while Domestic, or sentimental, novels occur largely in the home, with ideas of family acting as a locus for the novel's action (Alcott's *Little Women* being one famous example). By writing a story about what constitutes a family and about the Christian values attendant upon discovering one's place in the family structure, only setting that story in the dingiest mining camp in the Sierras and populating the camp with nothing but notorious male scoundrels, Harte takes a large step toward merging the vocabularies of Western and Domestic fiction as defined by Tompkins (see note 8). Moreover, Harte's stories are almost all about the "valorization of character over conduct" (122) that Lora Romero posits at the center of Domesticity's project ("Domesticity and Fiction," in *The Columbia History of the American Novel,* ed. Emory Elliot [New York: Columbia University Press, 1991]). Although Romero is predominantly concerned with the internal struggle

of female protagonists—the development of women's private Christian character versus the interpersonal battles of men's public discourse—her distinction could just as easily suit the inhabitants of Roaring Camp, whose preternatural greed and violent impulses are held in check by their love for Thomas.

16. As Schroeder contends, "Luck is an irrational value, and the final stages of civilization, the encouragement of man's higher faculties, cannot exist in a culture based on superstitious unreason" (201). In other words, the miners of Roaring Camp must recognize that they were "redeemed" not by Thomas's literal presence or death but by the self-generated exercise of those qualities for which they understood Thomas to stand and which he brought out in them.

17. See Tompkins, *West of Everything*, 34–39.

18. Bret Harte, *The Outcasts of Poker Flat and Other Tales* (New York: New American Library, 1961), 154. Subsequent citations will be made parenthetically in the text. Only citations from "Miggles" are taken from this Harte edition.

19. For a feminist spin on theories of gender inversion, see Elizabeth Grosz's "Irigaray's Notion of Sexual Morphology," in *Reimagining Women: Representations of Women in Culture,* ed. Shirley Neuman (Toronto: University of Toronto Press, 1993). Not only does Grosz's article offer a specific interpretation of one theorist's (Irigaray's) strategies for subverting the ostensible determinism of sexed bodies, but it also gives a useful synopsis of the way feminist theory overall has tended to deal with the cultural inscription of sex and sexuality throughout the twentieth century. To an extent, the ideas expressed in this article might be applied to "The Luck of Roaring Camp" as well, since it also works to break down ideas of gender absolutism, only from the other side—the men's side—of the issue.

20. Henry Nash Smith, *Virgin Land* (Cambridge: Harvard University Press, 1950). Chapter 10, in particular, discusses these masculine dime-novel heroines.

21. Refer back to the way Miggles is dressed when she meets the party originally, in an outfit culled equally from a man's and woman's wardrobe.

22. One can hardly make such a reading without noting the analogues to Harte's own unpleasant domestic experience, a fact that may have fundamentally impacted the way he thought about and presented family life in his fictions. Briefly, Harte's wife spent money recklessly and, according to some witnesses, was something of a shrew. She and Harte were separated approximately thirty years before his death, and though he continued to support her financially, they were never again on speaking terms. Most Harte biographies credit Anna Harte with the dissolution of the marriage, but these same biographies, written in the first several decades of this century, take such a vindictive view of the woman that it is difficult to know how unbiased they are being. Likewise, Harte's letters to her are mostly cordial and hardly revelatory. The facts, though, are simple: even before they were separated Harte spent much time away from his wife and family. His attention to domestic matters in his fiction, then, may be his attempt to compensate for his family's literal absence or, more intriguing, an attempt to imagine a domestic space different from, perhaps less limited and more palatable to him than, his real-world one.

23. Harte, *Luck of Roaring Camp,* 49. Subsequent citations will be made parenthetically in the text.

24. Linda Burton, "For Better or Worse: Tennessee and His Partner: A New Approach to Bret Harte," *The Arizona Quarterly* 36, no. 2 (1980): 212.

25. Burton, "For Better or Worse," 213.

26. Scharnhorst, *Bret Harte,* 29.

27. William F. Conner, "The Euchring of Tennessee: A Reexamination of Bret Harte's 'Tennessee's Partner,'" *Studies in Short Fiction* 17, no. 2 (1980): 113.

28. Ibid.

29. Burton and Conner both cite sources for these traditional readings, the most influential of which include T. Edgar Pemberton's *The Life of Bret Harte* (London: C. Arthur Pearson, Ltd., 1903); Richard O'Connor's *Bret Harte: A Biography* (Boston: Little, Brown, 1966); and Cleanth Brooks and Robert Penn Warren, eds., *Understanding Fiction* (New York: Crofts, 1943).

30. Granted, there are some exceptions to this rule, but speaking archetypically, the western usually works to constitute a sacred, closed, heterosexual, and single-raced domestic order. Take, for example, the action of two somewhat later but infinitely traditional westerns, Owen Wister's *The Virginian* and Zane Grey's *Riders of the Purple Sage.* In Wister's case, the first thing the Virginian and Molly Wood do after their wedding is retreat to a "bower" in the mountains "untouched by any human influence." In *Riders,* the couple's break with the rest of the world is even clearer. Seconds after Jane Withersteen declares her love for Lassiter, he rolls a boulder onto their pursuing enemies that seals them together into Surprise Canyon forever.

31. In *Between Men: English Literature and Male Homosocial Desire* (New York: Columbia University Press, 1985), Eve Sedgwick notes the way that in Anglo-American culture, the exercise of homosexuality has been strictly taboo for most men, even those who regularly engage in acts of male bonding such as the western institutions of working, drinking, gambling, and fighting. It is culturally abhorrent, then, to extrapolate a possible all-male sexual relationship from men's expressions of camaraderie or even "brotherly love." "Homosocial" and "homosexual" clearly mean two different things. However, the same assertion cannot be made of women, for, as Sedgwick notes, female sexuality operates on

> an intelligible continuum of aims, emotions, and valuations [which] links lesbianism with the other forms of women's attention to women: the bond of mother and daughter, for instance, the bond of sister and sister, women's friendship, "networking," and the active struggles of feminism. . . . Thus the adjective "homosocial" as applied to women's bonds . . . need not be pointedly dichotomized as against "homosexual"; it can intelligibly denominate the entire continuum. (2–3)

The schism between the relatively continuous spectrum of female homosocial-homosexual relations and its discontinuous male counterpart raises the immediate, if simple, question of why the difference. And while Harte would probably not have asked the question in exactly Sedgwick's terms, it is clear that he was concerned with the different kinds of cultural performance attributed to men and women. He would not have been exploring issues of homoeroticism, then, but questions of gender difference that ultimately suggested questions of sexuality and sexual performance.

32. Gayle Rubin, "The Traffic in Women: Notes toward a Political Economy of Sex," in *Toward an Anthropology of Women*, ed. Rayna R. Reiter (New York: Monthly Review Press, 1975), 180. As Rubin also writes, "Gender is not only an identification with one sex; it also entails that sexual desire be directed toward the other sex." Implicit in cultural constructions of gender, then, are constructions of sexuality as well. As Harte discovers, it is impossible to speak of one without eventually being forced into a discussion of the other.

33. Morrow, "Bret Harte, Mark Twain," 342.

34. Shirley Neuman, "'An appearance walking in a forest the sexes burn': Autobiography and the Construction of the Feminine Body," *Signature: A Journal of Theory and Canadian Literature* 2 (Winter 1989): 1–26.

35. See note 21.

36. While I have reduced the relationship of Chubbuck and Pet along anatomical lines, it is important to note that, culturally speaking and as Harte has portrayed it, their lesbian relationship can signify in a number of ways. Luce Irigaray, paraphrasing Freud, locates a female desire to be male at the base of lesbian impulses. As she writes,

> The extreme consequence of this masculinity complex can be found in the sexual economy and in the object choice of the female homosexual, who, having in most cases taken her father as 'object,' in conformity with the female Oedipus complex, then regresses to infantile masculinity owing to the inevitable disappointments that she has encountered in her dealings with her father. The desired object for her is from then on chosen according to the masculine mode, and 'in her behavior towards her love-object' she consistently assumes 'the masculine part.' (*The Irigaray Reader*, ed. Margaret Whitford [Oxford: Basil Blackwell, Ltd., 1991], 43)

Lesbian desire, that is, results from a woman's refusal to admit she is not a man and her stubborn insistence on taking women as love objects. By problematizing issues of gender, however, Harte breaks down the correlation of sexed bodies to gender performance and, in so doing, unfixes the Freudian certainty of Chubbuck's desire (is he a man in love with a woman? a woman in love with a woman? a woman in love with a man? a man in love with a man? and so forth). Even simpler is Irigaray's own objection to Freud, which asks, "*Why is the interpretation of female homosexuality, now as always, modeled on that of male homosexuality?*" (65). As he breaks down gender essentialism and the subordination of female/feminine to male/masculine, Harte would very likely ask the same question.

Chapter 3

1. Jane Gardiner, "'A More Splendid Necromancy': Mark Twain's *Connecticut Yankee* and the Electrical Revolution," *Studies in the Novel* 19, no. 4 (1987): 448. For further

discussion of this topic, see also Bruce Michelson's "Realism, Romance, and Dynamite: The Quarrel of *A Connecticut Yankee in King Arthur's Court*," *The New England Quarterly* 64, no. 4 (1991): 609–32.

2. Henry Nash Smith, *Mark Twain: The Development of a Writer* (Cambridge, Mass.: The Belknap Press, 1962), 157.

3. John Cawelti, *The Six-Gun Mystique* (Bowling Green, Ohio: Bowling Green State University Popular Press, 1977), 58.

4. Mark Twain, *A Connecticut Yankee in King Arthur's Court* (New York: Harper & Row, 1963), 19. Future references will be made parenthetically in the text.

5. Mark Twain, *Your Personal Mark Twain* (New York: International Publishers, 1969), 195.

6. Richard Slotkin, *The Fatal Environment: The Myth of the Frontier in the Age of Industrialization, 1800–1890* (New York: Atheneum, 1985), 524. Numerous critics sympathize with Slotkin's perspective. As Thomas Bulger attests in "Mark Twain's Ambivalent Utopianism":

There is considerable value in Hank Morgan's attempts to reform Arthurian civilization into a democratic utopia: slavery is abolished; the repressive institutions of the Catholic Church and of the British monarchy are being phased out in favor of an enlightened republicanism; nineteenth-century American technology improves the material well-being of the British nation as a whole. (*Studies in American Fiction* 17, no. 2 [1989]: 238)

This last statement especially strikes me as questionable, but true or not, Bulger's assessment is most in line with the reading of *A Connecticut Yankee* offered by fans of Morgan's intent, if not his actual successes.

7. For the best discussion of this idea, see both R. W. B. Lewis's *The American Adam: Innocence, Tragedy, and Tradition in the Nineteenth Century* (Chicago: University of Chicago Press, 1955) and Slotkin's *Regeneration Through Violence: The Mythology of the American Frontier, 1600–1860* (Middletown, Conn: Wesleyan University Press, 1973).

8. One of the funnier moments in the text comes when Hank reveals, "We had a steamboat or two on the Thames, we had steam warships, and the beginnings of a steam commercial marine; I was getting ready to send out an expedition to *discover* America" (*Connecticut Yankee*, 284, italics mine).

9. Stephen H. Sumida, "Re-evaluating Twain's Novel of Hawaii," *American Literature* 61, no. 4 (1989): 603.

10. I am thinking in particular of Natty Bumppo because his consummate efficiency in killing Natives is often accompanied by a panegyric of white morality, so much so that it becomes difficult to tell whether his philosophy gives rise to his actions or vice-versa. Twain's hatred of Cooper may be one reason why Hank Morgan comes off sounding like Bumppo at so many points and why Twain makes him look ridiculous for it.

11. In his afterword to *A Connecticut Yankee*, Edmund Reiss writes: "While extolling democracy and human equality, Hank sets himself up as The Boss, a dictator

who wants not only to rule the land but also to control nature, to make eclipses—to be, in other words, a god. And Hank Morgan is not to be a god of love" (324).

12. Slotkin, *Regeneration,* 517.

13. *Roughing It* (New York: Viking Penguin, 1981), 168–69.

14. Not that Slotkin is alone in his assessment. Robert F. Berkhofer Jr. writes that "The vitriolic racism of literary realism found no more bitter expression than in Mark Twain's description of the Gosiute in his *Roughing It*" (*The White Man's Indian* [New York: Vintage Books, 1979], 105). And, more generally, Wayne R. Kime notes that "As Twain represents him, . . . the Indian is 'ignoble—base and treacherous, and hateful in every way'" ("Huck among the Indians: Mark Twain and Richard Irving Dodge's *The Plains of the Great West and Their Inhabitants,*" *Western American Literature* 24, no. 4 [1990]: 322).

15. Slotkin, *Regeneration,* 522.

16. Importantly, I do not contend that Twain was a fan of Native culture or that he was even a proponent of greater Native rights. But I do think that his writing exhibits a profound skepticism toward American Indian policy, believing it to be misguided and often cruel. Apologists for the historical treatment of Natives have characterized his views as intolerably racist, in large part to validate their own position. Aside from the overly idyllic depiction of Native culture that these positions often produce, what such scholars also neglect is the correspondent condemnation of white society that always accompanies Twain's writing on Natives. Take, for example, a selection from his "The French and the Comanches," which Slotkin likewise cites:

> Now as to cruelty, savagery, and the spirit of massacre. These do not add grace to the world's partly civilized defects. They grow naturally out of the social system; the system could not be perfect without them. It is hard to draw a line here, with any great degree of exactness, between the French, the Comanches, and the several other nations existing upon the same moral and social level. It must in candor be admitted that in one point the Comanches rank higher than the French, in that they do not fight among themselves, whereas a favorite pastime with the French, from time immemorial, has been the burning and slaughtering of each other.
>
> I very much doubt if the French are more cruel than the Comanches; I think they are only more ingenious in their methods. (*Letters from the Earth* [New York: Harper & Row, 1938], 146)

Though the passage hardly idealizes Comanche society, Twain levels his central and most poignant criticisms at the French. As with *A Connecticut Yankee,* the intent of the piece is not to denigrate the Indians so much as to reveal how uncivilized Euro-American society remains and how similar it is, in ideology and method, to the supposed savage culture it holds in contempt. The onus is not upon the Indians at all, but on the vicious whites who wish to maintain their civility through superficial cultural veneer and dissembling rhetoric. Twain may be misanthropic, admittedly, but he is nothing if not even-handed.

17. Shortly after Twain, of course, Turner's Thesis would raise this concept to the

level of myth, confirming the frontier as America's ultimate site of social and economic equality.

18. Nancy S. Oliver has argued that American schemes of Manifest Destiny were always predicated on an ironic notion of individualism operating "under the protective direction of the federal government" ("New Manifest Destiny in *A Connecticut Yankee in King Arthur's Court,*" *Mark Twain Journal* 21, no. 4 [1983]: 28). Her thesis is that even as Western immigrants were touted as pioneers and self-made individuals, they almost always moved according to the edicts of Congress, their migrations and settlements directed to satisfy Washington's imperial concerns. While Oliver's comments have mostly to do with territorial expansion, her idea of government aspiration masquerading as the will of the people is most descriptive of Hank's project in Camelot and once again highlights his link to American modes of conquest in the nineteenth century.

19. Frederick Anderson, ed., *A Pen Warmed Up in Hell: Mark Twain in Protest* (New York: Perennial Library, 1972), 44.

20. Twain, not coincidentally, gained most of his early journalistic experience working for newspapers in the American West, where he refined most of the skills that would become trademarks of his writing: hyperbole, humor, dialect, and so forth. Early on, however, he demonstrated a certain discomfort with the liberties that such papers took with the truth. His final departure from journalistic life was in large part fueled by his distaste for such practices, despite his willingness to use similar techniques in other kinds of writing. For more on this subject, see Stephen Fender's "The Prodigal in a Far Country Chawing of Husks: Mark Twain's Search for a Style in the West," *Modern Language Review* 71 (1976): 737–56.

21. Francis Paul Prucha, ed., *Documents of United States Indian Policy* (Lincoln: University of Nebraska Press, 1990), 174–81.

22. Henry died in an explosion aboard the steamship *Pennsylvania*. For further details, as well as Twain's reaction to his brother's death, see Charles Neider, ed., *The Autobiography of Mark Twain* (New York: The Perennial Library, 1917), 107–11.

23. The tournament, of course, is that event driving the cultural identities of cowboy and knight irrevocably together. As Cawelti has noted of the knightly tradition in the western generally,

the Westerner's six-gun and his way of using it in individual combat was the closest thing in the armory of modern violence to the knight's sword and the duelist's pistol. Thus in a period when violence in war was becoming increasingly anonymous . . . the cowboy hero in isolated combat with Indian or outlaw seemed to reaffirm the traditional image of masculine strength, honor and moral violence. The cowboy hero with his six-gun standing between the uncontrolled violence of the savages and the evolving collective forces of the legal process played out in new terms the older image of chivalrous adventure. (*Six-Gun,* 86)

Even Owen Wister, in his "The Evolution of the Cow-Puncher" (1897), noted how "in personal daring and in skill as to the horse, the knight and the cowboy are nothing but the same Saxon of different environments . . . ; and no hoof in Sir Thomas Mallory shakes the crumbling plains with quadrupled sounds more valiant than the galloping that has echoed from the Rio Grande to the Big Horn Mountains" (in *Owen Wister's West, Selected Articles,* ed. Robert Murray Davis [Albuquerque: University of New Mexico Press, 1987]).

24. Richard S. Pressman, "A Connecticut Yankee in Merlin's Cave: The Role of Contradiction in Mark Twain's Novel," *American Literary Realism* 16, no. 1 (1983): 68.

Chapter 4

1. Lee Clark Mitchell, *Westerns: Making the Man in Fiction and Film* (Chicago: University of Chicago Press, 1996), 96. Robinson echoes this sentiment in "The Virginian and Molly in Paradise: How Sweet Is It?" *Western American Literature* 21, no. 1 (1986): 27–38 (revised and reprinted in Forrest G. Robinson, *Having It Both Ways: Self-Subversion in Western Popular Classics* [Albuquerque: University of New Mexico Press, 1993]). Moreover, male critics in abundance have seen the book in a positive light. Among others, Gary Scharnhorst explores the Virginian's relation to Washington and Jefferson ("The Virginian as a Founding Father," *Arizona Quarterly* 40, no. 3 [1984]: 227–41), while Sanford E. Marovitz has discussed more generally the brands of American patriotism constructed by the book ("Testament of a Patriot: The Virginian, The Tenderfoot, and Owen Wister," *Texas Studies in Literature and Language* 15, no. 3 [1973]: 551–73). J. Bakker reminds audiences that "the vision underlying [Wister's] work is affirmative and optimistic" ("The Western: Can It Be Great?" *Dutch Quarterly Review of Anglo-American Letters* 14, no. 2 [1984]: 140), and Neal Lambert concludes that "what Wister actually did was to lift out certain positive elements of [East and West] and synthesize these into a significant emblem" ("Owen Wister's Virginian: The Genesis of a Cultural Hero," *Western American Literature* 6 [1971]: 103–4).

2. Jane Tompkins, *West of Everything* (New York: Oxford University Press, 1992), 142. Tompkins devotes an entire chapter to Wister, raising interesting points about *The Virginian's* opposition to nineteenth-century women's fiction. At the same time, though, Tompkins's logic can be dangerously circular: she contends, in essence, that Wister wrote a sexist novel because he disliked his mother, but her only "proof" of Wister's feelings is the sexist program of the novel itself.

3. Christine Bold, *Selling the Wild West: Popular Western Fiction, 1860–1960* (Bloomington: Indiana University Press, 1987), 43–44.

4. John Seelye, introduction to *The Virginian* by Owen Wister (New York: Penguin, 1988), xxviii.

5. Bret Harte, *The Luck of Roaring Camp and Other Stories* (New York: Macmillan, 1928), 88. Future references to this volume will be made parenthetically in the text.

6. Miller acknowledged his connection to Harte in his preface to a reprint of the novel version. For more information, see A. V. D. Honeyman, ed., *The Danites: and Other Choice Selections, from the Writings of Joaquin Miller, "the Poet of the Sierras"* [online], the Making of America digital library: <http://moa.umdl.umich.edu/moa>.

7. Biographical information on Miller taken from Benjamin S. Lawson, "Joaquin Miller," in *Nineteenth-Century American Western Writers.* Vol. 186 of *Dictionary of Liter-*

ary *Biography*, ed. Robert L. Gale (Pittsburgh: The Gale Group, 1997), 238–46. It should also be noted, given this chapter's emphasis on the connection between literary and popular western writing, that Miller's novel contained an anti-Mormon bias prevalent throughout western texts, from Twain's *Roughing It* (1872) to Zane Grey's *Riders of the Purple Sage* (1912).

8. Seelye, introduction, xxix. Additionally, Wister would likely have been aware of Miller's play, as Seelye notes that it had "a long and successful stage history."

9. Take, for example, this speech by Miller's narrator:

Water will find its level. In this camp, in all new camps, in all new countries, new enterprises, wars, controversies—no matter what, there are certain men who come to the surface. These come to the front, and men stand aside, and they take their place. They stay there, for they belong there. They may not come immediately; but let any great question be taken up, let it be of enough consequence to stir up the waters, and the waters will find their level. (*First Fam'lies of the Sierras* [Chicago: Jansen, McClurg & Co., 1876], 74–75)

Subsequent references to this volume will be made parenthetically in the text.

10. It should also be noted that Miller's novel adopts a tone toward women, reverential but condescending, that could be taken straight from *The Virginian*. In one instance, the narrator emphatically announces that a "woman's weakness is her strength" (37), an observation that guides the protective stance taken toward women in the text. In another scene, where the Widow is ill, the miners give up their normal miscreant pursuits—gaming, whoring, and fighting—out of respect for the sick woman. This scene is repeated almost verbatim in *The Virginian,* where the boys stop drinking and playing cards in deference to the engineer's suffering wife.

How high and holy the influence of this one woman over these half-grizzlies, these hairy-faced men who had drunk water from the same spring with the wild beasts of the Sierras.

Now they would not drink, would hardly shout or speak sharp, while she lay ill. Whatever was the matter, or the misfortune, they had too much respect for her, for themselves, to carouse till she should again show her face, or at least while her life was uncertain. (Miller, *First Fam'lies,* 174)

11. All quotes of Crane taken from Stephen Crane, *The Red Badge of Courage and Other Stories,* ed. Pascal Covici Jr. (New York: Penguin, 1991).

12. Owen Wister, *The Virginian* (New York: Viking Penguin, 1988), 392. All further references to this volume will be noted parenthetically in the text.

13. *Henry V* (III, vi).

Chapter 5

1. Robert Erwin has noted the tremendous amount of Indian writing produced as early as the Revolutionary period, though none of it fiction: "Between 1772 and 1924 Indian authors published more than 6700 articles and books in English," and

"Ottawas, Mohawks, Cherokees, Micmacs, and Yaquis—people from every corner of the continent—created syllabaries and orthographies in which to write their own languages" ("Injuns," *The Virginia Quarterly Review* 72, no. 3 [1996]: 500).

2. Take, for example, Gerald Vizenor's description of the trickster—that comic and indeterminate figure central to Native oral discourse:

> The trickster is a sign, a communal signification that cannot be separated or understood in isolation; the signifiers are acoustic images bound to four points of view, and the signified, or the concept the signifier locates in language and social experience, is a narrative event or translation. The listeners and readers become the trickster, a sign, and semiotic being in discourse; the trickster is a comic holotrope in narrative voices, not a model or tragic figure in isolation. (*Narrative Chance* [Norman: University of Oklahoma Press, 1993] 189)

This explanation works to unsettle the "certainty" of written discourse that underscores most reading projects by making audience interaction the most crucial element of both literary interpretation *and* production. In short, while Vizenor is describing the way that the trickster figure is deployed in contemporary Native written discourse, he likewise demonstrates why—to practitioners of exclusively oral storytelling—the idea of "fixing" a trickster in written discourse would have been antithetical to the purposes of the text itself.

3. Accordingly Andrew Wiget (*Native American Literature* [Boston: Twayne, 1985]) can write at length about the various incarnations of Native nonfiction throughout the nineteenth century—under headings like "Religious and political writing," "The autobiographical tradition," and "The historical and ethnographic traditions"—but can find only one author, John Rollin Ridge, to consider critically when reviewing Native fiction written before 1900.

4. The relative dearth of Native fiction until the 1930s has been amply confirmed by a variety of scholars. Robert F. Berkhofer Jr. deals with no Native-authored fiction texts before 1932 in *The White Man's Indian* (New York: Vintage Books, 1978), and A. LaVonne Brown Ruoff, in a more exhaustive literary study, notes only two Native American novels produced in the nineteenth century: John Rollin Ridge's *The Life and Adventures of Joaquin Murieta* (1854) and Simon Pokagon's *O-gi-maw-kwe mit-i-gwa-ki (Queen of the Woods)* (1899) (*American Indian Literatures, an Introduction* [New York: Modern Language Association, 1990]). In other less specialized western texts, the case "against" Native fiction is even more extreme. For example, despite the inclusion of several transcribed creation myths, the first Native fiction writer to appear in James C. Work's somewhat exhaustive anthology of Western writing, *Prose and Poetry of the American West* (Lincoln: University of Nebraska Press, 1990), is N. Scott Momaday, who became famous in the 1960s.

5. Such ethnocentrism has become something of a critical commonplace, especially in Western/frontier studies. For two exhaustive explorations of how this issue played out in nineteenth-century literature, see Richard Slotkin's *The Fatal Environment: The Myth of the Frontier in the Age of Industrialization, 1800–1890* (New York: Atheneum,

1985) and Dana D. Nelson's *The Word in Black and White, Reading "Race" in American Literature, 1638–1837* (New York: Oxford University Press, 1992).

6. Indeed, as note 4 suggests, even at the turn of the century, when Zitkala-Sa produced the bulk of her work, she was one of only three Natives who had written or were writing fiction, Ridge and Pokagon being the others.

7. I would not want to suggest that the works to be discussed in this chapter are all that Ridge or Zitkala-Sa produced. Along with journalistic writing, Ridge was a poet of some note, and Zitkala-Sa's *Old Indian Legends* (1901) was one of the first attempts to translate Native myth into English literary form. Of their work overall, though, only a few volumes remain extant, which is perhaps one reason they have only recently started to receive serious critical attention.

8. The most complete publication history of Ridge's novel and the many texts it fostered can be found in Joseph Henry Jackson's introduction to *The Life and Adventures of Joaquin Murieta, the Celebrated California Bandit* (Norman: University of Oklahoma Press, 1955). Jackson notes that within five years of its original publication, Ridge's dime novel had been turned into a longer serialized novel in a California paper, and within a decade it had become the basis for a stage play in San Francisco and several longer novels published in Spain. In 1871, the original volume was reissued under Ridge's name but on a different dime-novel imprint, and by the 1880s Erasmus Beadle had published a number of versions of the story as part of Beadle's Dime Library, many of them purporting to be based on actual events. In the 1890s, several histories charting the "real" biography of Joaquin Murieta, with sections borrowed directly from Ridge's novel, began to appear. After the turn of the century, writers and scholars simply assumed Murieta had been an actual person. Stories and movies based on his life persisted well into the 1940s, as did reissues of the novel as a straightforward biography. Journalistic and even scholarly accounts wrote the bandit into the history of southern California, interviewing people who had actually "seen" Murieta or, later, interviewing the descendants of members of Murieta's gang, and so forth. As John Carlos Rowe puts it, "Scholars are fond of pointing out how Ridge's novel originated a legend that came to be taken for historical fact" ("Highway Robbery: 'Indian Removal,' The Mexican-American War, and American Identity in *The Life and Adventures of Joaquin Murieta*," *Novel: A Forum on Fiction* 31, no. 2 [1998]: 149–73).

9. The standard features of the dime-novel western are thoroughly explored in the following: Bill Brown's *Reading the West: An Anthology of Dime Westerns* (Boston, Mass.: Bedford, 1997); Daryl E. Jones's *The Dime Novel Western* (Bowling Green, Ohio: The Bowling Green State University Popular Press, 1978); Thomas L. Kent's "The Formal Conventions of the Dime Novel," *Journal of Popular Culture* 16, no. 1 (1982): 37–47; Michael K. Simmons "Nationalism and the Dime Novel," *Studies in the Humanities* 9, no. 1 (1981): 39–44; and Henry Nash Smith's *Virgin Land: The American West as Symbol and Myth* (Cambridge: Harvard University Press, 1950). While not all dime novels follow the exact same pattern, their similarities are pronounced enough to be grouped into several basic categories. *Joaquin Murieta* falls roughly under that dime-novel plot which Jones refers to as the "persecution and revenge" story and Kent refers to as "the wronged

man motif." Both of these plots involve a character who, through no fault of his own, is persecuted and made an "outsider." Often this outsider becomes a kind of "Robin Hood outlaw" whose crimes are committed on the grounds of survival and "moral" revenge for the injustices waged against him. Commonly, the protagonist's triumph at the end of these novels signals his reintegration into society, his adoption of an "insider" identity, and the generic triumph of justice over injustice.

10. John Rollin Ridge, *The Life and Adventures of Joaquin Murieta, the Celebrated California Bandit* (Norman: University of Oklahoma Press, 1955), 12–13. Subsequent citations of this volume will be made parenthetically in the text.

11. Joaquin's profound sense of justice is symbolically reinforced throughout the book. In one section, for instance, Ridge includes a poem on Mount Shasta that, as John Lowe points out, "ends, in fact, by transforming this 'blasphemous' babel-like natural phenomenon into a symbol of law, a pure white shaft that towers above man's activities as a moral guide. It is in the shadow of this peak that Joaquin and his men take refuge for several months, descending at intervals into the valley below to steal horses with the aid of the Indians." ("Space and Freedom in the Golden Republic: Yellow Bird's *The Life and Adventures of Joaquin Murieta, the Celebrated California Bandit*," *Studies in American Indian Literatures* 4, no. 2–3 [1992]: 113–14.) Lowe's observation highlights the frequent games of inversion that the book plays. Joaquin's placement on Mount Shasta makes him a legitimate interpreter of the "law" (like Moses), an identity inverted by his horse-stealing, inverted again by his rational justifications for turning outlaw. Thus the novel refuses to endorse a singular brand of "law" or "justice," the narrator's reservations about Joaquin's methods fiercely combated by the sense of righteous vengeance fueling Joaquin's crusade.

12. As the narrator comments after Joaquin's mining claim is usurped and his mistress is raped by whites, "It was the first injury he had ever received at the hands of the Americans, whom he had always hitherto respected, and it wrung him to the soul as a deeper and deadlier wrong from that very circumstance" (10).

13. This connection has been recognized by practically every Ridge scholar. In particular, see Joseph Henry Jackson's introduction to *Joaquin Murieta* and Karl Kroeber's "American Indian Persistence and Resurgence," *boundary 2* 19, no. 3 (1992): 1–25.

14. However Rowe, among other critics, is quick to point out that Joaquin's Robin Hood identity must be read with some skepticism. His overt brutality toward a number of poor victims undercuts any uniform class-based reading that the novel invites in other places. Clearly the frontier novel is a "darker" space than the Robin Hood legend, often valorizing violence—even unrighteous violence—for its own sake. Joaquin is both hero and villain here (like an early version of fictional renditions of Jesse James), and if he is at turns compassionate and sadistic, it is because the western form not only allows but also requires him to be both of those things. In a more allegorical sense, the concomitant desire for violent revenge and peaceful reconciliation are evident in Ridge's own life; perhaps what appears in the novel is as much psychological autobiography as it is a figurative statement about relations between different races or classes.

15. For a more extensive history of Ridge's life, see Rowe, "Highway Robbery,"

151–54. Per Rowe: "I argue . . . that Ridge's novel resolves the conflicting and traumatic experiences of his personal history as a Cherokee, of the U.S. conquest of California in the Mexican-American War, and of the social disorder in California during the Gold Rush in a narrative organized around the myth of progressive individualism, a crucial part of dominant cultural values in the United States in the 1850s" (150).

16. While Ridge elides Mexican and Indian identities to an extent, his pan-racial sentiment is problematized by Joaquin's patronizing attitude toward Digger Indians in California and his overt contempt for Chinese-Americans. As Peter G. Christensen argues, Ridge's design is not to draw all races together—he was proslavery, after all—but to glorify those races that he sees courageously resisting unfair treatment by whites ("Minority Interaction in John Rollin Ridge's *The Life and Adventures of Joaquin Murieta*," *MELUS* 17, no. 2 [1991–92]: 61–72).

17. While scholarship on Ridge is limited, the debate over his racial "intentions" is quite pronounced. A. LaVonne Brown Ruoff, for instance, assumes that his depiction of Mexicans is an unadulterated metaphor for Native peoples:

> Clearly Ridge chose to deal indirectly with the injustices suffered by Indians. The decreased interest of the public in the Indian as a subject for serious literature undoubtedly dictated this choice as did their increased interest in stories about the gold fields of California. This shift in popular taste undoubtedly explains the lack of emphasis on Indian subjects in Ridge's work because his letters reveal his commitment to the cause of the Cherokee people. (Andrew Wiget, ed., *Critical Essays on Native American Literature* [Boston: G. K. Hall, 1985], 198)

On the other hand, Christensen sees the novel as one which casts Natives in an unflattering light, allowing Ridge not only to erect a system of racial hierarchies but also to gain a symbolic revenge over his father's murderers.

18. Maria Mondragon, "'The [Safe] White Side of the Line': History and Disguise in John Rollin Ridge's *The Life and Adventures of Joaquin Murieta: The Celebrated California Bandit*," *American Transcendental Quarterly* 8, no. 3 (1994): 174.

19. Rowe writes that the novel "demands . . . a legal system that ignores different classes, races, and political or economic interests for the sake of judging the 'individual' alone according to his deficiencies or merits" (160).

20. More complete histories of Zitkala-Sa can be found in Mary Stout's "Zitkala-Sa: The Literature of Politics," in *Coyote Was Here: Essays on Contemporary Native American Literary and Political Mobilization*, ed. Bo Scholer, *The Dolphin* 9 (April 1984): 70–78); and Roseanne Hoefel's "Writing, Performance, Activism: Zitkala-Sa and Pauline Johnson," in *Native American Women in Literature and Culture*, ed. Susan Castillo and Victor DaRosa (Porto, Portugal: Fernando Pessoa University Press, 1997), 107–18.

21. Dorothea M. Susag, "Zitkala-Sa (Gertrude Simmons Bonnin): A Power(full) Literary Voice," *Studies in American Indian Literatures* 5, no. 4 (1993): 7.

22. Foreword to Zitkala-Sa, *American Indian Stories* (Lincoln: University of Nebraska Press, 1985), vii.

23. Susag, "Zitkala-Sa," 7. A similar assessment of Zitkala-Sa's frequent use of sentimentalism can be found in Patricia Okker's "Native American Literatures and the Canon: The Case of Zitkala-Sa," in *American Realism and the Canon,* ed. Tom Quirk and Gary Scharnhorst (Newark: University of Delaware Press, 1994), 87–101. The double-edged deployment of domestic themes is quite important here. No critic maintains that Zitkala-Sa is writing a straightforward domestic fiction reminiscent of white-authored texts (in which a special bond between women, often mother and daughter, is reflected in their mutual commitment to Christianity and to the peaceful process of saving souls). Rather, critics maintain that Zitkala-Sa uses the veneer of domestic fiction—the closeness of mother and daughter, the mother's apparent conversion to Christianity—to disguise the actual work of *American Indian Stories,* which is to supplant the supposedly Christian bonds between women with Native American beliefs and customs.

This reading is reinforced by Laura Wexler's "Tender Violence: Literary Eavesdropping, Domestic Fiction, and Educational Reform" (in *The Culture of Sentiment: Race, Gender, and Sentimentality in Nineteenth-Century America,* ed. Shirley Samuels [New York: Oxford University Press, 1992]), which contends that nineteenth-century domestic ideologies, far from merciful and benevolent, partook of the same kinds of racial coercion and forced acculturation as "white male" conquests. Contemporary critics, notes Wexler, have failed to consider

> the expansive, imperial project of sentimentalism. In this aspect sentimentalization was an *externalized* aggression that was sadistic, not masochistic, in flavor. The energies it developed were intended as a tool for the control of others, not merely as aid in the conquest of self. This element of the enterprise was not oriented toward white, middle-class readers and their fictional alter-egos at all. . . . Rather, it aimed at the subjection of different classes and even races who were compelled to play not the leading roles but the human scenery before which the melodrama of middle-class redemption could be enacted, for the enlightenment of an audience that was not even themselves. (15)

Wexler's observations point to the sinister nature of "domestic conversion" attempts which would have made Zitkala-Sa's resistance necessary. By exploring domesticity's imperial undercurrent, Wexler draws closer together women's and men's cultures of the nineteenth century, shrinking the gap between the types of "conquests" occurring in the home and on the battlefield. In this way, Zitkala-Sa's own quick transition from narratives appropriating the forms of sentimental (non)fiction to narratives appropriating the forms of frontier accounts makes sense, for she saw little difference between the racial ideologies and methodologies defining the two.

24. Of the handful of scholars (including those noted here) who have produced work on *American Indian Stories,* only one, Dexter Fisher, mentions the fiction included in the book—and even then only the stories' titles.

25. Zitkala-Sa, *American Indian Stories* (Lincoln: University of Nebraska Press, 1985), 112. Subsequent citations of this volume will be made parenthetically in the text.

26. For elaboration on this point, as well as for a more extensive discussion of frontier literature's relation to domestic discourses of the nineteenth century, see Tompkins's *West of Everything* (New York: Oxford University Press, 1992).

. I would not want to suggest that Zitkala-Sa is writing exclusively in the pattern of men like Remington and Wister, or even that she is conscious of *all* the resonances of traditional frontier literature in her work. Important to me, however, is the fact that such resonances do exist. Whether or not she intends every single echo of "the White West" in her fiction, Zitkala-Sa's appropriation, approximation, mutation, and inversion of such themes locate her at least in part in a mainstream frontier canon, where her resistance to stereotypical western ideas about race and gender works to challenge what critics have largely accepted as a monologic discursive space.

28. It should be noted that "The Trial Path" is a story within a story, where the main action is told to a girl by her grandmother, the ostensible wife of the slain man and (later) of his assailant. Vanessa Holford Diana suggests that this structure is designed to reinforce the liberating power of storytelling itself. The main action, she argues, should not be taken literally but as a metaphor for preserving oneself and one's family—much as storytelling preserves one's culture ("'Hanging in the Heart of Chaos': Bi-Cultural Limbo, Self-(Re)presentation, and the White Audience in Zitkala-Sa's *American Indian Stories,*" *Cimarron Review* 121 [October 1997]: 154–72). This reading, of course, does not contradict a more "frontier" interpretation of the story; the main action's emphasis on masculine physicality, violence, and trial by ordeal (not to mention the grandmother's celebration of these) still suggests a figurative desire for a world in which momentary physical performances have near-universal philosophical implications.

29. Jeanne Smith confirms that "Tusee's disguises skillfully manipulate gender roles. Because as a woman she is an observer at the victory dance rather than a participant, she can do what a man can't. No one would suspect that an appealing young woman at the edge of a campfire, or a wandering old woman humming to herself, is a murderous avenger" ("'A Second Tongue': The Trickster's Voice in the Works of Zitkala-Sa," in *Tricksterism in Turn-of-the-Century American Literature: A Multicultural Perspective,* ed. Elizabeth Ammons and Annette White Parks [Boston: Tufts University, 1994], 54).

30. For some perspective on just how radical this inversion is (not just for Native but all women in Zitkala-Sa's time), see Gayle Rubin's "The Traffic in Women: Notes toward a Political Economy of Sex," in *Toward an Anthropology of Women,* ed. Rayna Reiter (New York: Monthly Review Press, 1975), 157–210.

31. Extrapolating forward, Ridge and Zitkala-Sa ironically may have had their profoundest effect on white writers concerned with constructing legitimate and sympathetic portrayals of Native peoples. Two examples especially, Frank Waters's *The Man Who Killed the Deer* (Athens, Ohio: Swallow Press, 1985) and Oliver LaFarge's *Laughing Boy* (Boston: Houghton Mifflin, 1957), use a number of western literary conventions in their respective creations of an independent identity for Native protagonists trapped between cultures.

32. Making matters even more difficult in such discussions is a critical ignorance over how Ridge and Zitkala-Sa were being read in their own day. The various and long-standing history of *The Life and Adventures of Joaquin Murieta* makes it nearly impossible to say for sure who comprised Ridge's principal audience or how the novel was received. Nor is Zitkala-Sa's situation much clearer. Since she was published regularly in both *The Atlantic Monthly* and *Harper's*, it is safe to say that her audience was largely white, Eastern, and middle- to upper-class. Gendered readings are not so simple, however, because both *Harper's* and *The Atlantic* published a broad variety of fiction at the turn of the century, including popular western and domestic stories. Was Zitkala-Sa thus read more as a "woman" writer or a "Western" writer? Was she read as both? If the latter, how did her stories work to construct a public version of self? And how did this identity resolve the inherent tensions between western and domestic ideologies (as famously chronicled by writers like Frank Norris and Stephen Crane)? The number and depth of these questions suggest some interesting directions in which further discussions of Zitkala-Sa might proceed, but at the same time they largely close down the authority of critics to speak definitively about who was reading these and other Native American writers from 1854 to 1930, how, and why.

Chapter 6

1. This opinion is common to critics of all stripes. Sharon O'Brien confirms that *Archbishop* is "considered one of [Cather's] finest novels" ("Becoming Noncanonical: The Case Against Willa Cather," in *Reading in America: Literature and Social History,* ed. Cathy N. Davidson [Baltimore: Johns Hopkins University Press, 1989], 240). Joan Acocella writes that "Of [Cather's] novels, *Death Comes for the Archbishop* is the most celebrated, and perhaps justly—it is a nearly perfect piece of writing" ("Cather and the Academy," in *The Best American Essays 1996,* ed. Geoffrey C. Ward [New York: Houghton-Mifflin, 1996], 11). And John H. Randall III notes: "Of all the books Cather ever wrote, *Death Comes for the Archbishop* is by far the most popular. It ran through eleven editions, was translated into eight languages, and is known to people who have never read anything else of Willa Cather's. Many consider it to be the crowning glory of her achievement" ("Summary of *Death Comes for the Archbishop:* The Cathedral and the Stagecoach," in *Critical Essays on Willa Cather,* ed. John J. Murphy [Boston: G. K. Hall & Co., 1984], 250).

2. The novel's ties to more traditional westerns have been noted by other critics. John J. Murphy, for example, compares it to Owen Wister's *The Virginian,* noting how "Wister's tall stranger and Cather's young priest are knights-errant in the wilderness, rescuing those in need, righting wrongs, bringing law to lawless regions" (Murphy, *Critical Essays,* 259). And Susan J. Rosowski notes how Latour's early wanderings in the desert resemble scenes straight out of Wister or Cooper (*The Voyage Perilous: Willa Cather's Romanticism* [Lincoln: University of Nebraska Press, 1986], 162). Neither of these readings quite parallels my own, however. In Murphy's reading, Latour becomes a genuine hero, "saving" those people whom I would suggest he largely disregards. And

in Rosowski's reading, Latour becomes the antithesis of the traditional frontier protagonist, constantly emphasizing spiritual matters over worldly ones. For the most part, critics have been satisfied to read the novel much as Rosowski does: a version of the anti-western characteristic of Cather's other writing. John R. Milton's *The Novel of the American West* (Lincoln: University of Nebraska Press, 1980), Arnold Davidson's *Coyote Country* (Durham, N.C.: Duke University Press, 1994), and Max Westbrook's *A Literary History of the American West* (Fort Worth: Texas Christian University Press, 1987), among others, take the revisionist status of the novel for granted.

3. Cather offered this anecdote about popular fiction of her day when giving an address at Bowdoin in 1925: "The novel has resolved into a human convenience to be bought and thrown away at the end of a journey. . . . I tried to get Longfellow's *Golden Legend* in Portland this afternoon to send away to my niece. The bookseller said he didn't have it and would not sell it if he did. He said he was cutting out all his two dollar books because people wanted Zane Grey and such" (L. Brent Bohlke, ed., *Willa Cather in Person* [Lincoln: University of Nebraska Press, 1986], 155). Later, she would remark that "the novel, as we know it today, is the child of democracy, and is not a high form of art. A novel today partakes of all our infirmities. The novel is too easy to write and too easy to read" (Bohke, *Willa Cather*, 157).

4. Willa Cather, *Death Comes for the Archbishop* (New York: Vintage, 1971), 20. Subsequent references to this edition will be made parenthetically in the text.

5. Here it might be useful to reiterate—in their entirety—Jane Tompkin's distinctions between western and women's novels, parts of which feature in earlier chapters of this book.

Most of the action [in women's novels] takes place in private spaces, at home, indoors, in kitchens, parlors, and upstairs chambers. And most of it concerns the interior struggles of the heroine to live up to an ideal of Christian virtue—usually involving uncomplaining submission to difficult and painful circumstances, learning to quell rebellious instincts, and dedicating her life to the service of God through serving others. In these struggles, women give one another a great deal of emotional and material support. . . . Culturally and politically, the effect of these novels is to establish women at the center of the world's most important work (saving souls) and to assert that in the end spiritual power is always superior to worldly might.

The elements of the typical Western plot arrange themselves in stark opposition to this pattern, not just vaguely and generally but point for point. First of all, in Westerns (which are generally written by men), the main character is always a full-grown adult male, and almost all of the other characters are men. The action takes place either outdoors—on the prairie, on the main street—or in public spaces—the saloon, the sheriff's office, the barber shop, the livery stable. The action concerns physical struggles between the hero and a rival or rivals, and culminates in a fight to the death with guns. In the course of these struggles the hero frequently forms a bond with another man—sometimes his rival, more often a comrade—a bond that is more important than any relationship he has with a woman and is frequently tinged with homoeroticism. (38–39)

6. This position is also taken by Patrick Shaw ("Women and the Father: Psychosexual Ambiguity in *Death Comes for the Archbishop*," *American Imago* 46, no. 1 [1989]), who recalls Latour's similarities to his real-life model, Father Lamy: "Lamy was in fact a money-oriented Archbishop who alienated the people of New Mexico with his tithing demands and whose French cathedral thus stands more as a symbol of his French distaste for the Spanish adobe structures preferred by the populace" (74). Shaw's argument is adapted from E. A. Mares's view of the novel as "a historical and social anachronism tragically flawed by the narrowness of its ethnic and cultural biases" (Mares quoted in Shaw, 74).

7. The irony of Magdalena's self-directed escape is reiterated toward the end of the book when, seeing her at work in Latour's garden, Vaillant remarks, "Who would think, to look at her now, that we took her from a place where every vileness of cruelty and lust was practised!" (210). Even in retrospect, the priests maintain the rather egotistical and patently false portrait of themselves as Magdalena's deliverers.

8. Ann W. Fisher-Wirth, "Dispossession and Redemption in the Novels of Willa Cather," in *Cather Studies*, vol.1, ed. Susan J. Rosowski (Lincoln: University of Nebraska Press, 1990), 49.

9. As Tompkins notes, the popular western is riddled with heroes who must sometimes defy the wishes of their "purer" love interests in order to enact worldly change: the Virginian and Molly Wood in *The Virginian*, Lassiter and Jane Withersteen in *Riders of the Purple Sage*, and so forth.

10. Many of the articles protesting the racism of *Death Comes for the Archbishop* focus on Latour's patronizing (at best) relationship with the Mexicans whom he is trying to win back from the schismatic priests. In particular, scholars have questioned Cather's depiction of Padre Martinez, a priest who challenged Father Lamy and Kit Carson, among others, for political and religious control of the Taos region. Far from the hedonist depicted in the novel, Martinez was in fact a devoted spiritual leader who clashed with Lamy over a number of legitimate issues, most notably the imposition of tithes to support Lamy's construction of a cathedral. For further information, see the following: Rudolfo Acuna's *Occupied America: A History of Chicanos* (New York: Harper, 1981); Ted J. Warner's "*Death Comes for the Archbishop*: A Novel Way of Making History," in *Willa Cather: Family, Community, and History*, ed. John J. Murphy (Provo, Utah: Brigham Young University Humanities Publications Center, 1990); Lance Larsen's "Cather's Controversial Portrayal of Martinez," in Murphy, *Willa Cather*; Judith Beth Cohen's "Father Martinez: Folk Hero or Dangerous Infidel? Rereading Willa Cather's *Death Comes for the Archbishop*," in *Rethinking American Literature*, ed. Lil Brannon and Brenda M. Greene (Urbana, Ill.: National Council of Teachers of English, 1997); and David Lavender's "The Tyranny of Facts," in *Old Southwest, New Southwest: Essays on a Region and Its Literature*, ed. Judy Nolte Lensink (Tucson, Ariz.: The Tucson Public Library, 1987).

While the depiction of Martinez suggests a racist stripe to Cather's attitude toward

Mexicans, I am more concerned with her treatment of Indians because—in the stereo-typical frontier novel—Indians commonly represent the "savagery" that the "civilized" hero must combat. In this same manner, Indians in *Death Comes for the Archbishop* represent a foreign theological force (a "savagery") against which Latour is constantly pitting his pure Catholic faith; Mexicans, while outside the scope of Latour's immediate influence, are still part of the region's Catholic (hence "civilized") traditions, just following the wrong leader. In this vein, it matters little to my argument that Cather's ethnocentric treatment of Martinez is historically inaccurate. I would argue that *Archbishop* is a racist book even when read on its own terms, as fiction, with only modest recourse to the actual people on whom these characters are based.

11. This scene also recalls Antonia's battle with the snake in *My Antonia,* where her ability to kill it becomes a signal of her ability to survive on and even to master the frontier. Antonia's conquest, however, does not have the same ethnic undertones as Latour's, where killing the snake and mastering the frontier both stand in for a conquest of the Native peoples in whom the myth-symbols "snake" and "frontier" find physical expression.

12. The "Stone Lips" section forms one of the novel's scenes most contested among critics. While most critics see Latour as being horrified by his experience in the cave, a vocal minority believes that it reveals to him a side of spirituality (his own or the Indians') that he had never realized before. In the former camp, consider Deborah Williams's "Losing Nothing, Comprehending Everything: Learning to Read Both the Old World and the New in *Death Comes for the Archbishop*" (*Cather Studies* 4 [1999]: 80–96) and Audrey Goodman's "The Immeasurable Possession of Air: Willa Cather and Southwestern Romance" (*Arizona Quarterly* 55, no. 4 [1999]: 49–78). In an interesting spin on this theme, Steven P. Ryan argues that Latour's descent into the cave represents a battle with the beast; Latour's emergence the following morning suggests a victory that leaves him charged for further battle in the real world ("'Snake Root': Latour's Descent into Hell in *Death Comes for the Archbishop,*" *Willa Cather Pioneer Memorial Newsletter and Review* 41, no. 2 [1997]: 33–36).

13. Latour's cultural blind spots are noted by Rosowski as well: "Yet as Cather presents the sacramental quality of symbolization, she suggests also its limitations. *Agape* accompanies a trust in a world that is God's word; conversely, anything outside this pattern poses an immense threat" (*Voyage Perilous,* 172).

14. A similar point is made by Susie Thomas, who writes that "The emblematic tradition in Christianity allows Latour to sympathise with the Indians' belief that their gods are present in the landscape. Although, to Christians, the house of God is the church, in a broader sense He is present everywhere in creation" (*Willa Cather* [Savage, Md.: Barnes & Noble Books, 1990], 152). Paradoxically, though, Latour's sympathies often fail to influence his actions to any great degree. What elements of himself he recognizes in the Natives are usually suppressed in favor of his more rigid "Catholic" sensibilities (though here again it is often hard to distinguish the imperatives of his religion from those of his ego).

15. Latour himself occasionally speaks of his aloofness and melancholy, as in his

confession to Vaillant that "I am always a little cold—*un pedant*, as you used to say" (261–62).

16. I should note that there are a number of critics who do not see Cather as racist at all. Most of these scholars view Indians in the novel as a positive influence on Latour's own Catholicism, focusing the priest on the landscape itself and reminding him of the palpable connection to God offered in the earth. Such essays sometimes sound alarmingly apologist, though, as if trying to offer the Natives a spiritual presence that is literally undercut by the Navajo persecution and Latour's inaction at the novel's end. A few sample essays of this type include Evelyn Haller's "*Death Comes for the Archbishop:* A Map of Intersecting Worlds" (*Willa Cather Pioneer Memorial Newsletter and Review* 34, no. 3 [1990]: 15–21); Marilee Lindemann's "Con-quest or In-quest? Cather's Mythic Impulse in *Death Comes for the Archbishop*" (*Willa Cather Pioneer Memorial Newsletter and Review* 31, no. 3 [1987]: 15–18); Thomas M. Casey's "Mariology and Christology in *Death Comes for the Archbishop*" (*Willa Cather Pioneer Memorial Newsletter and Review* 35, no. 3 [1991]: 22–25); Guy Reynolds's "The Ideology of Cather's Catholic Progressivism: *Death Comes for the Archbishop*" (*Cather Studies* 3 [1996]: 1–30); Conrad Ostwalt's "Boundaries and Marginality in Willa Cather's Frontier Fiction" (in *Dissent and Marginality: Essays on the Borders of Literature and Religion,* ed. Kiyoshi Tsuchiya [New York: St. Martin's Press, 1997], 102–14); and Marilyn Arnold's "The Integrating Vision of Bishop Latour in Willa Cather's *Death Comes for the Archbishop*" (*Literature and Belief* 8 [1988]: 38–57).

17. Fisher-Wirth, "Dispossession and Redemption," 45.

18. David Stouck, *Willa Cather's Imagination* (Lincoln: University of Nebraska Press, 1975), 139.

19. J. Gerard Dollar, "Desert Landscapes and the 'Male Gaze': Cather's *Death Comes for the Archbishop,*" *Willa Cather Pioneer Memorial Newsletter and Review* 42, no. 1 (1998): 8.

Chapter 7

1. The Modern Language Association Bibliography does show eighty publications on Waters in the last ten years. But it bears noting that all but nine of these publications were either proceedings from the annual *Studies in Frank Waters/Frank Waters Society Conference Papers* or entries in *Frank Waters: Man and Mystic* (ed. Vine Deloria Jr. [Athens, Ohio: Swallow Press, 1993]). Waters still has a following, in other words, but it is not one that has generated much interest in more mainstream critical circles.

The same might be said for earlier decades. John R. Milton notes that Waters was virtually unknown until around 1970, when there was a surge of interest in his work, concurrent with public interest in the American Indian (*The Novel of the American West* [Lincoln: University of Nebraska Press, 1980], 264). In critical terms, though, this surge did not attract significant interest from a broad base of readers. In fact, the vast majority of writing on Waters during this period was still confined to *Studies in Frank Waters* and three other Western literary journals. (To wit, four articles on Waters appeared in

Western American Literature between 1968 and 1987; the *South Dakota Review* devoted a special issue to him in 1977; and *Writers' Forum* ran a special section on him in 1985.) It is also worth mentioning that the same four men—John R. Milton, Thomas J. Lyon, Alexander Blackburn, and Charles L. Adams—authored many of these articles. And while their work on Waters has been compelling, it did not seem to generate a concomitant interest among non-Western regional critics and journals, even at the height of Waters's popularity.

2. Most recently, Blackburn has published *A Sunrise Brighter Still: The Visionary Novels of Frank Waters* (Athens: Swallow Press/Ohio University Press, 1991), and Adams, in addition to editing *Studies in Frank Waters,* has published the entries on Waters in the definitive reference volumes *A Literary History of the American West,* edited by Max Westbrook et al. (Fort Worth: Texas Christian University Press, 1987) and *Updating the Literary West,* also edited by Westbrook (Fort Worth: Western Literature Association/Texas Christian University Press, 1997).

3. Biographical information on Waters, here and later, is taken primarily from Thomas J. Lyon's *Frank Waters* (New York: Twayne, 1973) and the Gale Group's Literature Resource Center (online).

4. Per the Modern Language Association Bibliography again, Jackson's *Ramona* has fostered twenty critical treatments over the last ten years, including five dissertations and articles in the prestigious mainstream journals *American Literature* and *Studies in American Fiction.* La Farge's *Laughing Boy,* by contrast, has generated one publication, a single chapter in a dissertation on Southwestern writers.

5. Frank Waters, *The Man Who Killed the Deer* (Athens, Ohio: Swallow Press, 1985), 64. Subsequent references to this volume will be made parenthetically in the text.

6. For more on this kind of character, see the section on Zitkala-Sa's "The Soft-Hearted Sioux" in chapter 5.

7. See Jane Tompkins's *West of Everything* (New York: Oxford University Press, 1992). The issue of pain so permeates Tompkins's book that it has its own extensive entry in the index.

8. Occasionally the narrator cannot help making an overt statement in this regard. Before the pine pole incident, he offers these observations.

> The Pueblo Indian is invariably patient and charitable to summer visitors. Yet in the antics of the Chiffonetas are revealed his acute perception and sly humor. One wears strapped to his arm a battered alarm clock. He looks at it. "It is time to be hungry!"—and he snatches from a bystander a bag of popcorn. Another owlishly puffs a pipe. Still another grabs a woman's hat for his own head, and as though on high heels minces off wiggling his naked hips. Civilization slapped on a savage who shows its ludicrous aspects. (189)

9. The fact that Byers cannot completely qualify his relationship to the Pueblo people in words becomes an oft-repeated refrain in the novel, to wit:

> That, he decided, . . . was the damned catch when you tried to think intelligently about Indians. They couldn't be thought about intelligently. They had to be

either dismissed or taken on their own ground. And their premises of life were based not on the rational, the reasoning, evaluating approach, but wholly on the instinctive and intuitive. Things came or they didn't; they didn't proceed logically from point to point. So you had to take them or leave them as they were in fact, not theory. (40)

10. It should be noted that, in his role as witness, Byers is as keenly aware of the Pueblo people's potential flaws as their attributes, a quality that deflects any hint of romanticism from the novel:

> Often during his lonely life he had cursed the chance which had made him an Indian trader. No man knew better these people who had drained his youth, shaped his life and thought, and stamped on him forever their racial traits. He knew their surface indolence and cunning, their dirt and filth and lice, their secretiveness, barbarity, ignorance and stubborn denial of change. And so no man could better refute the sickly sentimentalism of lady tourists, the pampering enthusiasm of museum collectors, the false idealism of escapists and the mock gravity of anthropologists, ethnologists, and myth-mongers toward them—all the whining, shouting voices that proclaimed the Indian as nature's pet, a darling of the gods, and the only true American. Sometimes he damned them all to hell, swore that he would close up his post and go off to live, in white collars and shined shoes, the life of "a respectable white man." (39)

Unlike more traditional frontier narratives, Byers's observations about Indians do not advance a claim of cultural superiority. The quick juxtaposition of Pueblo Indians and white outsiders suggests a concomitant honesty on Byers's part, his calling both worlds as he sees them. In this regard, his threat to "live . . . the life of 'a respectable white man'" rings hollow, because even as that threat momentarily idealizes the white world into which the trader pretends he could slip, his observations about white culture instantly remind him of the different problems that would exist wherever he might go.

11. The narrator explicitly links childbirth, Pueblo belief, and a universal spirituality in a comparison of Juan de Bautista, Napaita, and Martiniano himself:

> The child born by woman out of the formless mystery of everlasting life into the narrow confines of human flesh, linked to the boundless universe with the first breath he draws, but constricted for awhile within the personal, individual image.
>
> The boy born by ceremonial out of the long initiate wherein he has been awakened out of the long narrow world of the flesh into the greater world of the spirit, into that conception of his oneness with the cosmic whole, the breathing mountains, the living stones, the young corn plant and the deer, all that life which has gone before and will follow after, and which exists at once in one perpetual time.
>
> And the man reborn, as men are ever reborn out of their dead selves, by life itself. For as there are many faiths and many conceptions of the one paradox by

which man exists as transient flesh and enduring spirit, all these faiths stem from the one faith, the one wonder and mystery of which we are an inseparable part. Let each man, though bereft of teacher, priest and preceptor, but depend upon this faith, and so be reborn by life itself into the greater whole. And so see before him at last, through the cycles of his widening perception, the one road which is his to tread with all. (256–57)

12. This sexist sensibility is exacerbated by the ceremonial commission that the fathers offer their sons as they leave them in the kiva: "*Now I, the father, having deposited his seed, withdraw from this womb*" (100).

Epilogue

1. This period was arguably the first in which critics broke substantially with Turnerian ideas about the importance of the frontier. For more on this era of Western scholarship, see Fred Erisman's "Early Western Literary Scholars" in Westbrook's *A Literary History of the American West* (303–16).

2. The importance of Bakhtin to recent criticism of Western literature should not be underestimated. *Western American Literature,* for one, ran a 1998 issue (33, no. 2) featuring Bakhtinian approaches to the frontier, a methodology summarized in the introduction to the issue by Reuben Ellis:

> This view of language has important implications for how we approach reading. A literary text—in particular the novel, for Bakhtin, is not a monologue directed at passive readers but, as he puts it, "a rejoinder in a given dialogue" with them. More significantly, the text is itself internally dialogic. Bakhtin notices that Dostoevsky's characters habitually alter and qualify their thoughts and remarks, sometimes in reaction to other characters and sometimes, it seems, in self-consciousness about what a reader might say in response. For Bakhtin, the incessant shuffling of Dostoevsky's characters suggests more broadly the essential nature of literature. "No living word relates to its object in a *singular* way," he writes; "between the word and its object, between the word and the speaking subject, there exists an elastic environment of other, alien words about the same subject, the same theme." In this view of the literary text, the author loses the role of grand impressario and becomes just another speaker in the dialogue or *polyphony* of the text. Ideas compete, characters become larger and more surprising than the author's original vision of them, and the world of the book becomes an unpredictable conversation. For Bakhtin, polyphony is more than a description of style or an account of how the creative process enlarges an author's original design. Polyphony suggests more broadly a sense of ethics that, like characters in a novel or perhaps any object of our perception, should not so readily be predicted, controlled, or typed; they are, as Bakhtin puts it, "unfinalized." (121–22)

3. Forrest G. Robinson, "The New Historicism and the Old West," in *New West— Old West: Centennial Essays,* ed. Barbara Howard Meldrum (Moscow: University of Idaho Press, 1993), 80.

4. On this point, Richard Aquila succinctly describes the multifarious nature of the popular western. In *Wanted Dead or Alive: The American West in Popular Culture* (Urbana: University of Illinois Press, 1996), he writes that

the Western has served as a record of American attitudes. For the most part these are conflicting attitudes: nostalgia and progress, individualism and community, violence and love, hatred and respect for Native Americans, and action and order. As a cultural form the Western thrust simultaneously forward and backward, was both progressive and regressive, prompted the advance of civilization while celebrating a primitive past. Moreover, it was an adaptable form; once established, the Western fit the needs of different writers and different audiences. . . . The mythic nature of the Western lies less in any godlike quality of the hero or any legendary attributes of setting or plot than in its deep and often contradictory appeals to American readers. (65)

WORKS CITED

Acocella, Joan. "Cather and the Academy." In *The Best American Essays 1996,* edited by Geoffrey C. Ward, 1–31. New York: Houghton-Mifflin, 1996.

Acuna, Rudolfo. *Occupied America: A History of Chicanos.* New York: Harper, 1981.

Adams, Charles L. "Frank Waters." In *A Literary History of the American West,* edited by Max Westbrook et al., 935–57. Fort Worth: Texas Christian University Press, 1987.

———. "Frank Waters." In *Updating the Literary West,* edited by Max Westbrook, 854–60. Fort Worth: Western Literature Association/Texas Christian University Press, 1997.

Anderson, Frederick, ed. *A Pen Warmed Up in Hell: Mark Twain in Protest.* New York: Perennial Library, 1972.

Aquila, Richard. *Wanted Dead or Alive: The American West in Popular Culture.* Urbana: University of Illinois Press, 1996.

Arnold, Marilyn. "The Integrating Vision of Bishop Latour in Willa Cather's *Death Comes for the Archbishop.*" *Literature and Belief* 8 (1988): 38–57.

Bakhtin, Mikhail. *The Bakhtin Reader.* Edited by Pam Morris. New York: Edward Arnold, 1994.

———. *The Dialogic Imagination: Four Essays.* Austin: The University of Texas Press, 1990.

Bakker, J. "The Western: Can It Be Great?" *Dutch Quarterly Review of Anglo-American Letters* 14, no. 2 (1984): 140–63.

Barthes, Roland. *A Barthes Reader.* New York: Hill and Wang, 1987.

Beale, Howard K. *Theodore Roosevelt and the Rise of America to World Power.* Baltimore: The Johns Hopkins Press, 1956.

Berkhofer, Robert F. Jr. *The White Man's Indian.* New York: Vintage Books, 1979.

Blackburn, Alexander. *A Sunrise Brighter Still: The Visionary Novels of Frank Waters.* Athens: Swallow Press/Ohio University Press, 1991.

Boggan, J. R. "The Regeneration of 'Roaring Camp.'" *Nineteenth-Century Fiction* 22, no. 3 (1967): 271–80.

Bohlke, L. Brent, ed. *Willa Cather in Person.* Lincoln: University of Nebraska Press, 1986.

Bold, Christine. "How the Western Ends: Fenimore Cooper to Frederic Remington." *Western American Literature* 17, no. 2 (1982): 117–35.

———. *Selling The Wild West: Popular Western Fiction, 1860 to 1960.* Bloomington: Indiana University Press, 1987.

Brooks, Cleanth, and Robert Penn Warren, eds. *Understanding Fiction.* New York: Crofts, 1943.

Brown, Allen S. "The Christ Motif in 'The Luck of Roaring Camp.'" *Papers of the Michigan Academy of Science, Arts, and Letters* 46 (1961): 629.

Brown, Bill. *Reading the West: An Anthology of Dime Westerns.* Boston: Bedford, 1997.

Bulger, Thomas. "Mark Twain's Ambivalent Utopianism." *Studies in American Fiction* 17, no. 2 (1989) 235–42.

Burton, Linda. "For Better or Worse: Tennessee and His Partner: A New Approach to Bret Harte." *The Arizona Quarterly* 36, no. 2 (1980): 211–16.

Casey, Thomas M. "Mariology and Christology in *Death Comes for the Archbishop.*" *Willa Cather Pioneer Memorial Newsletter and Review* 35, no. 3 (1991): 22–25.

Cather, Willa. *Death Comes for the Archbishop.* New York: Vintage, 1971.

———. *My Antonia.* Boston: Houghton Mifflin, 1946.

———. *Willa Cather on Writing.* New York: Knopf, 1949.

Cawelti, John G. *The Six-Gun Mystique.* Bowling Green, Ohio: Bowling Green State University Popular Press, 1984.

———. *The Six-Gun Mystique Sequel.* Bowling Green, Ohio: Bowling Green State University Popular Press, 1999.

———. "What Rough Beast—New Westerns?" *ANQ: A Quarterly Journal of Short Articles, Notes, and Reviews* 9, no. 3 (1996): 4–15.

Chessman, C. Wallace. *Theodore Roosevelt and the Politics of Power.* Boston: Little, Brown and Company, 1969.

Child, Lydia Maria. *Hobomok and Other Writings on Indians by Lydia Maria Child.* Edited by Carolyn Karcher. New Brunswick, N.J.: Rutgers University Press, 1986.

Christensen, Peter G. "Minority Interaction in John Rollin Ridge's *The Life and Adventures of Joaquin Murieta.*" *MELUS* 17, no. 2 (1991–92): 61–72.

Cohen, Judith Beth. "Father Martinez: Folk Hero or Dangerous Infidel? Rereading Willa Cather's *Death Comes for the Archbishop.*" In *Rethinking American Literature,* edited by Lil Brannon and Brenda M. Greene, 146–59. Urbana, Ill.: National Council of Teachers of English, 1997.

Conner, William F. "The Euchring of Tennessee: A Reexamination of Bret Harte's 'Tennessee's Partner.'" *Studies in Short Fiction* 17, no. 2 (1980): 113–20.

Cooper, James Fenimore. *The Complete Works of J. Fenimore Cooper.* New York: G. P. Putnam's Sons, 1893.

Crane, Stephen. *The Red Badge of Courage and Other Stories.* Edited by Pascal Covici Jr. New York: Penguin, 1991.

Danziger, Marlies K., ed. *An Introduction to Literary Criticism.* Boston: D. C. Heath, 1961.

Davidson, Arnold E. *Coyote Country.* Durham, N.C.: Duke University Press, 1994.

Davis, David B. "Ten-Gallon Hero." In *The Western: A Collection of Critical Essays,* edited by James K. Folsom, 15–30. Englewood Cliffs, N.J.: Prentice-Hall, 1979.

Davis, Robert Murray, ed. *Owen Wister's West, Selected Articles.* Albuquerque: University of New Mexico Press, 1987.

Deloria, Vine Jr., ed. *Frank Waters: Man and Mystic.* Athens, Ohio: Swallow Press, 1993.

DeVoto, Bernard. "Birth of an Art." In *Western Writing,* edited by Gerald W. Haslam, 9. Albuquerque: University of New Mexico Press, 1974.

Diana, Vanessa Holford. "'Hanging in the Heart of Chaos': Bi-Cultural Limbo, Self-(Re)presentation, and the White Audience in Zitkala-Sa's *American Indian Stories.*" *Cimarron Review* 121 (October 1997): 154–72.

DiNunzio, Mario R., ed. *Theodore Roosevelt: An American Mind: A Selection from His Writings.* New York: St. Martin's Press, 1994.

Dollar, J. Gerard. "Desert Landscapes and the 'Male Gaze': Cather's *Death Comes for the Archbishop.*" *Willa Cather Pioneer Memorial Newsletter and Review* 42, no. 1 (1998): 6–9.

Duckett, Margaret. "Bret Harte and the Indians of Northern California." *Huntington Library Quarterly* 18 (November 1954): 59–83.

———. "Bret Harte's Portrayal of Half-Breeds." *American Literature* 25 (May 1953): 193–212.

———. "Plain Language from Bret Harte." *Nineteenth Century Fiction* 11 (March 1957) 241–60.

Dyer, Thomas G. *Theodore Roosevelt and the Idea of Race.* Baton Rouge: Louisiana State University Press, 1980.

Egbert, Oliver S. "The Pig-Tailed China Boys Out West." *Western Humanities Review* 12 (Spring 1958): 175–77.

Ellis, Reuben. "A Thousand Frontiers: An Introduction to Dialogue and the American West." *Western American Literature* 33, no. 2 (1998): 117–24.

Erisman, Fred. "Early Western Literary Scholars." In *A Literary History of the American West,* edited by Max Westbrook et al., 303–16. Fort Worth: Texas Christian University Press, 1987.

Erwin, Robert. "Injuns." *The Virginia Quarterly Review* 72, no. 3 (1996): 493–502.

Etulain, Richard W. "The Historical Development of the Western." In *The Popular Western: Essays toward a Definition,* edited by Richard W. Etulain and Michael T. Marsden, 75–84. Bowling Green, Ohio: Bowling Green State University Popular Press, 1974.

———. "Origins of the Western." In *Critical Essays on the Western American Novel,* edited by William T. Pilkington, 56–60. Boston, Mass.: G. K. Hall & Co., 1980.

———. "Riding Point: The Western and Its Interpreters." In *The Popular Western: Essays toward a Definition,* edited by Richard W. Etulain and Michael T. Marsden, 5–9. Bowling Green, Ohio: Bowling Green State University Popular Press, 1974.

Etulain, Richard W., and Michael T. Marsden, eds. *The Popular Western: Essays toward a Definition.* Bowling Green, Ohio: Bowling Green State University Popular Press, 1974.

Fender, Stephen. "The Prodigal in a Far Country Chawing of Husks: Mark Twain's Search for a Style in the West." *Modern Language Review* 71 (1976): 737–56.

Fetterly, Judith. "'My Sister! My Sister!': The Rhetoric of Catharine Sedgwick's *Hope Leslie.*" *American Literature* 70, no. 3 (1998): 491–516.

Fiedler, Leslie. *Love and Death in the American Novel.* New York: Criterion, 1960.

———. *The Return of the Vanishing American.* New York: Stein and Day, 1969.

Fisher, Dexter. "Zitkala Sa: The Evolution of a Writer." *American Indian Quarterly* 5, no. 3 (1979): 229–38.

Fisher-Wirth, Ann W. "Dispossession and Redemption in the Novels of Willa Cather." In *Cather Studies.* Vol. 1, edited by Susan J. Rosowski, 36–54. Lincoln: University of Nebraska Press, 1990.

Folsom, James K., ed. *The Western: A Collection of Critical Essays.* Englewood Cliffs, N.J.: Prentice-Hall, 1979.

Fruss, Phyllis, and Stanley Corkin. "Willa Cather's 'Pioneer' Novels and [Not New, Not Old] Historical Reading." *College Literature* 26, no. 2 (1999): 36–58.

Gallagher, Tag. "Shootout at the Genre Corral: Problems in the 'Evolution' of the Western." In *Film Genre Reader II,* edited by Barry Keith Grant, 246–60. Austin: University of Texas Press, 1995.

Gardiner, Jane. "'A More Splendid Necromancy': Mark Twain's *Connecticut Yankee* and the Electrical Revolution." *Studies in the Novel* 19, no. 4 (1987): 448–58.

Garland, Hamlin. *Main-Travelled Roads.* New York: Holt, Rinehart and Winston, 1967.

Gatewood, William B. Jr. *Theodore Roosevelt and the Art of Controversy: Episodes of the White House Years.* Baton Rouge: Louisiana State University Press, 1970.

Goodman, Audrey. "The Immeasurable Possession of Air: Willa Cather and Southwestern Romance." *Arizona Quarterly* 55, no. 4 (1999): 49–78.

Gould, Lewis L. *The Presidency of Theodore Roosevelt.* Lawrence: University Press of Kansas, 1991.

Grey, Zane. *Riders of the Purple Sage.* New York: Pocket Books, 1912.

Grosz, Elizabeth. "Irigaray's Notion of Sexual Morphology." In *Reimagining Women: Representations of Women in Culture,* edited by Shirley Neuman, 182–95. Toronto: University of Toronto Press, 1993.

Gussman, Deborah. "Inalienable Rights: Fictions of Political Identity in *Hobomok* and *The Scarlet Letter.*" *College Literature* 22, no. 2 (1995): 58–80.

Gutierrez-Jones, Carl. "Haunting Presences and the New Western History: Reading Repetition, Negotiating Trauma." *Arizona Quarterly* 53, no. 2 (1997): 134–51.

Haller, Evelyn. "*Death Comes for the Archbishop:* A Map of Intersecting Worlds." *Willa Cather Pioneer Memorial Newsletter and Review* 34, no. 3 (1990): 15–21.

Harrison, Dick. *Unnamed Country: The Struggle for a Canadian Prairie Fiction.* Edmonton: University of Alberta Press, 1977.

Harte, Bret. *The Luck of Roaring Camp and Other Stories.* New York: Lancer Books, Inc., 1968.

———. *The Outcasts of Poker Flat and Other Tales.* New York: New American Library, 1961.

——. *Condensed Novels. New Burlesques.* New York: Collier, 1902.

Harte, Geoffrey Bret, ed. *The Letters of Bret Harte.* Boston: Houghton Mifflin, 1926.

Haslam, Gerald W., ed. *Western Writing.* Albuquerque: University of New Mexico Press, 1974.

Heyne, Eric, ed. *Desert, Garden, Margin, Range: Literature of the American Frontier.* New York: Twayne, 1992.

Hoefel, Roseanne. "Writing, Performance, Activism: Zitkala-Sa and Pauline Johnson." In *Native American Women in Literature and Culture,* edited by Susan Castillo and Victor DaRosa, 107–18. Porto, Portugal: Fernando Pessoa University Press, 1997.

Honeyman, A. V. D., ed. *The Danites: and Other Choice Selections from the Writings of Joaquin Miller, 'the Poet of the Sierras.'* [online] The Making of America digital library: <http://moa.umdl.umich.edu/moa>.

Hutchinson, W. H. "Virgins, Villains, and Varmints." In *The Western: A Collection of Critical Essays,* edited by James K. Folsom, 31–49. Englewood Cliffs, N.J.: Prentice Hall, 1979.

Irigaray, Luce. *The Irigaray Reader.* Edited by Margaret Whitford. Oxford: Basil Blackwell, Ltd., 1991.

Jackson, Helen Hunt. *Ramona.* Boston: Little, Brown, 1921.

Jackson, Joseph Henry. Introduction to *The Life and Adventures of Joaquin Murieta, the Celebrated California Bandit.* Norman: University of Oklahoma Press, 1955.

Jefferson, Thomas. *Writings.* New York: The Library of America, 1984.

Johnson, Susan Lee. "Gift Horses: Influence, Insurgence, Interdisciplinarity in Western Studies." *Western American Literature* 34, no. 1 (1999): 78–91.

Jones, Daryl E. *The Dime Novel Western.* Bowling Green, Ohio: Bowling Green State University Popular Press, 1978.

Karcher, Carolyn. *The First Woman in the Republic: A Cultural Biography of Lydia Maria Child.* Durham, N.C.: Duke University Press, 1994.

Kent, Thomas L. "The Formal Conventions of the Dime Novel." *Journal of Popular Culture* 16, no. 1 (1982): 37–47.

Kime, Wayne R. "Huck Among the Indians: Mark Twain and Richard Irving Dodge's *The Plains of the Great West and Their Inhabitants. Western American Literature* 24, no. 4 (1990): 321–33.

Kirkland, Carolyn. *A New Home, Who'll Follow?* New Brunswick, N.J.: Rutgers University Press, 1990.

Kolodny, Annette. *The Land Before Her: Fantasy and Experience of the American Frontiers, 1630–1860.* Chapel Hill: University of North Carolina Press, 1984.

Kowalewski, Michael, ed. *Reading the West: New Essays on the Literature of the American West.* New York: Cambridge University Press, 1996.

Kroeber, Karl. "American Indian Persistence and Resurgence." *boundary 2* 19, no. 3 (1992): 1–25.

LaFarge, Oliver. *Laughing Boy.* Boston: Houghton Mifflin, 1957.

Lambert, Neal. "Owen Wister's Virginian: The Genesis of a Cultural Hero." *Western American Literature* 6 (1971): 99–107.

Larsen, Lance. "Cather's Controversial Portrayal of Martinez." In *Willa Cather: Family, Community, and History,* edited by John J. Murphy, 275–80. Provo, Utah: Brigham Young University Humanities Publications Center, 1990.

Lavender, David. "The Tyranny of Facts." In *Old Southwest, New Southwest: Essays on a Region and Its Literature,* edited by Judy Nolte Lensink, 63–73. Tucson, Ariz.: The Tucson Public Library, 1987.

Lawrence, D. H. *Studies in Classic American Literature.* New York: Penguin, 1961.

Lawson, Benjamin S. "Joaquin Miller." In *Dictionary of Literary Biography.* Vol. 186, *Nineteenth-Century American Western Writers,* edited by Robert L. Gale, 238–46. Pittsburgh: The Gale Group, 1997.

Lee, L. L., and Merrill Lewis, eds. *Women, Women Writers, and the West.* Troy, N.Y.: The Whitson Publishing Company, 1979.

Lewis, R. W. B. *The American Adam: Innocence, Tragedy, and Tradition in the Nineteenth Century.* Chicago: University of Chicago Press, 1955.

Limerick, Patricia Nelson. "Layer Upon Layer of Memory in the American West." *The Chronicle of Higher Education* 3 (March 2000): B4–B7.

Lindemann, Marilee. "Con-quest or In-quest? Cather's Mythic Impulse in *Death Comes for the Archbishop.*" *Willa Cather Pioneer Memorial Newsletter and Review* 31, no. 3 (1987) 15–18.

London, Jack. *Martin Eden.* New York: Penguin, 1984.

Lowe, John. "Space and Freedom in the Golden Republic: Yellow Bird's *The Life and Adventures of Joaquin Murieta, the Celebrated California Bandit.*" *Studies in American Indian Literatures* 4, no. 2–3 (1992): 106–22.

Lyon, Thomas J. *Frank Waters.* New York: Twayne, 1973.

Maguire, James H. "Fictions of the West." In *The Columbia History of the American Novel,* edited by Emory Elliot, 437–64. New York: Columbia University Press, 1991.

Marks, Frederick W. III. *Velvet on Iron: The Diplomacy of Theodore Roosevelt.* Lincoln: University of Nebraska Press, 1979.

Marovitz, Sanford E. "Testament of a Patriot: The Virginian, The Tenderfoot, and Owen Wister." *Texas Studies in Literature and Language* 15, no. 3 (1973): 551–73.

Marx, Leo. *The Machine in the Garden: Technology and the Pastoral Idea in America.* New York: Oxford, 1964.

McCullough, David. *Brave Companions: Portraits in History.* New York: Prentice Hall Press, 1992.

Meldrum, Barbara Howard, ed. *Old West—New West: Centennial Essays.* Moscow: University of Idaho Press, 1993.

Meltzer, Milton, and Patricia G. Holland, eds. *Lydia Maria Child: Selected Letters, 1817–1880.* Amherst: University of Massachusetts Press, 1982.

Michelson, Bruce. "Realism, Romance, and Dynamite: The Quarrel of *A Connecticut Yankee in King Arthur's Court.*" *The New England Quarterly* 64, no. 4 (1991): 609–32.

Miller, Joaquin. *First Fam'lies of the Sierras.* Chicago: Jansen, McClurg and Co., 1876.

Miller, Perry. *Errand into the Wilderness*. Cambridge: The Belknap Press of Harvard University Press, 1956.

Milton, John R. *The Novel of the American West*. Lincoln: University of Nebraska Press, 1980.

Mitchell, Domhnall. "Acts of Intercourse: 'Miscegenation' in Three 19th Century American Novels." *American Studies in Scandinavia* 27 (1995): 126–41.

Mitchell, Lee Clark. *Westerns: Making the Man in Fiction and Film*. Chicago: University of Chicago Press, 1996.

Mondragon, Maria. "'The [Safe] White Side of the Line': History and Disguise in John Rollin Ridge's *The Life and Adventures of Joaquin Murieta: the Celebrated California Bandit*." *American Transcendental Quarterly* 8, no. 3 (1994): 173–87.

Morley-Gaines, Ann-Janine. "Of Menace and Men: The Sexual Tensions of the American Frontier Metaphor." *Soundings: An Interdisciplinary Journal* 64, no. 2 (1981): 132–49.

Morrow, Patrick D. "Bret Harte, Mark Twain, and the San Francisco Circle." In *A Literary History of the American West*, edited by Max Westbrook et al., 339–58. Fort Worth: Texas Christian University Press, 1987.

Murphy, John J., ed. *Critical Essays on Willa Cather*. Boston: G. K. Hall and Co., 1984.

Neider, Charles, ed. *The Autobiography of Mark Twain*. New York: The Perennial Library, 1917.

Nelson, Dana D. *The Word in Black and White, Reading "Race" in American Literature, 1638–1837*. New York: Oxford University Press, 1992.

Nemerov, Alexander. *Frederic Remington and Turn-of-the-Century America*. New Haven: Yale University Press, 1995.

Neuman, Shirley. "'An appearance walking in a forest the sexes burn': Autobiography and the Construction of the Feminine Body." *Signature: A Journal of Theory and Canadian Literature* 2 (Winter 1989): 1–26.

Norris, Frank. *McTeague: a Story of San Francisco*. New York: Norton, 1977.

O'Brien, Sharon. "Becoming Noncanonical: The Case Against Willa Cather." In *Reading in America: Literature and Social History*, edited by Cathy N. Davidson, 240–58. Baltimore: Johns Hopkins University Press, 1989.

O'Connor, Richard. *Bret Harte: A Biography*. Boston: Little, Brown, 1966.

Okker, Patricia. "Native American Literatures and the Canon: The Case of Zitkala-Sa." In *American Realism and the Canon*, edited by Tom Quirk and Gary Scharnhorst, 87–101. Newark: University of Delaware Press, 1994.

Oliver, Nancy S. "New Manifest Destiny in *A Connecticut Yankee in King Arthur's Court*." *Mark Twain Journal* 21, no. 4 (1983): 28–32.

Ostwalt, Conrad. "Boundaries and Marginality in Willa Cather's Frontier Fiction." In *Dissent and Marginality: Essays on the Borders of Literature and Religion*, edited by Kiyoshi Tsuchiya, 102–14. New York: St. Martin's Press, 1997.

Pemberton, T. Edgar. *The Life of Bret Harte*. London: C. Arthur Pearson, Ltd., 1903.

Pilkington, William T., ed. *Critical Essays on the Western American Novel*. Boston: G. K. Hall and Co., 1980.

Pokagon, Simon. *O-gi-maw-kwe mit-i-gwa-ki (Queen of the Woods)*. Hartford, Mich.: C. H. Engle, 1899.

Powell, Timothy B. *Beyond the Binary: Reconstructing Cultural Identity in a Multicultural Context*. New Brunswick, N.J.: Rutgers University Press, 1999.

Pressman, Richard S. "A Connecticut Yankee in Merlin's Cave: The Role of Contradiction in Mark Twain's Novel." *American Literary Realism* 16, no. 1 (1983): 58–72.

Prucha, Francis Paul, ed. *Documents of United States Indian Policy*. Lincoln: University of Nebraska Press, 1990.

Randall, John H. III. "Summary of *Death Comes for the Archbishop:* The Cathedral and the Stagecoach." In *Critical Essays on Willa Cather*, edited by John J. Murphy, 250–53. Boston: G. K. Hall and Co., 1984.

Reiss, Edmund. Afterword to *A Connecticut Yankee in King Arthur's Court*. New York: Harper and Row, 1963.

Remington, Frederic. *Frederic Remington: Paintings and Sculpture*. New York: Wings Books, 1993.

Reynolds, Guy. "The Ideology of Cather's Catholic Progressivism: *Death Comes for the Archbishop*." *Cather Studies* 3 (1996): 1–30.

Ricou, Laurence. *Vertical Man, Horizontal World: Man and Landscape in Canadian Prairie Fiction*. Vancouver: University of British Columbia Press, 1973.

Ridge, John Rollin. *The Life and Adventures of Joaquin Murieta, the Celebrated California Bandit*. Norman: University of Oklahoma Press, 1955.

Robinson, Forrest G. *Having It Both Ways: Self-Subversion in Western Popular Classics*. Albuquerque: University of New Mexico Press, 1993.

———. "The Virginian and Molly in Paradise: How Sweet Is It?" *Western American Literature* 21, no. 1 (1986): 27–38.

Romero, Lora. "Domesticity and Fiction." In *The Columbia History of the American Novel*, edited by Emory Elliot, 110–29. New York: Columbia University Press, 1991.

———. "Vanishing Americans: Gender, Empire, and New Historicism." *American Literature* 63, no. 3 (1991): 385–404.

Roosevelt, Theodore. *Autobiography*. New York: Charles Scribner's Sons, 1929.

———. *The Roosevelt Book: Selections from the Writings of Theodore Roosevelt*. New York: Charles Scribner's Sons, 1909.

Rosowski, Susan J. *The Voyage Perilous: Willa Cather's Romanticism*. Lincoln: University of Nebraska Press, 1986.

———. "The Western Hero as Logos, or, Unmaking Meaning." *Western American Literature* 32, no. 3 (1997): 269–92.

Rousch, Jan. "Research in Western American Literature, 1997–1998." *Western American Literature* 34, no. 1 (1999): 4–5.

Rowe, John Carlos. "Highway Robbery: 'Indian Removal,' The Mexican-American War, and American Identity in *The Life and Adventures of Joaquin Murieta*." *Novel: A Forum on Fiction* 31, no. 2 (1998): 149–73.

Rubin, Gayle. "The Traffic in Women: Notes toward a Political Economy of Sex." In *Toward an Anthropology of Women*, edited by Rayna R. Reiter. New York: Monthly Review Press, 1975.

Ruoff, A. LaVonne Brown. *American Indian Literatures, an Introduction*. New York: Modern Language Association, 1990.

Ryan, Steven P. "'Snake Root': Latour's Descent into Hell in *Death Comes for the Archbishop*." *Willa Cather Pioneer Memorial Newsletter and Review* 41, no. 2 (1997): 33–36.

Samuels, Peggy, and Harold Samuels, eds. *The Collected Writings of Frederic Remington*. Garden City, N.Y.: Doubleday and Company, 1979.

Schaefer, Jack. *Shane*. New York: Bantam Books, 1983.

Scharnhorst, Gary. *Bret Harte*. New York: Twayne, 1992.

———. "The Virginian as a Founding Father." *Arizona Quarterly* 40, no. 3 (1984): 227–41.

Schroeder, Fred E. H. "The Development of the Super-ego on the American Frontier." *Soundings* 57 (Summer 1974): 189–205.

Scott, Sir Walter. *Kenilworth*. New York: A. L. Burt Co., 1900.

Sedgwick, Eve. *Between Men: English Literature and Male Homosocial Desire*. New York: Columbia University Press, 1985.

Seelye, John. Introduction to *The Virginian*, by Owen Wister. New York: Penguin, 1988.

———. *Stories of the Old West: Tales of the Mining Camp, Cavalry Troop, & Cattle Ranch*. New York: Penguin, 1994.

Shakespeare, William. *The Complete Pelican Shakespeare*. New York: The Viking Press, 1969.

Shaw, Patrick. "Women and the Father: Psychosexual Ambiguity in *Death Comes for the Archbishop*." *American Imago* 46, no. 1 (1989): 61–76.

Simmons, Michael K. "Nationalism and the Dime Novel." *Studies in the Humanities* 9, no. 1 (1981): 39–44.

Slotkin, Richard. *The Fatal Environment: The Myth of the Frontier in the Age of Industrialization, 1800–1890*. New York: Atheneum, 1985.

———. *Gunfighter Nation: The Myth of the Frontier in Twentieth-Century America*. New York: Harper Perennial, 1993.

———. *Regeneration Through Violence: The Mythology of the American Frontier, 1600–1860*. Middletown: Conn.: Wesleyan University Press, 1973.

Smith, Jeanne. "'A Second Tongue': The Trickster's Voice in the Works of Zitkala-Sa." In *Tricksterism in Turn-of-the-Century American Literature: A Multicultural Perspective*, edited by Elizabeth Ammons and Annette White-Parks. Boston: Tufts University, 1994.

Smith, Henry Nash. *Mark Twain: The Development of a Writer*. Cambridge, Mass.: The Belknap Press, 1962.

———. *Virgin Land: The American West as Symbol and Myth*. Cambridge: Harvard University Press, 1950.

Stauffer, Helen Winter, and Susan Rosowski, eds. *Women and Western American Literature*. Troy, N.Y.: The Whitson Publishing Company, 1982.

Stegner, Wallace. Introduction to *The Outcasts of Poker Flat and Other Tales*, by Bret Harte. New York: New American Library, 1961.

Stewart, George R. Jr. *Bret Harte: Argonaut and Exile.* Boston: Houghton Mifflin, 1931.

Stouck, David. *Willa Cather's Imagination.* Lincoln: University of Nebraska Press, 1975.

Stout, Mary. "Zitkala-Sa: The Literature of Politics." In *Coyote Was Here: Essays on Contemporary Native American Literary and Political Mobilization,* edited by Bo Scholer. *The Dolphin* 9 (April 1984): 70–78.

Sumida, Stephen H. "Re-evaluating Twain's Novel of Hawaii." *American Literature* 61, no. 4 (1989): 586–609.

Susag, Dorothea M.. "Zitkala-Sa (Gertrude Simmons Bonnin): A Power(full) Literary Voice." *Studies in American Indian Literatures* 5, no. 4 (1994): 3–24.

Thomas, Susie. *Willa Cather.* Savage, Md.: Barnes and Noble Books, 1990.

Tompkins, Jane. *West of Everything: The Inner Life of Westerns.* New York: Oxford University Press, 1992.

Turner, Frederick Jackson. *The Significance of the Frontier in American History.* New York: Holt, Rinehart, and Winston, 1920.

Twain, Mark. *The Autobiography of Mark Twain.* New York: The Perennial Library, 1917.

———. *A Connecticut Yankee in King Arthur's Court.* New York: Harper & Row, 1963.

———. *Letters from the Earth.* New York: Harper & Row, 1938.

———. *A Pen Warmed Up in Hell: Mark Twain in Protest.* Edited by Frederick Anderson. New York: Perennial Library, 1972.

———. *Roughing It.* New York: Viking Penguin, 1981.

———. *Your Personal Mark Twain.* New York: International Publishers, 1969.

Utley, Robert M. *The Indian Frontier of the American West, 1846–1890.* Albuquerque: University of New Mexico Press, 1984.

Vizenor, Gerald. *Narrative Chance.* Norman: University of Oklahoma Press, 1993.

Vorpahl, Ben Merchant. "Roosevelt, Turner, Wister, and Remington." In *Literary History of the American West,* edited by Max Westbrook et al., 276–302. Fort Worth: Texas Christian University Press, 1987.

———, ed. *My Dear Wister: The Frederic Remington–Owen Wister Letters.* Palo Alto, Calif.: The American West Publishing Company, 1972.

Walker, Don D. "Notes toward a Literary Criticism of the Western." In *The Popular Western: Essays toward a Definition,* edited by Richard W. Etulain and Michael T. Marsden, 86–100. Bowling Green, Ohio: Bowling Green State University Popular Press, 1975.

Warner, Ted J. "*Death Comes for the Archbishop:* A Novel Way of Making History." In *Willa Cather: Family, Community, and History,* edited by John J. Murphy, 265–73. Provo, Utah: Brigham Young University Humanities Publications Center, 1990.

Waters, Frank. *The Man Who Killed the Deer.* Athens, Ohio: Swallow Press, 1985.

Westbrook, Max et al., eds., *A Literary History of the American West.* Fort Worth: Texas Christian University Press, 1987.

———. *Updating the Literary West.* Fort Worth: Texas Christian University Press, 1997.

Wexler, Laura. "Tender Violence: Literary Eavesdropping, Domestic Fiction, and Educational Reform." In *The Culture of Sentiment: Race, Gender, and Sentimentality in*

Nineteenth-Century America, edited by Shirley Samuels, 3–38. New York: Oxford University Press, 1992.

White, G. Edward. *The Eastern Establishment and the Western Experience: The West of Frederic Remington, Theodore Roosevelt, and Owen Wister.* New Haven: Yale University Press, 1968.

Wiget, Andrew. *Native American Literature.* Boston: Twayne, 1985.

———, ed. *Critical Essays on Native American Literature.* Boston: G. K. Hall, 1985.

Williams, Deborah. "Losing Nothing, Comprehending Everything: Learning to Read Both the Old World and the New in *Death Comes for the Archbishop.*" *Cather Studies* 4 (1999): 80–96.

Williams, William Carlos. *In The American Grain.* New York: New Directions, 1956.

Wister, Owen. *Roosevelt.* New York: Macmillan, 1930.

———. "The Evolution of the Cow-Puncher." In *Owen Wister's West, Selected Articles,* edited by Robert Murray Davis. Albuquerque: University of New Mexico Press, 1987.

———. *The Virginian.* New York: Viking Penguin, 1988.

Work, James C. *Prose and Poetry of the American West.* Lincoln: University of Nebraska Press, 1990.

Wright, Will. *Sixguns and Society: A Structural Study of the Western.* Berkeley: University of California Press, 1975.

Zitkala-Sa. *American Indian Stories.* Lincoln: University of Nebraska Press, 1985.

———. *Old Indian Legends.* Boston: London, Ginn and Company, 1901.

INDEX

American Adam. *See* Garden myth
American Indian tribes and cultures, as rendered in fiction
Cherokee, 120–21
Comanche, 86, 202 n. 16
Gosiute, 84–85
Mohican, 46–48
Navajo, 146–48, 149, 151
Pueblo, 144–45, 157–71
Sioux (Dakota), 124–32
Wampanoag, 37–48
See also Cather, Willa; Child, Lydia Maria; Cooper, James Fenimore; Ridge, John Rollin; Sedgwick, Catharine; Waters, Frank; Zitkala-Sa
American Indians, 23, 25, 35, 74–76, 84–86, 88–89, 112–33, 142–48, 151, 194 n. 6
earliest writing in English by, 112–13, 205 n. 1
in early frontier novels, 36–49
end of federal wars with, 7
mixed blood, and liminal cultural status, 120, 124–25, 157–59, 162
as represented by Frederic Remington, 8
role in TV westerns, ix
in Turner's Frontier Thesis, 3
Anglo-Saxonism, 9–14, 15, 16, 79–80
anti-western, x
Austen, Jane, 104–5
Austin, Mary, xii
authorial intention, interpretive problems related to, xiv

Bakhtin, Mikhail, xviii, 36, 174–75, 182 n. 8, 219 n. 2
Barthes, Roland, 193 n. 54
Beadle, Alfred, xix
Bold, Christine, xi, 12, 97, 192 n. 48

Canadian Western writing, x, 181 n.
Cather, Willa, xii, 134–53, 174
  Death Comes for the Archbishop, 134–53
    Indian perspective in, 142–48, 151
    role of women in, 136–42
    treatment of schismatic priests, 135
  My Ántonia, 136
  O, Pioneers!, 136
Cawelti, John, xi, 24–25, 84, 183 n. 12
Child, Lydia Maria, xii, 34–49, 174
  "An Appeal for the Indians," 45
  Hobomok, 37–45
  views on American Indians, 45–46
childbirth, 67, 100, 165
chivalric tradition, relation to popular west, 1, 13, 83, 92, 97, 203 n. 23
"civilization versus savagery," xi, xiv, 3, 24–28, 41–43, 48, 74, 92–93, 103, 113, 151, 161
  as central frontier paradigm, x, 24–25
  relationship to Garden myth, 25–26
  in works of Frederic Remington, 8–12
Cody, Buffalo Bill, 90–91
Cooper, James Fenimore, xii, xix, 1, 15, 16, 25, 28, 38–39, 96–97, 104, 105, 109, 123, 143, 152, 194 n. 11

233

The Last of the Mohicans, 46–48
The Pioneers, 48
The Wept of Wish-ton-Wish, 47
Crane, Stephen, xii, 15, 101–3
"The Bride Comes to Yellow Sky," 101–3
cross-dressing, 58–59, 67–71
Cultural Studies, xx, 182 n. 10
Custer, George Armstrong, 84

Davidson, Arnold E., x, 156
dime novels, 34, 97, 101, 114, 115, 207 n. 9
domestic fiction. *See* sentimental fiction

Etulain, Richard, xiv, 190 n. 40, 191 n. 46, 195 n. 1

family, 56, 61–62, 65–66, 93–94, 165–71
Faulkner, William, 155
Fetterley, Judith, 35–36
Fiedler, Leslie, xi, 181 n. 2, 196 n. 9
film, western, 173, 184 n. 21
    relation to western literature, xix
Ford, John, xix, 173
formula western. *See* popular western
frontier, xvii, 8–9, 11, 75–77, 83, 93, 185 nn. 2–5
    Frederick Jackson Turner's thesis about, xviii, 2–5, 176–77
    historical closing of, 4–5
    relation to geographic West, xviii

Garden myth, 26, 54–55, 77–78, 81–82, 148–51, 192 nn. 49–51
Garland, Hamlin, xiii–xiv
    Main-Travelled Roads, xiii–xiv
gender roles, ix, xvi–xvii, 21, 40, 45, 48, 110, 125, 136–42, 165–71, 196 n. 7
    construction of, in popular western writing, ix, xvi–xvii, 52, 95–96, 104–5
    and cultural constructions of homosociality/homosexuality, 52, 62–72, 134
    subversion of traditional, 52–62, 114–15, 127–28, 130–32
    See also Cather, Willa; Child, Lydia Maria; Harte, Bret; Waters, Frank; Wister, Owen; Zitkala-Sa
Grey, Zane, 27, 141, 213 n. 3

Harte, Bret, xii, 50–73, 98–100, 174
    gender inversion in, 52–62, 68–72
    homoeroticism in, 62–72

The Luck of Roaring Camp and Other Sketches, 51
    "The Idyl of Red Gulch," 98–100
    "The Luck of Roaring Camp," 53–56
    "Miggles," 57–62
    "The Outcasts of Poker Flat," 98
    "The Poet of Sierra Flat," 67–72
    "Tennessee's Partner," 62–67
    "Muck-a-Muck," 51
    as a popular western writer, 50–51
Hawkes, Howard, xix, 173
homosexuality, 52, 62–72, 134, 196 n. 9
    in the popular western, 66
    relation to homosociality, 66, 70, 107, 135, 151
hygiene, in popular western ideology, 83–85

Indians. *See* American Indians
Irigaray, Luce, 200 n. 36

Jackson, Helen Hunt, 155–56
James, Henry, 104

Karcher, Carolyn, 36, 37, 45
Kirkland, Caroline, 34–35

La Farge, Oliver, 155–56
Limerick, Patricia Nelson, xi
London, Jack, 101, 103–4, 108
lynching, 106–10

Manifest Destiny, x, 81–82, 124, 203 n. 18
marriage, 17, 37–41, 61, 63, 65–66, 93, 99–101, 102–3, 110, 199 n. 30
Mexicans, ix, x, 114, 116–18, 120, 135, 143, 162–63
Miller, Joaquin, 98, 99–101, 104, 109
    The Danites of the Sierras, 99
    First Fam'lies in the Sierras, 99–101
Milton, John R., xi, 156, 216 n. 1
miscegenation, 37–41, 46–47, 71
Mitchell, Lee Clark, xvi, 95–96
morality, as defined in popular western, 30–32, 78, 195 n. 1
Moran, Thomas, 188 n. 22
Mormonism, 99, 141, 204 n. 7

Native Americans. *See* American Indians
New Western History, xv, xvi, 182 n. 11
Norris, Frank, 15, 101, 103–4, 108

Parkman, Francis, 34
patriotism, 88
polyphony, xiv–xv, xviii, 36, 174–75, 182 n.
    8, 219 n. 2
popular western, x–xi, xiv, xvii, 24, 96–97,
    100, 109, 111, 113, 119, 123, 135, 137,
    141–42, 151–52, 159, 163, 181, 220 n. 4
    defined, x–xi, 52–53
    evolution of, 1–2
    major themes in, 24–32
    relation to frontier novel, xviii
primitivism, 75, 84–85

"regeneration through violence." See Garden myth
Remington, Frederic, 5, 6–13, 21, 91, 123,
    124, 127
    artistic technique, 12–13
    John Ermine of the Yellowstone, 25
    praise for frontier violence, 8–12
    racism in works by, 9–11, 187 n. 12
revisionist western. See anti-western
Ridge, John Rollin, 113–23, 130, 132–33
    ambivalence toward Cherokee heritage,
        120
    influence on later writers, 123, 132–33
    The Life and Adventures of Joaquin Murieta, 115–23
        call for "individual" tolerance in,
            121–23
        pan-racialism in, 114, 121–22
        publication history, 115–16, 207 n. 8
        treatment of Mexicans, 116–18, 120
    racism in, 120
Robinson, Forrest G., 95–96, 178
Roosevelt, Theodore, 5, 6, 18–24, 189 n. 35,
    190 nn. 37–39, 191 n. 45
    "The Strenuous Life," 19–21
    views on race, 22–23
Russell, Charles, 188 n. 22

Schaefer, Jack, xiii–xiv
    Shane, xiii–xiv, 27
science fiction, as extension of popular
    frontier, 174
Scott, Sir Walter, 1, 39, 105, 107–8, 111
    Kenilworth, 105, 107–8
Sedgwick, Catharine, 34–35
    Hope Leslie, 47–48
Sedgwick, Eve, 70, 199 n. 31
sentimental fiction, 93, 101, 110, 125, 136–37,
    166, 197 n. 15, 210 n. 23

overtures to, in western novels, 17, 100
    popular western reaction to, 28
    relation to Bret Harte, 56
    and "separate spheres" model, 34–36
Shakespeare, William, 104–7, 111
    Henry IV, 104–6
    Henry V, 106–7
    Romeo and Juliet, 104, 107
Sherman, William T., 7, 186 n. 11
Short, Luke, xii
silence, function of, in popular western,
    28–30
Slotkin, Richard, xi, 80–81, 84–85
Smith, Henry Nash, xi, 76, 186 nn. 7, 9
Stephens, Ann S., 34–35
superpower, American image as, figured in
    the popular west, 173

television westerns, ix–x
Tompkins, Jane, xvi, 93, 95–96, 109, 128,
    159, 178, 196 n. 8
Turner, Frederick Jackson, 2–5, 6, 26–27,
    92, 176–77, 182 n. 11, 185 nn. 2–5
Twain, Mark, 15, 74–94
    The Adventures of Huckleberry Finn, 75
    A Connecticut Yankee in King Arthur's
        Court, 74–94
    ideas on patriotism in, 79–80, 88
    representation of Indians in works by,
        84–86
    Roughing It, 75, 84–85

Vietnam War, 173–74
violence, in popular western. See "civilization versus savagery"; popular western,
    major themes in

Waters, Frank, 154–72
    The Man Who Killed the Deer, 157–71
        as an anti-frontier narrative, 160–65
        as "domestic" fiction, 165–71
        importance of female characters in,
            165–71
        racial complexity of, 161–65
        reverence for landscape in, 161, 165
        as a traditional frontier novel, 157–60
Westbrook, Max, 184 n. 19
Western Studies, field of, xi–xiii, xv–xvi, xx,
    175, 177–79
    major themes in, xvi
    polarization of popular and literary writing in, xi–xiii

relation to contemporary American politics, xii–xiii, xv–xvi
Wister, Owen, xii, xix, 5, 6, 13–18, 21, 95–111, 124, 127, 152, 174
"The Evolution of the Cow-Puncher," 13–14
Lin McLean, 108
The Virginian, 14–18, 25, 31, 78–79, 95–111
British literary antecedents, 104–9
marriage in, 103
place in American frontier tradition, 98–104

transregionalism in, 16
women. *See* gender roles

Zitkala-Sa, 113–15, 124–33
American Indian Stories, 124–32
emphasis on physical conflict in, 128–32
failure of sentimental culture in, 124–28
gender inversion in, 127–28, 130–32
influence on later writers, 132–33
position between white and Sioux cultures, 124–25